World Religions

Biographies

World Religions

Biographies VOLUME 2

Michael J. O'Neal and J. Sydney Jones
Neil Schlager and Jayne Weisblatt, Editors

U·X·L
An imprint of Thomson Gale,
a part of The Thomson Corporation

Detroit • New York • San Francisco • New Haven, Conn. • Waterville, Maine • London

THOMSON
GALE

World Religions: Biographies

Written by Michael J. O'Neal and J. Sydney Jones
Edited by Neil Schlager and Jayne Weisblatt

Project Editor
Nancy Matuszak

Editorial
Julie L. Carnagie

Rights and Acquisitions
Edna Hedblad, Emma Hull, and Sue Rudolph

Imaging and Multimedia
Lezlie Light, Michael Logusz,
Christine O'Bryan, and Robyn Young

Product Design
Jennifer Wahi

Composition
Evi Seoud

Manufacturing
Rita Wimberley

LIBRARY OF CONGRESS CATALOGING-IN-PUBLICATION DATA

Jones, J. Sydney.
  World religions reference library / edited by Neil Schlager and Jayne Weisblatt;
written by J. Sydney Jones and Michael O'Neal; Nancy Matuszak, content project editor.
    p. cm. -- (World religions reference library)
  Includes bibliographical references and index.
  ISBN-13: 978-1-4144-0227-7 (Almanac : set : alk. paper) --
  ISBN-10: 1-4144-0227-9 (Almanac : set : alk. paper) --
  ISBN-13: 978-1-4144-0228-4 (Almanac : vol. 1 : alk. paper) --
  ISBN-10: 1-4144-0228-7 (Almanac : vol. 1 : alk. paper) --
  [etc.]
    1. Religions.I. O'Neal, Michael, 1949-II. Schlager, Neil, 1966-III. Weisblatt, Jayne.
IV. Title.V. Series.
  BL74.J66 2006
  200--dc22
                                                                            2006012295

ISBN-13:

978-1-4144-0229-1
  (Almanac vol. 2)
978-1-4144-0230-7
  (Biographies set)
978-1-4144-0231-4
  (Biographies vol. 1)

978-1-4144-0232-1
  (Biographies vol. 2)
978-1-4144-0232-8
  (Primary Sources)
978-1-4144-0234-5
  (Cumulative Index)

ISBN-10:

1-4144-0229-5
  (Almanac vol. 2)
1-4144-0230-9
  (Biographies set)
1-4144-0231-7
  (Biographies vol. 1)

1-4144-0232-5
  (Biographies vol. 2)
1-4144-0233-3
  (Primary Sources)
1-4144-0234-1
  (Cumulative Index)

This title is also available as an e-book.
ISBN-13: 978-1-4144-0232-1, ISBN-10: 1-4144-0612-6
Contact your Thomson Gale sales representative for ordering information.
Printed in the United States of America

10 9 8 7 6 5 4 3 2

Contents

Religion influences the views and actions of many people in the world today in both political and personal ways. In some instances religious fervor compels people to perform selfless acts of compassion, while in others it spurs them to bitter warfare. Religion opens some people to all humanity but restricts others to remain loyal to small groups.

In general, religion can be described as a unified system of thought, feeling, and action that is shared by a group and that gives its members an object of devotion—someone or something sacred to believe in, such as a god or a spiritual concept. Religion also involves a code of behavior or personal moral conduct by which individuals may judge the personal and social consequences of their actions and the actions of others. Most of the time, religion also deals with what might be called the supernatural or the spiritual, about forces and a power beyond the control of humans. In this function, religion attempts to answer questions that science does not touch, such as the meaning of life and what happens after death.

Perhaps one of the most amazing things about religion is that there is no commonly held way of looking at it. Yet most of the world's population participates in it in one way or another. Though hard to define, religion seems to be a universal experience and need. Of the nearly 6.5 billion people on Earth, only about 16 percent (about 1.1. billion) say they do not believe in a god or do not believe in a specific religion. The rest of the world's population belongs to one of more than twenty different major religions.

Features and Format

World Religions: Biographies presents the biographies of fifty men and women who have played a critical role in the world's religions throughout history. Among those profiled are Abraham, whose influence is seen in three of the modern world's most dominant religions: Judaism, Christianity, and Islam; Muhammad, considered the final and most important prophet by Muslims; and Siddhartha Gautama, who became known as the Buddha. More modern figures are also included, from the Hindu teacher Swami Vivekananda to Bahá'u'lláh, who founded the Bahá'í faith. Women who made significant impacts on religion are also featured, including Mother Teresa, the Buddhist nun Dipa Ma, and the ancient Mesopotamian priestess Enheduanna.

Nearly one hundred black-and-white photos and maps illustrate the text, while sidebars highlight interesting concepts and fascinating facts connected to the individuals being profiled. The set also includes a glossary, a timeline, sources for further reading, and a subject index.

World Religions Reference Library

World Religions: Biographies is only one component of the three-part World Religions Reference Library. The set also includes two almanac volumes and one volume of primary source documents:

- *World Religions: Almanac* (two volumes) covers the history, traditions, and worldviews of dominant and less prominent religions and their sects and offshoots. This title examines the development of religions throughout history and into modern times: their philosophies and practices, sacred texts and teachings, effects on everyday life, influences on society and culture, and more. The set features eighteen chapters on today's prominent world religions and also explores ancient beliefs, such as those of Egypt and Mesopotamia; smaller movements like that of neo-paganism and Bahá'í; and philosophies, including those of ancient Greece and Rome, agnosticism, and atheism. In addition, an introductory chapter explores the concept of religion in more depth.

- *World Religions: Primary Sources* (one volume) offers eighteen excerpted writings, speeches, and sacred texts from across the religious spectrum. These include selections from the Bible, including both the Old and New Testament (Judaism and Christianity); the Qur'an (Islam); and the Dhammapada (Buddhism). Among the other selections are the Daoist text Dao De Jing; the Avesta, the sacred scripture of Zoroastrianism; the Sikh sacred scripture, Shri Guru Granth Sahib; and Thomas Henry Huxley's essay "Agnosticism and Christianity."

Acknowledgments

U • X • L would like to thank several individuals for their assistance with the *World Religions: Biographies*. At Schlager Group, Jayne Weisblatt and Neil Schlager who oversaw the writing and editing, while Michael J. O'Neal and J. Sydney Jones wrote the text. Thanks also to Shannon Kelly, who assisted with copyediting, Nora Harris for indexing, and Gloria Lam for proofing.

Special thanks are due for the invaluable comments and suggestions provided by U • X • L's World Religions Reference Library advisors and consultants:

- George Alscer, Associate Professor and Chair of Religious Studies, Philosophy and Pastoral Ministry, Marygrove College, Detroit, Michigan.

- Janet Callahan, Ford Interfaith Network, Dearborn, Michigan.

- Mary Ann Christopher, Librarian, Yellow Springs High School, Yellow Springs, Ohio.

- Margaret Hallisey, Retired library media specialist and former board member of the American Association of School Librarians; the Massachusetts School Library Media Association; and the New England Educational Media Association.

- Fatima al-Hayani, Professor of Religious Studies, University of Toledo, Toledo, Ohio.

- Madan Kaura, Bharatyia Temple, Ford Interfaith Network, Dearborn, Michigan.
- Ann Marie LaPrise, Huron School District, Monroe, Michigan.
- Ann W. Moore, Librarian, Schenectady County Public Library, Schenectady, New York.
- Chuen Pangcham, Midwest Buddhist Meditation Center (Buddha Vihara Temple), Warren, Michigan.
- Gene Schramm, Retired professor of Semitic Languages and Near Eastern Studies, University of Michigan, Ann Arbor, Michigan.

- Cheryl Youse, Media specialist, Hatherly Elementary School, Plymouth, Michigan.

Comments and Suggestions

We welcome your comments on *World Religions: Biographies* and suggestions for other topics in history to consider. Please write to Editors, *World Religions: Biographies,* U•X•L, 27500 Drake Road, Farmington Hills, Michigan 48331-3535; call toll-free 800-877-4253; send faxes to 248-699-8097; or send e-mail via http://www.gale.com.

Timeline of Events

c. 2300–c. 2260 BCE Life span of **Enheduanna.** The daughter of the Sumerian ruler Sargon of Akkad, Enheduanna is made High Priestess to the Sumerian Moon God, Nanna, beginning a tradition that will last for the next five hundred years among the princesses of the kings of the Middle Eastern region of Mesopotamia. Enheduanna also establishes the religious cult of Inanna, the daughter of the Moon God.

c. 2050–c. 1950 BCE Life span of **Abraham,** a central figure in three major religions: Judaism, Christianity, and Islam.

1353 BCE **Akhenaten,** also known as Amenhotep IV, becomes pharaoh of Egypt.

c. thirteenth century BCE According to Judeo-Christian belief, **Moses** leads the Israelites, the Jewish people, out of slavery from Egypt.

c. 1200 BCE Date perhaps marking the life of **Zarathushtra,** the founder of Zoroastrianism.

c. 604 BCE **Laozi,** considered the founder of Daoism, is born in China.

c. 569 BCE Vardhamana, who later takes the name **Mahavira** and is considered the founder of Jainism, gives up all of his worldly possessions to live a life of piety.

c. 551–479 BCE Life span of the scholar Kong zi, who is known in the West by his Latinized name, **Confucius.**

528 According to Buddhist belief, Siddhartha Gautama achieves enlightenment after a night of meditation, thus becoming **the Buddha.**

c. 483 BCE Death of the Buddha.

c. 476 BCE Greek philosopher **Anaxagoras** produces his major work *On Nature.*

c. 390 BCE The Greek philosopher **Plato** writes his most influential work, *The Republic.*

384–322 BCE Life span of the Greek philosopher **Aristotle.** Believing that achieving happiness is humanity's chief goal, he organizes all human behavior into a pyramid of actions that all lead to one supreme activity or goal for the individual.

c. 6 BCE **Jesus Christ,** also known as Jesus of Nazareth, is born.

c. 30 CE Jesus Christ is put to death by crucifixion by Roman authorities in Jerusalem.

c. 35 Saul of Tarsus, later known as **Saint Paul,** converts to Christianity.

610 According to Islamic belief, **Muhammad** begins receiving revelations and prophecies from the archangel Jabra'il (Gabriel).

661 'Alī ibn Abī Tālib, the fourth caliph, or leader, of Islam, is murdered. His followers, part of the Shi'a sect, believe that 'Ali is the first imam, or leader with divinely inspired powers.

c. 717–c. 801 Life span of **Rābi'ah al-Adawiyah,** a poet and a founding member of the mystical branch of Islam called Sufism. Her verses and prayers will become part of the literature and oral tradition of Islam.

1017–1137 Life span of **Ramanuja,** one of the great Hindu teachers of medieval India.

c. 1105 The Islamic philosopher **Abu Hāmid Muhammad al-Ghazālī** publishes his greatest work, *The Revival of the Religious Sciences.* The book explains the doctrines or rules and practices of Islam, especially Sufi Islam.

1177 **Moses Maimonides,** a Jewish scholar best known for his "thirteen principles of faith," is officially appointed head of Cairo's Jewish community.

c. 1199–c. 1287 Life span of **Madhva,** the founder of a sect of Hinduism called Madhvism.

1253 Japanese Buddhist monk **Nichiren** claims that the only true Buddhist religion is Nichiren Buddhism.

c. 1270 The Sufi Muslim poet **Jalāl ad-Dīn ar-Rūmī** finishes his most important work, the *Masnavi*. After his death in 1273, his name becomes associated with the Muslim sect known as the Whirling Dervishes, who are noted for their ecstatic body movements or dances as they chant the many names of Allah.

1377 The Muslim historian **Ibn Khaldūn** publishes his *Muqaddima,* in which he presents his theory for the rise and fall of civilizations.

1517 The German Augustinian monk **Martin Luther** launches the Protestant Reformation, which divides Christianity into two denominations, or branches: Catholicism and Protestantism.

1534 The Spanish nobleman **Ignatius of Loyola** establishes the Society of Jesus, or the Jesuit order, in 1534.

1536 **John Calvin** publishes the first edition of *Institutes of the Christian Religion*. In it, he argues that the authority of the pope should be rejected, that all humans are sinful and without any free will, and that eternal life is predetermined by God.

1698–1760 Life span of **Israel ben Eliezer,** the founder of Hasidism, a Jewish mystical movement that emphasizes a direct connection to God through prayer and through joyous experiences such as music and dance.

1699 The Sikh leader **Gobind Singh** founds the Khalsa, a militant brotherhood that gives identity to Sikhism and empowers Sikhs to resist persecution.

1783 Publication of *Jerusalem; or, On Religious Power and Judaism,* by the German Jewish scholar **Moses Mendelssohn.** In the book, Mendelssohn calls for freedom of conscience and argues that the state should play no role in determining the religious beliefs of its citizens.

1804 The Islamic leader **Usuman dan Fodio** leads a successful *jihad* (holy war) to become the ruler of the Fulani Empire in West Africa.

1844 The Communist philosopher **Karl Marx** publishes *Critique of the Hegelian Philosophy of Public Law.* In it, he explains his atheist views, writing that "Man makes religion, religion does not make man."

1866 **Baháʾuʾlláh,** founder of the Baháʾí faith, publicly declares himself the Messenger of God.

1873 Jewish rabbi **Isaac Mayer Wise** forms the Union of American Hebrew Congregations; two years later he forms Hebrew Union College. In so doing, Wise becomes a key figure in the development of Reform Judaism in the United States.

1875 **Dayananda Sarasvati** founds the Arya Samaj, a Hindu reform movement. This organization will play a major part in the growth of Indian nationalism.

1893 The paper "What Is Hinduism?" by **Swami Vivekananda,** presented at the World Parliament of Religions in Chicago, exposes many Westerners to Hinduism for the first time. Also in Chicago at this conference, **Anagarika Dharmapala** speaks movingly of his religion, Theravada Buddhism. He gains converts in the United States and opens a U.S. chapter of the Maha Bodhi Society.

1911–1989 Life span of **Dipa Ma,** who becomes a beloved Buddhist teacher.

1932 **Black Elk** works with poet John G. Neihardt to write the work *Black Elk Speaks.* This book brought the traditional religious practices of the Lakota Sioux tribe to a wider audience.

1942 Israeli scholar **Nechama Leibowitz** begins providing weekly lessons about the Torah to students via the mail. She will continue the lessons for fifty years.

1945 **Mother Maria Skobtsova,** a nun in the Eastern Orthodox Church, dies in the concentration camp at Ravensbrück in Germany.

1947 India gains its independence from Britain, due in large part to the nonviolent protest movement led by **Mahatma Gandhi,** a devout Hindu.

1950 In Calcutta, India, **Mother Teresa** founds a new order of Catholic nuns, eventually called the Missionaries of Charity. Mother

Teresa and the order establish hospices, orphanages, and schools throughout India and eventually throughout the world.

1954 **Gerald Brousseau Gardner** publishes *Witchcraft Today,* which places witchcraft as the surviving piece of pagan or pre-Christian religion in the modern world. With the book's popularity, Gardner is dubbed by the English media as "Britain's Chief Witch."

1966 The Buddhist teacher **Thich Nhat Hanh** is exiled from Vietnam.

1986 The Anglican priest **Desmond Mpilo Tutu** becomes the Archbishop of Cape Town, South Africa. He continues his efforts to gain civil rights for South Africa's black population.

1989 The **Dalai Lama** wins the Nobel Peace Prize for his work on behalf of his homeland, Tibet, which has been under Chinese control since 1950.

1994 **Malidoma Patrice Somé** publishes his autobiography, *Of Water and the Spirit.* In it, he describes his youth as a member of the Dagara tribe in West Africa.

Words To Know

A

acupuncture: Traditional Chinese medical treatment that uses needles inserted into the body at specific locations to stimulate the body's balanced flow of energy.

adur aduran: The "fire of fires" that burns in Zoroastrian temples.

agnosticism: The view that the existence or nonexistence of God is unknown and is probably unknowable.

ahimsa: The principle of nonviolence, or not doing harm to any living creature.

Ahura Mazda: The supreme God of Zoroastrianism.

Akaranga Sutra: One of the sacred texts of Jainism, which contains the teachings of Mahavira.

Akhand Paath: Any occasion, such as a marriage or a death, when the Granth Sahib is read in its entirety.

alchemy: An ancient science that aimed to transform substances of little value into those of greater value, such as lead into gold.

Allah: The name of God in Islam, derived from the Arabic word *al-ilah*, meaning "the One True God."

Amaterasu: The Sun-goddess.

Amesha Spentas: The "Bounteous Immortals," aspects, or sides, of Ahura Mazda.

amrit: A solution of water and sugar, used in the ceremony when Sikhs are initiated into the faith.

Amrit Sanskar: The initiation ceremony for young Sikhs.

Anand Karaj: The Sikh wedding ceremony.

animism: The worship of trees, rocks, mountains, and such, which are believed to have supernatural power.

anthropomorphism: Attributing human shape or form to nonhuman things, such as the gods.

apathia: Stoic belief that happiness comes from freedom from internal turmoil.

apeiron: Anaximander's term for the first principle, an undefined and unlimited substance.

archē: The beginning or ultimate principle; the stuff of all matter, or the building block of creation.

arihant: An enlightened person.

Ark of the Covenant: A cabinet in which the Ten Commandments were kept in the First Temple of Jerusalem.

artha: Prosperity and success in material affairs.

Asatru: A neo-pagan religion based on worship of the Norse (Scandanavian) gods.

ascetic: A person who practices rigid self-denial, giving up all comforts and pleasures, as an act of religious devotion. Jain monks and nuns are ascetics.

asha: Righteousness that derives from natural law.

Ashkenazic: Term used to refer to Jews of France, Germany, and Eastern Europe.

astrology: The study of the movement of the planets and stars in relation to one another in order to predict future events.

ataraxia: Serenity, tranquility, or peace of mind.

atheism: A disbelief in the existence of God or a belief that there is no God.

atomism: The belief that matter is composed of simple, indivisible, physical particles that are too tiny to be observed by human beings.

atonement: In Christianity, the sacrifice and death of Jesus to redeem humankind from its sins.

aum: Often spelled Om, the sacred syllable and symbol of Hinduism; a symbol of the unknowable nature of Brahma.

Avesta: The chief sacred scripture of Zoroastrianism.

B

baptism: A religious ceremony in which a person is dipped in or sprinkled with water as a sign of being cleansed of sin.

bar mitzvah: The Jewish coming-of-age ceremony for boys.

bat mitzvah: The Jewish coming-of-age ceremony for girls.

belief: A conviction of the truth of a proposition either by close examination or trust.

Beltane (Beltaine): Neo-pagan holiday on April 30.

benevolence: The tendency to do good and to be kind to others.

Bhagavad Gita: A Sanskrit poem regarded as a Hindu scripture; part of the epic *Mahabharata,* which means "Great Epic of the Bharata Dynasty"; examines the nature of God and how mortals can know him.

bhakti: Devotion.

blasphemy: Disrespectful comments or actions concerning a religion or its God.

bodhisattva: A person who has attained enlightenment but, rather than entering a state of nirvana, chooses to stay behind to help others reach enlightenment.

Bon: An indigenous religion of Tibet.

Brahma: The creator-god.

The Buddha: The title of Siddhartha Gautama after he attained enlightenment.

C

caliph: One of Muhammad's successors as leader of the faith.

Candomblé: A South American religion with many similarities to Santería, often used synonymously with Santería.

canon: The official, sacred texts of a religion.

caste: Social classes in Hinduism, the dominant religion in India.

Celtic: A term referring to an ethnic group that spread throughout Europe, particularly the British Isles, and is the source of many modern neo-pagan movements.

church: From the Greek, this word refers to the community of all Christians. It is also the place where Christians go to worship.

consciousness: The condition of being aware of one's thoughts, feelings, and existence.

conservative: A movement in modern Judaism that tries to strike a balance between Orthodox and Reform Judaism.

conversion: A change in which a person adopts a new set of religious beliefs.

coven: A group of neo-pagans, such as Wiccans. Alternately referred to as circles, groves, kindreds, garths, hearths, and other terms.

covenant: In religion, a covenant refers to an agreement between God or a messenger of God and his followers.

creed: A statement of belief or basic principles.

crucifixion: The suffering and death by nailing or binding a person to a cross.

cuneiform: Sumerian writing, so-called because of its wedge-shaped marks.

daevas: Ancient Persian deities.

Dao: The path or way; the rhythmic balance and natural, flowing patterns of the universe.

de: Political power that is the result of a ruler's virtue and honesty.

deity: A god or goddess.

dharma: Righteousness in one's religious and personal life.

Diaspora: The scattering of the Jews throughout the world.

Digambara: Literally "sky-clad"; one of the two major sects of Jainism.

disciple: A person who accepts and assists in spreading the teachings of a leader. In the Bible, a follower of Jesus.

doctrine: A set of ideas held by a religious group.

druidism: A neo-pagan religion based in the Celtic region of the British Isles.

dynasty: A sequence of rulers from the same family.

Eightfold Path: The path of the Buddha's teachings that can lead to the end of suffering.

Ek Onkar: The "True God" of Sikhism.

emanation: That which inevitably flows outward from the transcendental (spiritual, beyond human experience) central principle of reality, "the One," in the Neoplatonic philosophy of Plotinus.

empiricism: Belief that knowledge comes through the senses.

enlightenment: The state of realization and understanding of life, a feeling of unity with all things.

Epicureanism: The philosophy of Epicurus and others that states that the highest good is pleasure and the avoidance of pain.

equinox: Either of two points during the year when the Sun crosses the equator and the hours of day and night are equal. The spring, or vernal, equinox occurs generally on March 21 and the autumn equinox occurs on or about September 23.

Esbat: Wiccan celebration of the full Moon.

ethics: The study of moral values and rules or a guide to such values and rules.

etiquette: Proper behavior; good manners.

Evangelical: Describing a Protestant group that emphasizes the absolute authority of the Bible and forgiveness of sin through belief in Jesus.

excommunicate: To exclude or officially ban a person from a church or other religious community.

faith: Belief and trust in God, accompanied by a sense of loyalty to the traditional doctrines, or principles, of religion.

Faravahar: A figure of a bird with its wings spread that is a chief symbol of Zoroastrianism.

filial piety: The respect and devotion a child shows his or her parents.

fitrah: An inborn tendency to seek the creator.

Five Classics: The original texts used by Confucius in his practices and teachings: *Liji, Shijing, Shujing, Chunqui,* and *Yijing.*

Five Pillars: The core of Islamic belief referring to declaring faith, daily prayer, charitable giving, fasting, and pilgrimage.

folk beliefs: The beliefs of the common people.

Folk (*Minzoku*) Shinto: Shinto that emphasizes folk beliefs, or common beliefs, of rural agricultural laborers.

Four Affirmations: A code of conduct by which Shintoists live, including emphases on tradition and family, nature, cleanliness, and worship of the kami.

Four Books: The most prominent of Confucian sacred texts, established by Zhu Xi: the Analects, the Mencius, *Da Xue* (Great Learning), and *Zhongyong* (Doctrine of the Mean).

Four Noble Truths: The foundations of the Buddhist religion: that all life is suffering, that desire causes suffering, that suffering can end, and that ending suffering happens by following the path of the Buddha's teachings.

Gahambars: Seasonal festivals.

Gathas: A portion of the Zend-Avesta that contains holy songs; believed to be the words of Zarathushtra himself.

God: The supreme or ultimate being or reality; creator of the universe.

Goddess worship: Term that refers generally to any neo-pagan practice that elevates the status of goddesses over that of gods.

Golden Temple: The chief Sikh temple, located in the city of Amritsar in India; more formally, the Sri Harmandir Sahib.

gurdwara: A Sikh temple or place of worship.

guru: A religious teacher.

Ha-ne-go-ate-geh: The "Evil-Minded," the evil spirit of the Iroquois nation.

Ha-wen-ne-yu: The Great Spirit of the Iroquois nation.

hadiths: The sayings of the prophet Muhammad recorded by his followers.

Haj: Pilgrimage to the holy city of Mecca.

halal: Permissible activities for Muslims.

Hanukkah: The Jewish Festival of Lights commemorating the rededication of the First Temple.

haram: Prohibited activities for Muslims.

heretic: A person whose beliefs oppose his or her religion's official doctrines, or defining principles.

Ho-no-che-no-keh: The Invisible Agents, or lesser spirits, of the Iroquois.

Holocaust: The systematic slaughter of Jews by the Nazi regime in Germany before and during World War II (1939–45).

householders: Laypeople; Jains who are not monks or nuns.

idol: A statue or other image that is worshipped as a god.

Imbolc: Neo-pagan holiday generally held on February 2 to mark the lengthening of the days and the emergence of the world from winter.

Immaculate Conception: The principle of the Roman Catholic Church that Mary, the mother of Jesus, was conceived with a soul free from original sin.

incarnation: In Christianity, the belief that God took on bodily form through Jesus, making Jesus fully human and fully divine.

indigenous: A word that describes a people, culture, or religion that is native to a particular geographical region.

indulgence: In the Roman Catholic Church, the belief that paying money to the Church would allow a person to get into heaven or be forgiven for sins that were not yet committed.

Izanagi: The male figure in the Shinto creation myth.

Izanami: The female figure in the Shinto creation myth.

jinja: Shrine.

jinn: Evil spirits that tempt a person away from dedication to Allah.

jinn: Literally, "conquerors"; the great teachers of Jainism who have conquered their earthly passions.

jiva: The soul.

junzi: A gentleman or superior man.

Ka'aba: The shrine built by the prophet Abraham in the holy city of Mecca and the focal point of pilgrimages to the city.

kama: Gratification of the senses.

kami: The gods or divinities of Shinto; the life force or spirit associated with places, natural objects, and ancestors.

kami-dana: A "kami shelf" or altar in a private home.

kara: A steel bracelet, worn by Sikhs as a symbol of God.

karma: The result of good or bad actions in this lifetime that can affect this or later lifetimes.

kasha: The white shorts worn by Sikhs as a symbol of purity.

kesh: Uncut hair, a symbol of Sikhism.

kevalnyan: Enlightenment.

Khalsa: The militant "brotherhood" of Sikhism, founded by Guru Gobind Singh.

Khanda: The emblem of Sikhism.

kirpan: A sword or dagger worn by Sikhs as a symbol of their willingness to fight to defend their faith.

Kojiki: The chief text of Shinto, a work that combines history, myth, and folk belief.

kosher: Dietary laws, referred to in Hebrew as *kashrut*.

kungha: The wooden comb used to groom hair, a symbol of Sikhism.

kushti: The sacred cord, or belt, that Zoroastrians wear.

kusti: The "holy path" one has to follow to be a Zoroastrian.

laity: Body of worshippers who are not members of the clergy.

li: The rules of behavior a person must follow to reach the Confucian ideal of correct living.

Logos: Word, logic, or defining pattern of the universe, similar to the Dao in Chinese philosophy.

Lughnasadh: Neo-pagan harvest festival on August 1.

maat: Divine order and justice; a central concept in the religion of ancient Egypt.

Mabon: Neo-pagan celebration of the autumn equinox; the completion of the harvest season.

Magen David: The so-called Star of David, a symbol of the Jewish faith and nation.

magick: The ability to focus mental and physical energies to affect the natural world or to achieve a goal.

Mahavira: The twenty-fourth tirthankara often regarded as the founder of Jainism.

Mahavira jayanti: Mahavira's birthday, an important holy day for Jains.

mantra: A formula repeated over and over to create a trancelike state.

materialism: A belief that matter and the motion of matter constitute the universe. All phenomena, even those of mind, are the result of material interactions.

matsuri: Festival.

Mecca: A city in present-day Saudi Arabia, the holiest site of Islam, where the religion was founded.

meditation: Quiet reflection on spiritual matters.

menorah: A seven-branched candelabrum; at Hanukkah, a nine-branched candelabrum is used.

Messiah: The expected deliverer and king of the Jews, foretold by the prophets of the Old Testament; used by Christians to refer to Jesus Christ.

metaphysical: Having to do with the philosophical study of the nature of reality and existence.

metaphysics: The branch of philosophy that deals with explanations for the most general questions of being, such as what brought the world into being, and the nature of space, time, God, and the afterlife.

metempsychosis: Transmigration of souls, or the migration of the soul into a different form, animal, or object after death.

mezuzah: A small case containing Torah passages that observant Jews attach to the doorposts of their houses.

midrashim: Stories that expand on incidents in the Hebrew Bible.

Mishnah: The written text of the Talmud.

mitzvoth: The laws of Judaism contained in the Torah.

moksha: Salvation; liberation from rebirth.

monastery: A place where religious people such as monks live, away from the world and following strict religious guidelines.

monotheism: Belief in one supreme being.

morality: Following the rules of right behavior and conduct.

Moshiach: The expected Messiah in Jewish belief.

***muezzin*:** The person who issues the call to prayer.

murti: Image of a god.

Muslim: A follower of Islam, from the Arabic phrase *bianna musliman,* meaning "submitted ourselves to God."

myth: A legendary story, often with no basis in historical fact, that frequently tells of the actions of deities and helps to explain some naturally occurring event or some supernatural occurrence.

mythology: The collected stories of a culture or religion, especially those dealing with the origins, heroes, gods, and beliefs of a group of people.

Naam Karam: The naming ceremony for children.

namaskar: The basic prayer of Jainism, recited each morning and at night before bedtime.

Neo-paganism: A term referring to modern religions based on ancient pagan religions.

nirvana: The end of suffering, beyond time and space; the goal of all Buddhists.

nivritti: People who choose to withdraw from the world to lead a life of renunciation and contemplation.

***norito*:** Prayers to the kami.

Offering of Eightfold Puja: An important Jain temple ritual in which the worshipper makes eight offerings to the tirthankara.

Olódùmarè: The name of the supreme god in Santería.

Om: Often spelled Aum; the sacred syllable and symbol of Jainism (and Hinduism), used for purposes of meditation.

Oral Torah: Interpretations of the Torah and ways to apply their laws.

orders: Religious communities.

Original Sin: The sin that fell upon humankind when Adam and Eve ate of the forbidden fruit in the Garden of Eden; this act, in turn, led to the separation of humans from God.

orishas: Name given to the lesser gods of Santería.

orthodox: The name of one of the sects of Judaism, generally referring to traditional Jews who are conservative in their outlook.

Oshogatsu: The Shinto new year.

Ostara: Neo-pagan holiday held at the time of the spring equinox.

pagan: Pre-Christian or non-Christian; also referring to those who worship many gods.

pantheon: The class or collection of all gods and goddesses in a system of belief.

Parshva: The twenty-third tirthankara, who lived about 250 years before Mahavira.

Parsis (Parsees): Zoroastrians who live in India.

Paryushana: An eight-day festival, the most important holy observance for Jains during the year.

Pesach: The feast of Passover, commemorating the flight of the Jews from Egypt.

philosophical Daoism: A form of Daoism by which followers seek knowledge and wisdom about the unity of everything in existence and how to become closer to it.

philosophy: The study of morals and reality by logical reasoning to gain a greater understanding of the world.

polytheism: A religion worshiping many gods.

pravritti: People who choose to live in the world rather than withdraw from it.

prophecy: Prediction of future events.

prophet: A person chosen to serve as God's messenger.

pu: Uncarved or unformed; the state of simplicity to which Daoists try to return.

puja: Worship.

purusharthas: The four aims of Hinduism or "the doctrine of the four-fold end of life."

Purva: The original Jain sacred texts, now lost.

pyramid: A stone tomb constructed to house a deceased pharaoh of Egypt.

qi: The breath of life or vital energy that flows through the body and the earth.

Qur'an: The sacred scriptures of Islam; contains the revelations given to the prophet Muhammad revealed to him beginning in 610.

ra'kah: A unit of prayer.

rationalism: Belief that knowledge can come exclusively from the mind.

reform: One of the sects of Judaism, generally used to refer to the less traditional branch of the faith.

Regla de Ocha: The formal name for the Santerían religion.

Rehit Maryada: The Sikh code of ethical conduct.

religious Daoism: A form of Daoism that recognizes gods, ancestor spirits, and life after death.

ren: Empathy, the ability to feel for and sympathize with others; the highest Confucian ideal.

Resurrection: The rising of Jesus Christ from the dead three days after his Crucifixion, or death on a cross.

Rig Veda: The central scripture of Hinduism, a collection of inspired hymns and songs.

Rosh Hoshanah: The Jewish "New Year."

Sabbat: Holidays practiced by Wiccans throughout the year, including the summer and winter solstices, the vernal and autumnal equinoxes, and four additional holidays between these four.

sacrament: A sacred rite, or ceremony.

sadhana: Ascetic person.

saint: A deceased person who has been recognized for living a virtuous and holy life.

salat: Daily prayer.

salvation: The deliverance of human beings from sin through Jesus Christ's death on the cross.

Samhain (Samhuinn): Neo-pagan holiday celebrated on October 31.

samsara: The ongoing cycle of birth, life, death, and rebirth.

Samyak charitra: Right conduct; one of the Three Jewels of Jain ethical conduct.

Samyak darshana: Right faith, or right perception; one of the Three Jewels of Jain ethical conduct.

Samyak jnana: Right knowledge; one of the Three Jewels of Jain ethical conduct.

Sanskrit: An ancient Indo-European language that is the language of Hinduism, as well as of much classical Indian literature.

Santería: The "way of the saints"; an African-based religion practiced primarily in Cuba and other Central and South American countries.

Santero: A practitioner of Santería.

saum: Fasting.

sect: A small religious group that has branched off from a larger established religion.

Sect (*Kyoha*) Shinto: Shinto as it is practiced by a number of sects, or groups, formed primarily in the nineteenth century.

secular: Worldly things, of the physical world, as opposed to religious and spiritual.

Sedreh-pushi: The Zoroastrian initiation rite.

Sephardic: Term used to refer to Jews of North Africa, the Middle East, Spain, and Portugal.

Shahadah: The Islamic declaration of faith. It consists of the words "*Ashahadu an la ilaha ill Allah wa ashahadu ann Muhammadar Rasulullah*," or "I declare there is no god except God, and I declare that Muhammad is the Messenger of God."

shaman: In indigenous tribes, an intermediary between the gods and the tribal members; also one who controls various spiritual forces, can look into the future, and can cure the ill with magic.

shamanism: A term used generally to refer to indigenous religions that believe in an unseen spirit world that influences human affairs.

shariʾah: Islamic law.

Shiʾite: One of the main sects of Islam; from the phrase *Shiʾat Ali,* or the party of ʿAli.

Shinbutsu bunri: The separation of Shinto and Buddhism when Shinto was declared the official state religion.

Shinbutsu shugo: The combination of Shinto and Buddhism.

Shinto: Literally, "the way of the gods" or "the way of the kami."

Shiva: The destroyer god, embodying the erotic and sexual.

Shivaism: A major sect of Hinduism, which sees Shiva ("the Destroyer") as the central god.

Shrine (*Jinja*) Shinto: The traditional, mainstream practice of Shinto, with emphasis on the local shrine.

skepticism: Doubt or disbelief toward a particular proposition or object.

Skepticism: A philosophical system that doubted the possibility of ever discovering real truth through the senses.

Socratic: Having to do with the philosopher Socrates and his method of asking questions of students to develop an idea.

solstice: The points in the year when the day is longest (the summer solstice, generally on June 21) and the shortest (the winter solstice, generally on December 21).

Sophists: A group of traveling teachers in ancient Greece who doubted the possibility of knowing all the truth through the physical senses.

State Shinto: Shinto as it was practiced after it was declared the official state religion in the late nineteenth century until 1945.

Stoicism: The philosophical system that holds that people should pursue the knowledge of human and divine things through the use of logical systems. It also says that humans may not be able to control natural events, but that they can control the way they react to them.

stupas: Originally a mound marking the spot where the Buddha's ashes were buried. Rock pillars carved with the words of the Buddha are also sometimes called stupas.

Sufism: A trend in or way of practicing Islam; characterized by an ecstatic, trancelike mysticism.

Sunnah: The example of the prophet Muhammad, containing the hadiths, or sayings; provides guidance to everyday questions of faith and morality.

Sunni: The main sect of Islam.

supernatural: That which is beyond the observable world, including things relating to God or spirits.

supreme being: The central God responsible for creating the cosmos.

sura: Any chapter in the Qur'an.

Susano-o: The Shinto god of violence and the ruler of the oceans.

Svetambara: Literally, "white-clad"; one of the two main sects of Jainism.

swastika: A pictorial character that symbolizes the eternal nature of Brahma because it points in all directions; also used as the official emblem of the Nazi Party during World War II (1939–45).

takhts: Seats of spiritual authority in Sikhism. The "Five Takhts" are gurdwaras located in India.

Talmud: Traditions that explain and interpret the Torah.

Tanakh: The chief Jewish scripture; the Hebrew Bible.

tawba: Repentance.

theism: Belief in the existence of gods or God.

theocracy: A form of government in which God or some supreme deity is the ruler. God's laws are then interpreted by a divine king or by a priest class.

theology: The study of God and of religions truths.

Three Jewels: The Jain code of ethical conduct, consisting of right faith, right knowledge, and right conduct.

Tian: Heaven, or the principle of ordering the universe.

Tipitaka: The Buddhist sacred texts accepted by all branches of Buddhism.

tirthankara: Literally, "makers of the ford,"; those souls who have attained enlightenment and have been freed from the cycle of death and rebirth; the twenty-four leaders of Jainism.

Torah: The first five books of the Tanakh: Genesis, Exodus, Leviticus, Numbers, and Deuteronomy.

tori: The gate that marks the entrance to a shrine. Its shape is regarded as a symbol of Shinto.

totem: Some sort of object or, perhaps, animal that assumes a spiritual symbolism for a clan or tribe.

transcendent: Going beyond the ordinary, beyond the universe and time, into spiritual dimensions.

Trinity: In Christianity, the union of the Father, Son, and Holy Spirit as three divine persons in one God.

Tsukiyomi: The Shinto moon-god and the ruler of night.

ujiko: A "named child" whose name is entered at birth at the local Shinto shrine.

Upanishads: The core of Hindu philosophy; collections of texts, originally part of the Vedas, that explain such core Hindu beliefs as karma, reincarnation, nirvana, the soul, and Brahman.

urvan: The soul.

Vaishnavaism: A major sect of Hinduism, which sees Vishnu ("the Preserver") as the central god.

Vedas: The chief sacred scriptures of Hinduism; knowledge, wisdom, or vision.

Virgin Birth: The Christian belief that Jesus Christ was the Son of God and born of a virgin mother.

Vishnu: Also called Krishna; the preserver-god.

Vodou: An African-based religion practiced primarily in Haiti and in other Central and South American countries.

Vodouisant: An uninitiated practitioner of Vodou.

Wakan: The incomprehensibility of life and death for the Sioux.

Wakan tanka: The world's motivating force for the Sioux.

wen: The arts of music, poetry, and painting.

Wicca: The name of a neo-pagan religion that generally worships the God and the Goddess.

wu wei: Nonaction, or deliberate and thoughtful action that follows the Dao.

Yahweh: One of the names for God in the Tanakh.

yazata: Guardian angel.

Yin and yang: Literally, "shady" and "sunny"; terms referring to how the universe is composed of opposing but complementary forces.

Yom Kippur: The Day of Atonement.

zakat: Annual charitable giving.

ziggurat: A stepped foundation or structure that held a shrine or temple in the Mesopotamian religion.

Zionism: A movement that began in the nineteenth century to find a permanent home for Jews.

Laozi

BORN: C. 604 BCE • Chu, China

Chinese philosopher

Laozi.
HULTON ARCHIVE/
GETTY IMAGES.

"The Dao that can be told is not the eternal Dao; / The name that can be named is not the eternal name. / The Nameless is the origin of Heaven and Earth."

Laozi (also spelled Lao Tzu or Lao-tzu) is the founder of the philosophical system called Daoism (Taoism), one of the three primary religions of China. The other two are Confucianism and Buddhism. Little is known about Laozi, who lived during the sixth century BCE. In fact, many historians claim that he was actually a mythical character or a mixture of several individuals. Nevertheless, Laozi is traditionally given credit for writing the primary text of Daoism, the Dao De Jing (also Tao Te Ching), often translated as "The Book of the Way and Its Virtue." This text teaches that one needs to copy the simplicity and calm of nature and attempt to harmonize one's life with the *Dao (Tao)*, the eternal path of the universe, often referred to as the Way.

Historical and mythical Laozi

There are several sources of information about Laozi. The one most biographies begin with is the Shiji (Shih-chi), or Records of the Historian, written by the Han dynasty court historian, Sima Qian (Ssu-ma Ch'ien). Many question the accuracy of Sima Qian's information, however, as his book was written several centuries after Laozi's death. According to Sima Qian, Laozi was born around 604 BCE in a small village in the state of Chu, which is the modern-day Chinese province of Henan (Honan). His original surname, or family name, was supposedly Li, and his given name was Er, but he was also sometimes called Dan (Tan). Li Er or Li Dan later became known as a great thinker and was given the honorary title of Laozi, meaning "old man" or "old master." Sima Qian's source for this information appears to have been a tutor for the imperial household whose family name was Li and who traced his ancestry back to Laozi.

At this point, myth and legend attempt to fill in some of the historical gaps. Laozi was said to have had a miraculous birth. In one story his mother was reported to have carried him in her womb for sixty-two years. In another story, it was seventy-two (a magical number in Chinese folk belief). One legend claims Laozi's mother gave birth to him while leaning against a plum tree, and at birth he was already white-haired and wise. The baby's first words supposedly referred to his origins: He declared that he would take his family name from the word for plum (*li* in Chinese) and then add the given name of the word for ear (*er,* or *erh*), because his ears were already very large, like those of all wise men.

Sima Qian noted that Laozi traveled to the capital city of the Zhou (Chou) Dynasty (1025–250 BCE), Luoyang (Loyang), which was established in 770 BCE. In the city he became the keeper of archival records at the court of the Zhou. In addition to compiling historical documents, he also made astrological calculations and cared for the sacred books of Chinese thought. Due to this most historians assume that Laozi was familiar with all of China's past religious traditions. Laozi married while in Luoyang, and he and his wife had a son named Tsung. Laozi's reputation as a wise man began to spread, and people from all parts of China soon sought his guidance.

Tradition holds that Laozi once met with another great Chinese philosopher, **Confucius** (c. 551–c. 479 BCE; see entry). This was recorded by Sima Qian and also in the Zhuangzi, another important early Daoist text. According to these sources, Laozi and Confucius met twice. At the end of their second interview, Laozi dismissed the younger philosopher with words that questioned all of his beliefs in family, social order, ritual, and education. As Sima Qian noted, Laozi supposedly told Confucius,

"The man who is intelligent and clear-sighted will soon die, for his criticisms of others are just; the man who is learned and discerning risks his life, for he exposes others' faults. The man who is a son no longer belongs to himself; the man who is a subject no longer belongs to himself."

Confucius reportedly later said to his own students that he knew how to trap a wild animal and how to net a fish, but Laozi was a dragon, and he did not know how to catch or understand a dragon. Several other times, according to the Zhuangzi, Confucius consulted Laozi on the Dao, or the Way, and each time he left the older master's company confused and mystified. Further evidence that the two were possibly connected can be found in one of the classic Chinese texts, the Liji (Record of Rites). It speaks of a Lao Dan, or "Old Dan," who acted as a mentor or teacher to Confucius. Dan was one of the names by which Laozi was known.

Journey to the west

According to Sima Qian's account, Laozi grew dissatisfied with the state of society and the decline of Zhou power. The sixth century BCE was a time of disorder in China, with local nobles challenging each other and the central power of the Zhou. Warfare was a nearly permanent feature of life. This decline in societal values was what prompted Confucius to develop his ethical philosophy, through which he hoped to reconstruct society morally. To Laozi, however, no such reconstruction seemed possible. Instead, legend says that he gave up his court position and headed west, riding atop a water buffalo, in search of a better kingdom. He rode through the desert regions of the state of Qin (Ch'in) and crossed the central plains to the Hangu Pass, at the border separating China from the outside world. There, the border guard Yin Xi (Yin Hsi) stopped him.

Aware of Laozi's fame, Yin Xi begged the elderly philosopher to write down his wisdom before leaving his native country. This Laozi did over the course of several days, creating a work of five thousand Chinese characters, divided into eighty-one chapters. This work was what would become known as the Dao De Jing. After completing the book, Laozi reportedly left China and was never heard from again. While Sima Qian never suggested Laozi had divine powers, he recorded the philosopher's life span as between 160 and 200 years. Sima Qian claimed Laozi's extremely long life was a result of his beliefs and meditation practices.

Some historians believe that the mythical person of Laozi is actually three historical figures combined into one. The first of these is Sima Qian's Li Er. The second is someone with a similar name, Lao Laizi (Lao Lai-tzu), also born in Chu. Little is known about this man except that he was about the same age as Confucius and is said to be the author of a book on Daoist teachings. The third person was born more than a century after the death of Confucius. A historian of the Zhou, he went by the name of Dan (Tan).

The Dao De Jing

The Dao De Jing is the primary Daoist text. The earliest discovered copies, which were written on bamboo strips, date to about 300 BCE. It is one of the most often translated books in world literature and also one of the most confusing. According to tradition, the book was composed by Laozi some time in the sixth century BCE, as he was about to leave China forever. Research has shown, however, that the work was probably not that of one person but of many. Literary scholars have observed that a book authored by one person can be expected to show a consistent style of writing, but many different styles exist in the Dao De Jing. In addition, the sayings gathered within do not necessarily reflect the historical period of the sixth century BCE.

Scholars maintain several different opinions on the date and authorship of the Dao De Jing, ranging from the third century BCE to the fifth or sixth century BCE. Most scholars, however, agree that the text was put together by several people.

The Dao De Jing is divided into two parts. Chapters one through thirty-seven deal with the Dao, while chapters thirty-eight through eighty-one deal with de, or "virtue." The work is difficult to understand partly because of the dual meanings of many of its key concepts and terms. For example, the title itself is one problem. *Dao* means "path," or "way," but the Dao is also the essential and unnamable process of the universe. *De* can mean "virtue" or "righteousness," but it can also refer to "power." *Jing,* at least simply means "doctrine," "book," "scripture," or "classic."

There are more than one hundred translations of the work in English alone. The book is short. Each chapter is about eight to twenty lines that are written like prose but are closer to poetry. Beyond the Dao, the text deals with the concepts of nothingness; eternal return, or the cycle of nature; and detachment, or being reserved and not overly involved in trying to control life. The text also focuses on *yin,* or passive energy, often using water metaphors to show the adaptability and enduring strength of the Dao. Self-knowledge is another common theme.

Laozi's teachings

The term *dao* had been used for the way of thinking taught by many schools in Chinese tradition before Laozi. In those cases the word simply referred to their doctrine, or way of teaching. In the Dao De Jing, an attempt was made to give greater meaning to the word. In the text, the Dao, or Way, is said to have several levels. At the highest level it is the invisible force behind all creation. This constant force is the beginning and end of everything. The Dao creates everything, and everything returns to the Dao in an eternal cycle.

On another level is the Dao of nature, the rhythm of the natural world and the universe. A third level is how the Dao exists in each individual and how one's internal energy, or *qi (ch'i)*, is kept in balance. Laozi, as well as many earlier Chinese thinkers, noted the power between opposites and the need to balance the active male energy, or *yang,* with the inactive female energy, or *yin.* To Laozi, becoming one with the Dao was the mark of an enlightened person.

For Laozi, another major principle in Daoism is the concept of *de,* which translates as "virtue," or sometimes as "power." Several chapters in the Dao De Jing are devoted to explaining how de, specifically virtuous behavior and intelligent action, are significant in one's life. An important Daoist concept regarding personal behavior is that of *wu wei,* which can be translated as "inaction" or even "actionless action." Wu wei says that action should be taken at the proper time and for the proper reasons, and should be effortless.

Three types of virtue are associated with the concept of *de:* compassion, moderation, and humility. By practicing these three virtues, a person can grow closer to becoming one with the Dao, from which all people came and to which all will return. Simplicity and spontaneity (impulsiveness; acting without thought) are essential beliefs of the Daoist system. Following all of these principles leads to living in harmony with the Dao. Over time, the philosophy of Daoism, or Dao *jia* (*chia*), evolved into Dao *jiao* (*chiao*), a religion associated with many divine beings and immortals.

For More Information

BOOKS

Boltz, Judith Magee. "Laozi." In *Encyclopedia of Religion.* 2nd ed. Edited by Lindsay Jones. Detroit, MI: Macmillan Reference USA, 2005, 5315–20.

Chan, Wing-Tsit. *The Way of Lao-Tzu.* Indianapolis, IN: Bobbs-Merrill, 1963.

Cleary, Thomas F. *The Essential Tao: An Initiation into the Heart of Taoism through the Authentic Tao Te Ching and the Inner Teachings of Chuang Tzu.* San Francisco, CA: HarperSanFrancisco, 1991.

Kaltenmark, Max. *Lao-Tzu and Taoism.* Stanford, CA: Stanford University Press, 1969.

Laozi. *Tao Te Ching: A New English Version.* Edited and translated by Stephen Mitchell. New York, NY: HarperCollins, 1988.

Oldstone-Moore, Jennifer. *Taoism: Origins, Beliefs, Practices, Holy Texts, Sacred Places.* New York, NY: Oxford University Press, 2003.

Smith, Huston. "Taoism." In *The Religions of Man.* New York, NY: Harper/Colophon Books, 1958, 175–92.

Waley, Arthur. *The Way and Its Power: A Study of the Tao Te Ching and Its Place in Chinese Thought.* New York, NY: Grove Press, 1958.

WEB SITES

Chan, Alan. "Laozi." *Stanford Encyclopedia of Philosophy.* http://plato.stanford.edu/entries/laozi/ (accessed on June 5, 2006).

"The Tao-Te Ching and Lao-tzu." *Overview of World Religions.* http://philtar.ucsm.ac.uk/encyclopedia/taoism/laotzu.html (accessed on June 5, 2006).

Nechama Leibowitz

BORN: September 3, 1905 • Riga, Latvia
DIED: April 12, 1997 • Jerusalem, Israel

Latvian Bible scholar

"The light that had become reduced to nothing more than a tiny dot in a world of darkness now shines brighter and brighter. . . . Now we are shown a tranquil world adorned with the rainbow . . . as a sign of surety of life and peace for the coming generations."

N echama Leibowitz was a noted biblical scholar, teacher, and radio commentator in Israel. She was a professor at Tel Aviv University and wrote many books on Judaism, the religion of the Jewish people. She was best known for her weekly lessons on the Torah (the first five books of the Bible) and for her efforts to educate Jews about their religion. She created *gilyonot,* or study pages, with information about the faith that were printed and mailed to thousands of students of Judaism around the world. In 1956 she was awarded the Israel Prize for Education and is recognized as one of the leading Torah teachers of the twentieth century. The Torah refers to the first five books of the Tanakh, also known as the Hebrew Bible, the sacred text of Judaism. To Christians, the Tanakh is known as the Old Testament.

From Latvia to Israel

Leibowitz was born in 1905 in Riga, Latvia, a country in north-central Europe. Her family was Orthodox Jewish, the branch of Judaism that holds to the faith's traditional practices. Orthodox Judaism includes a devotion to and study of the Torah, dietary rules such as avoiding pork, and daily attendance at the synagogue, the Jewish house of

Nechama Leibowitz

Nechama Leibowitz was best known for her teachings on the Torah, the first five books of the Bible. She sought to educate Jews about their religion. © ROSE HARTMAN/ CORBIS.

worship. Nechama was the younger sister of the well-known philosopher Yeshayahu Leibowitz (1903–1994). A philosopher is someone who studies art, science, and other subjects in an effort to gain greater understanding on the workings of the world. The family left Latvia in 1919 and settled in Berlin, Germany, where Leibowitz studied. She earned a doctorate from the University of Berlin in 1930, after completing her thesis, or long paper, on Bible translations. The Bible contains the Old Testament, a sacred text in the Jewish faith, and the New Testament, which is accepted by the Christian faith alongside the Old Testament.

The political climate in Germany by 1930 was not favorable to Jews. The Nazis, members of the National Socialist Workers Party led by Adolf Hitler (1889–1949), were blaming Jews for many of the country's problems. Anti-Semitism, or discrimination against Jews, was becoming more and more common. As a result, after she earned her doctorate Leibowitz immigrated to Palestine, which was then under British control. Palestine is considered by many Jews to be their ancestral homeland. There she lectured for twenty-five years at a school that trained religious teachers. Her subject was the methodology (techniques) of teaching the Hebrew language and the Hebrew Bible.

212

Begins her weekly lessons

Leibowitz also began to give lessons outside the school on various topics in the Bible. In 1942 she was asked to teach a group of women from a *kibbutz*, an agricultural collective or commune, who were on a break for educational purposes. She agreed to lead the six-month class. When it was over, the women were so interested in their studies that they asked Leibowitz if they could continue the class by mail. She began sending them weekly lessons, questions that required the women to examine and analyze parts of the Bible. Then she received their answers back by return mail, corrected and graded them, and sent them back to the kibbutz. She called these lessons simply *gilyonot,* or "pages." Soon others began requesting these weekly lessons. In 1943 there were fifty people taking part in the mailings. The next year the list grew to three hundred, and still Leibowitz was personally preparing the weekly worksheets, copying them, mailing them, and then correcting each one.

In 1954 Leibowitz began publishing her "Studies" series, which included many of the questions from her weekly lessons. In 1971 she stopped writing new material but continued to correspond with those who wrote to her with their own religious study. A wide variety of people took part in these lessons, which were translated into many different languages and sent to countries around the world. Before finally giving up the weekly lessons in 1992, Leibowitz estimated that she had corrected approximately forty thousand such lessons, and that some of her students had been with her for more than thirty years.

An example of one of her gilyonot concerns the first book of the Torah, called Bereshit. Discussing the great flood that God sent to Earth, and which Noah survived by building an ark and populating it with one of each gender of animal and man, Liebowitz provides commentary and interpretation. She draws attention to the symbolism within the story, from the darkness of the rains that killied all except those in the ark with Noah, to the renewal of life that occurs once the rains stop. She explains that the flood washed away the sins of man, such as the decline in moral behavior and the increasing glorification of things such as warfare and other violence. The Jewish Agency for Israel has reproduced her lessons online, where she says:

> The light that had become reduced to nothing more than a tiny dot in a world of darkness now shines brighter and brighter, till it once again illuminates the whole of our canvas. Now we are

The First Female Rabbi

The first woman to be ordained, or officially made, a *rabbi* (the chief official in a synagogue) was Regina Jonas (1902–1944). Jonas, unlike Nechama Leibowitz, was almost a forgotten figure in twentieth-century Judaism. She was a victim of the Holocaust, the mass murder of the Jews by the Nazis during World War II (1939–45; a war in which Great Britain, France, the United States, and their allies defeated Germany, Italy, and Japan), and died in the Auschwitz concentration camp. Concentration camps were camps where Jews and others were imprisoned. Millions of these prisoners were either killed or died of disease and lack of food. After the fall of the German Democratic Republic (East Germany) in 1989, secret state archives were opened and new information was discovered about this first female rabbi.

Jonas was born in Berlin in 1902, and after her school years she taught for a time. She then attended the Higher Institute for Jewish Studies in Berlin and graduated in 1930. She took further classes at a seminary, a college for those going into religious professions. Eventually she decided that she wanted to become a rabbi, but no woman had ever done this before. She went through all the course work necessary to become a rabbi and wrote the thesis, or long research paper, necessary to earn her degree. Her thesis topic was whether a woman could become a

rabbi according to the Talmud, the collection of Jewish law and traditions.

She concluded that, according to Jewish law, a woman could become a rabbi. At first, however, she could find no Jewish scholars or rabbis who would ordain her and officially give her this title. Many were afraid of the negative reactions of more conservative Orthodox Jews. Finally she found a rabbi who ordained her in 1935, but Jonas could still find no synagogue where she could function as its rabbi. Instead she worked as a chaplain, or religious counselor, for Jewish social clubs and institutions.

As World War II approached and persecution (mistreatment and harassment) of the Jews worsened, many rabbis left Germany. Jonas decided to stay and, because of the lack of male rabbis, was finally able to preach in a synagogue. In 1942 she was sent by the Nazis to the Theresienstadt concentration camp, and in 1944 she was transferred to Auschwitz, where she was killed in the gas chambers. Jonas left behind several lectures on the history of Jewish women and other subjects. It was not until 1972 that less traditional Jewish groups in the United States again began to ordain female rabbis. The first female rabbi since Jonas to be ordained in Germany was in 1995.

shown a tranquil world adorned with the rainbow, reflecting its spectrum of colour through the clouds, as a sign of surety of life and peace for the coming generations.

The state of Israel had been created in 1948 out of much of the land that was Palestine. Leibowitz became a regular commentator on the Voice of Israel radio station, and in 1956 she won the Israel Prize for her efforts in religious education. The following year she began lecturing at the University of Tel Aviv, and in 1968 she was made a full professor there. Yet she always preferred the more humble title, *morah,* or "teacher."

Methodology

Leibowitz claimed there were several goals to achieve when studying religion. She believed that first, and least important, was to gain knowledge of the facts. Next was the development of independent learning skills. Most important to Leibowitz were a love of learning and a love of the Bible. In order to reach these goals, Leibowitz proposed a method called active learning. In this kind of teaching there is no formal lecture and no introduction to the material to be studied. Leibowitz thought teachers should not ask questions to which there are obvious answers that can be memorized. She further believed teachers should avoid lessons that are always organized in the same way. She claimed both of these methods only lead to students learning by rote, or by memory, and not really thinking for themselves. Instead, she said students should be encouraged to think independently and actually analyze the material they are studying rather than merely memorizing it. Finally Leibowitz believed the teacher should be a role model and should display the sort of love of learning that he or she wants to instill or place in his or her students.

Leibowitz used this active learning method in her gilyonot and in the courses she taught at the university. She helped produce a new generation of religious scholars and gave a deeper understanding of the religious works of Judaism to all levels of Israeli society. When she died in Jerusalem in 1997, she was buried with a tombstone that read simply "Nechama Leibowitz 'Morah.'" As Moshe Sokolow noted on the Web site *Remembering Nehama Leibowitz,* "Nehama Leibowitz did not open new windows on the Torah; she simply polished the glass so we could all see inside much more clearly."

For More Information

BOOKS

Abramowitz, Leah. *Tales of Nehama: Impressions of the Life and Teaching of Nehama Leibowitz.* New York, NY: Gefen Publishing House, 2003.

Peerless, Shmuel. *To Study and to Teach: The Methodology of Nechama Leibowitz.* Jerusalem, Israel: Urim Publications, 2005.

PERIODICALS

Bonchek, Avigdor. "Professor Nechama: Teacher of Israel." *Jewish Action* (fall 1993). Also available online at http://www.ou.org/yerushalayim/lezikaronolam/nehama/ja93.html.

"In Remembrance: Nechama Leibowitz z'tl (1902–1997)." *Jewish Action* (summer 1997). Also available online at http://www.ou.org/yerushalayim/lezikaronolam/nehama/ja97.htm.

Sokolow, Moshe. "Nehama Leibowitz: The "Compleat" Didact. *Jerusalem Report* (May 15, 1997). Also available online at http://www.ou.org/yerushalayim/lezikaronolam/nehama/rememberingnehama.html.

WEB SITES

Leibowitz, Nechama. "Lesson of The Flood." *The Jewish Agency for Israel.* Department for Jewish Zionist Education. http://www.jafi.org.il/education/torani/NEHAMA/indexgil.html (June 5, 2006).

"Leibowitz, Nechama (1905–1997): Bible Scholar, Commentator, and Teacher." *Jewish Agency for Israel.* http://www.jafi.org.il/education/100/people/BIOS/nleib.html/ (accessed on June 5, 2006).

"Nechama Leibowitz (1905–1997)." Jewish Virtual Library. http://www.jewishvirtuallibrary.org/jsource/biography/nleib.html (accessed on June 5, 2006).

"Nechama Leibowitz." *Torah Community Connections.* http://www.moreshet.net/oldsite/nechama/gilayonarchives.htm/ (accessed on June 5, 2006).

"Nechama Leibowitz's Methodology: An Overview." *Lookstein Center for Jewish Education in the Diaspora.* http://www.lookstein.org/nechama_methodology.htm (accessed on June 5, 2006).

Sokolow, Moshe. "The Korban Pesha: Prerequisite to Geulah: A Shiur in Memory of Nehama Leibowitz" *Orthodox Union.* http://www.ou.org/yerushalayim/lezikaronolam/nehama/pesach58.html (accessed on June 5, 2006).

Ignatius of Loyola

BORN: December 24, 1491 • Azpeitia,
Guipuzcoa, Spain

DIED: July 31, 1556 • Rome, Italy

Spanish religious leader; soldier

"For the greater glory of God."

I gnatius of Loyola was a Spanish nobleman who began a career as a military man. After he was wounded in battle, he converted to Catholicism, a branch of Christianity, and became a "soldier" for the pope, the leader of the Catholic Church. The wars he then fought were not on the battlefield but against the Protestant Reformation, a sixteenth century religious movement that began as an attempt to reform the Roman Catholic Church and resulted in the creation of Protestant churches. He argued that the only way to salvation, or life after death, was through total obedience to the church. He established the Society of Jesus, also known as the Jesuit order, in 1534. His book, *Spiritual Exercises,* served as a guide for leading a Jesuit life in particular and a Christian one in general. For his service to the church, he was declared a saint after his death and is often called St. Ignatius of Loyola.

From soldier to religious convert

Ignatius of Loyola.
NEW YORK PUBLIC LIBRARY
PICTURE COLLECTION.

Ignatius of Loyola was born in 1491, in the family castle near the small village of Azpeitia in northern Spain. He was the youngest of thirteen

217

children, and his name at birth was Iñigo. His father was a soldier. His mother died when he was still a baby. As his father was frequently absent on military campaigns, young Ignatius was often cared for by a neighbor woman who impressed on him the basic qualities of faith and loyalty. As a child Ignatius wanted to be a military man like his father, but the large family lacked the necessary resources to allow him to receive good training. Instead, when he was sixteen, Ignatius was sent to serve at the residence of the treasurer of the kingdom of Castile. This man, Juan Velasquez, was a friend of Ignatius father and promised to help the youth find a career.

The journey from Ignatius's home to the Velasquez household was a hard one. Ignatius covered the 400 miles (644 kilometers) on the back of a mule. Once he arrived, he was educated in the dress and ceremonies of the Spanish court. He learned how to use a sword and how to dance and play cards. Gambling, in fact, became a favorite pastime for the young man. He enjoyed fine clothes and riding expensive horses.

After the death of his sponsor, Velasquez, in 1517, Ignatius joined the Spanish army. The Duke of Najera (Najera is a province of Spain), took the young man on as his personal aide, although Ignatius had never had any formal military training. When war broke out with France in 1520 over a territory in the north of Spain that France had claimed, Ignatius had to learn his new trade quickly. In 1521, at the age of thirty, he was an officer helping to defend the town of Pamplona in northern Spain against the French. The Spaniards were outnumbered and wanted to surrender, but Ignatius talked them into continuing the fight for the glory of their country. During the battle a French cannonball passed through his legs, smashing his right shin and tearing the flesh off his left leg. The town fell to the French, but Ignatius was treated with respect. The French did as much as they could to set his broken bones, and he was sent home to recover.

Back at his family's castle, Ignatius began a long healing process. His injuries had been so serious that his bones needed to be rebroken and set twice. He almost died in the process. To pass the time while waiting for his legs to mend, he read. The only books available to him were religious ones that dealt with **Jesus Christ** (c. 6 BCE–c. 30 CE; see entry) and various saints. These books, *The Life of Christ* and *The Flower of the Saints,* provided him with a new set of goals. He was inspired by the lives of the men in these books, men who had sought to improve the world. For the next five months, Ignatius read these books many times. By the time his injuries had healed, he had determined to give up soldiering and to devote his life to God.

Years of wandering

By March 1522 Ignatius had recovered enough to leave the family castle and set out on a religious journey that would last the rest of his life. He first went to a monastery, or religious center for study, at Montserrat, Spain, where he placed his military armor and sword in front of an image of the Virgin Mary, the mother of Jesus Christ. Thereafter he dressed in sandals and a rough cloth shirt or robe. He spent several months living in a cave near the town of Manresa, Spain, practicing what is known as religious asceticism. Ascetics lead a simple life of prayer, frequently fast (go without food), and devote all of their time to religious matters. During this time Ignatius began to write his *Spiritual Exercises*. These writings ultimately took the form of a guide to a thirty-day program of prayer and focus on God that is still used by the Jesuit order in the early twenty-first century. Ignatius was often invited to the homes of other noblemen, for even though he had given away all of his possessions to follow the path of God, the nobles still considered him to be one of their own. He gave religious lessons to some of these nobles but would always sleep in their barns or in the houses of poor people.

At the beginning of his religious journey, Ignatius of Loyola gave up his military armor and sword in front of a statue of the Virgin Mary like the one pictured here. This signaled his new devotion to God. PUBLIC DOMAIN.

After many months of traveling Ignatius decided to go to the Holy Land of Jerusalem, where Christ had lived and was crucified (killed by being nailed to a cross). Once he made his way on foot to Barcelona, Spain, he was able to board a ship bound for Italy and Jerusalem, despite the fact that he had no money. Ignatius had become like a wandering holy person, and people often gave him food and tried to help him. He did not stay long in Jerusalem, as the city and region were under the control of Muslims, followers of the religion of Islam. Ignatius was supposedly given a sign that he was on a divine mission when he attempted to return to Italy and was refused passage on two ships. These ships later sank in a storm. A third ship finally took him back to Venice, Italy.

Ignatius, now thirty-three years old, decided that he wanted to study to become a priest in the Catholic Church. In order to do that, he first had to learn Latin, the language used by educated people of the time. He went back to Barcelona and studied Latin while begging for food and shelter. He also gathered crowds to discuss religious matters and to teach them how to pray with feeling. This was during the Protestant Reformation, however, a period when followers of a reform movement that started in Germany were attempting to change some practices of the Catholic Church. The movement sought to put more power into the hands of the individual believer rather than in the officers of the church headquartered in Rome. Therefore, any sort of outside religious teaching that took place alarmed the church leaders. The Inquisition, an office set up by the Catholic Church to punish those going against its teachings, arrested Ignatius and sent him to prison for six weeks. When he was released, he was told not to teach until he became a priest. He moved on to Salamanca, Spain, where again he was thrown into prison for teaching. He did not try to defend himself when he was arrested and never complained. In fact, on one occasion, all the other prisoners broke out of prison, but Ignatius stayed behind.

In 1528 Ignatius moved on to Paris, France, and began to study for the priesthood. He remained in Paris for seven years. In addition to taking classes, he tried to teach other students his *Spiritual Exercises*. His roommates, Francis Xavier and Peter Faber, became close friends of his and his first converts. He began teaching these two his system of prayer and soon gathered six close followers around him. These young men all gave away their possessions as Ignatius had and begged for their food and lodging. Together they founded the Society of Jesus, or the Jesuit order, on August 15, 1534. The goal of the order was to serve in hospitals or as missionaries (people who try to convert nonbelievers) or to do whatever the pope in Rome might ask of them.

Ignatius's years of asceticism, however, had ruined his health. He went back to his home in Spain to recover, making the difficult journey by donkey. At Azpeitia he stayed at a poorhouse rather than at his family's castle. His health soon improved slightly, although he was never completely healthy again. By 1535 he was attracting large crowds to his teachings on the Bible (the sacred text of Christianity) and his *Spiritual Exercises*. Soon after, he left Spain and met up with his fellow Jesuits in Italy.

Although the Jesuits had gathered in Italy in preparation for a trip to Jerusalem, wars in the region prevented the group from traveling there. They remained in Italy doing charitable work and preaching. At this point he changed his given name, Iñigo, to Ignatius, after Saint Ignatius of Antioch (50– c. 107), who gave his life for his faith.

In 1537 Pope Paul III (1468–1549) heard of the Jesuits and gave his spoken approval to their mission. After reading Ignatius's *Spiritual Exercises,* the pope was convinced that the Jesuits could be helpful in combating the Reformation. For example, one section of the *Spiritual Exercises* is a list of rules that Jesuits must follow. As quoted on the Web site *Medieval Sourcebook* of Fordham University, rule thirteen states in part, "To be right in everything, we ought always to hold that the white which I see, is black, if the . . . Church decides it." This encouragement of such absolute obedience to the Catholic Church was appealing to the pope.

Head of the Jesuits

Ignatius presented a constitution, or basic set of rules, for his new religious order to the pope in 1538. In 1540 the new order was accepted as a legitimate Catholic group, and Ignatius was elected as its first Superior General or Father General. He then sent his followers throughout Europe and other regions to find new recruits, work in hospitals, and train the local people in correct religious practices, as laid out in the *Spiritual Exercises.* The motto of the Jesuits became "for the greater glory of God."

The Jesuits are somewhat different than other Catholic religious orders such as the Benedictines, Franciscans, or Dominicans. They demonstrate unquestioning loyalty to the pope and vow to take on any job he asks of them. This was particularly important during the years of what became known as the Counter-Reformation, or the reform movement that grew within the Catholic Church in an attempt to counteract the Reformation. The Jesuits also pledge to serve in the world, instead of living away from society, such as in monasteries, to concentrate on prayer.

Becoming a Saint

In Christianity a saint is someone who is judged to be particularly holy and worthy. Many of the early saints, such as Saint Ignatius of Antioch, were martyrs, or people who gave their lives for their faith. Other saints, such as Loyola, were people who were strong supporters of the religion. The word *saint* comes from the Latin *sanctus,* meaning "holy."

People become saints through a long and complex process called canonization. First, at least five years must pass from the time of a person's death until the beginning of the proceedings. Then witnesses are called to show that the person in question displayed heroic Christian virtues, such as faith, hope, and charity, and values, such as a sense of justice and caution. After this step the person is called a Servant of God. Next the person must be beatified, or blessed. For this to happen, it must be shown that the Servant of God performed a miracle *after* his or her death. Then the Servant of God takes on a new title, the Blessed. To be fully canonized a second miracle must occur after the beatification. Then the Blessed officially becomes a saint.

Ignatius eventually had to devote himself full time to directing his growing Society of Jesus as its missionaries were sent around the world. He made his home in Rome, where he wrote thousands of letters on behalf of the organization during the next fifteen years. He opened schools in Italy, Portugal, the Netherlands, Spain, Germany, and India. These schools, however, were intended primarily for the education of new Jesuits that might be recruited in those countries, as Ignatius never thought of his society as a teaching order. Despite this, rulers and church officials throughout Europe were soon asking for Jesuit schools in their areas in order to teach what they considered the proper principles of Christianity. This led to the Jesuits gaining a reputation as educators in Catholicism.

Ignatius worked twenty hours a day despite his constant ill health. Ever since his school days in Paris he had suffered from stomach pains and fever. (After his death a surgeon would discover this was caused by buildups of minerals, called stones, in his kidneys and other organs.) In the summer of 1556 his usual poor health grew even worse, and on July 31 of that year he died. His legacy has lived on in the Society of Jesus, still one of the strongest orders in the Catholic Church in the early twenty-first century. In 1609 he was beatified, or declared blessed, and in 1622 he was canonized, or made a saint. The former soldier found his place not at the front of an army but in the records of church history.

For More Information

BOOKS

Brodick, James. *Saint Ignatius Loyola: The Pilgrim Years.* New York, NY: Farrar, Straus, 1956.

Caraman, Philip. *Ignatius Loyola: A Biography of the Founder of the Jesuits.* San Francisco, CA: Harper & Row, 1990.

Janda, J. *Iñigo: The Life of St. Ignatius Loyola for Young Readers.* Mahwah, NJ: Paulist Press, 1994.

Loyola, Ignatius. *A Pilgrim's Journey: The Autobiography of St. Ignatius of Loyola.* Ft. Collins, CO: Ignatius Press, 2001.

Sklar, Peggy A., and Patrick Kelley. *St. Ignatius of Loyola: In God's Service.* Mahwah, NJ: Paulist Press, 2001.

WEB SITES

"Life of St. Ignatius Loyola." *Loyola University of Chicago Web site.* http://www.luc.edu/jesuit/ignatius.bio.html (accessed on June 5, 2006).

Loyola, St. Ignatius. "St. Ignatius Loyola: Spiritual Exercises." *Medieval Sourcebook.* http://www.fordham.edu/halsall/source/loyola-spirex.html (accessed on June 5, 2006).

O'Neal, Norman, S. J. *The Life of St. Ignatius of Loyola.* http://www.stignatiussf.org/himself.htm/ (accessed on June 5, 2006).

Pollen, J. H. "St. Ignatius Loyola." *Catholic Encyclopedia Online.* http://www.newadvent.org/cathen/07639c.htm (accessed on June 5, 2006).

World of Ignatius of Loyola. http://www.ignatiushistory.info/ (accessed on June 5, 2006).

Martin Luther

BORN: November 10, 1483 • Eisleben, Saxony-Anhalt, Germany

DIED: February 18, 1546 • Eisleben, Saxony-Anhalt, Germany

German theologian; monk; religious reformer

"My conscience is captive to the Word of God. I cannot and will not recant anything, for to go against conscience is neither right nor safe."

Martin Luther was a Catholic monk whose teachings helped inspire and define the Protestant Reformation in sixteenth-century Europe. The movement he sparked brought huge political and religious changes to the continent and made him an important figure in Western history. Those who knew him personally, however, regarded him as a thoroughly unlikable person. He was rude, self-important, insulting to opponents, and given to horrible outbreaks of temper. Many of his students found him amusing, as he punctuated classroom lectures with jokes and gross bodily noises. Members of the Lutheran Church throughout the world honor his memory and respect his teachings, but few, perhaps, would have wanted him as a houseguest.

A change of course

Martin Luther.

© DAVE BARTUFF/CORBIS.

Martin Luther was born in the town of Eisleben, Germany, on November 10, 1483. At the time Germany was a loose collection of independent

225

states, each ruled by a noble. Shortly after Luther's birth, his father, Hans, moved the family to Mansfeld and took up the copper trade. Hans and his wife, Margaretha, wanted Martin to succeed in the civil service, so they sent him to schools in Mansfeld, Magdeburg, and Eisenach. In 1501 Luther entered the University of Erfurt, where he completed a bachelor's degree in 1502 and a master's degree in 1505. He then enrolled in the university's college of law.

On July 2, 1505, Luther's well-ordered life changed suddenly. According to legend, he was returning to school from a visit home when a storm struck and he was knocked off his horse by a lightning bolt. Grateful that his life had been spared, he cried out, "Help, Saint Anne! I'll become a monk." To the great anger and disappointment of his parents, Luther then entered the Erfurt monastery of the Augustinian monks, an order founded in 1256 and formally referred to as the Hermits of Saint Augustine. A monastery is a place set away from the distractions of the world where one goes to focus on spiritual pursuits.

When Luther became a student at the monastery, his good-humored nature began to change as he searched for an understanding of God. He devoted himself to fasting (going without food), prayers, the confessions of his sins, pilgrimages, and self-flagellation, or whipping himself as punishment. His superior decided that his excessive devoutness was a product of having too little to occupy his mind, so Luther was ordered to pursue an academic career. After being ordained (invested with the authority of) a Catholic priest in 1507, Luther earned bachelor's degrees in theology in 1508 and 1509 and a doctorate in theology in 1512. (Theology is the study of religion.) Shortly after completing his doctorate, he joined the faculty at Wittenberg University. In addition to teaching theology he served as a parish priest at the Castle Church in Wittenberg.

Controversy

Over the next five years Luther grew to believe that the Catholic Church had become dishonest and overly involved with worldly, rather than spiritual, matters. He also believed that it had gone astray on a number of basic theological principles. The chief point of the church's theology that Luther disagreed with was how people achieved salvation, or life after death, in heaven. The Catholic Church taught that a person could earn a place in heaven in part through good works, but Luther believed that this was untrue. Based on his reading of the Bible, the sacred book of Christianity, he emphasized justification by grace through faith, often phrased more simply as justification through faith. This doctrine, or principle, says that salvation is an unconditional gift of God's love and grace that one receives through his son Jesus Christ, and that this gift is based on faith alone. This doctrine became one of the most important of the Protestant Reformation, a movement that saw the rejection of many of the teachings of Catholicism and led to the formation of many different Protestant churches, including the Lutheran Church.

Luther's beliefs regarding indulgences, however, were what attracted the attention of church authorities. According to Catholic theology, when a person confesses a sin to a priest and receives absolution, or forgiveness, from God through the priest, the sin is removed. The person is then in a state of grace and is eventually eligible to enter heaven at death. The Catholic Church, however, teaches that the stain of the sin is not fully removed, even after confession. Rather, after death, a person's soul must spend time in purgatory, a midway dwelling place between Earth and heaven. In purgatory, people are denied the presence of God until they redeem themselves for past sins and become fit to enter heaven. Indulgences, granted by the church, typically in the form of prayers, can shorten the time a person's soul must spend in purgatory. A plenary, or complete, indulgence takes away all of the time a person's soul would have otherwise spent in purgatory.

In Luther's era the practice of granting indulgences was much abused. The Catholic Church often simply sold them, granting letters of indulgence to those who contributed money. One of the worst offenders was a Dominican friar named Johann Tetzel (c. 1465–1519), who traveled around selling indulgences to raise funds for the renovation of Saint Peter's Basilica in Rome, Italy. Tetzel was reported to have often said, "As soon as the coin in the coffer rings, the soul from Purgatory springs." Luther was deeply offended by this practice, as well as by other indications that the church had grown greedy, and preached sermons against it. He feared that Catholics would feel they did not need to confess their sins and ask for God's forgiveness when they could simply buy their way into heaven.

The Ninety-five Theses

In 1517 Luther wrote out a number of statements, called the Ninety-five Theses, about the sale of indulgences and other matters regarding

Religious reformer Martin Luther posting his Ninety-five Theses on the door of All Saints Church in Wittenberg, Germany. This event helped spark the Protestant Reformation. THE GRANGER COLLECTION. REPRODUCED BY PERMISSION.

faith and salvation. According to legend, on October 31 of that year Luther nailed the Ninety-five Theses to the door of the Castle Church, probably hoping to open a public debate on the issue. Many people would later view this dramatic, defiant act as the symbolic start of the Protestant Reformation. Yet most historians say that he did not actually nail the document to the church door, but instead sent it to a small number of bishops. Importantly, none of the Ninety-five Theses questioned the right of the pope (the head of the Roman Catholic Church) to grant indulgences, nor did they in any way question the pope's authority. Soon Luther's work was translated from Latin and distributed throughout Germany and all of Europe, which was made possible by the recent invention of the printing press. The publication of the Ninety-five Theses started a great debate in the Catholic Church.

The pope at the time, Leo X (1475–1521; served 1513–21), thought that Luther was just "a drunken German" and ordered a well-known Italian theologian, Sylvester Mazzolini (1460–1523), to investigate the matter. Mazzolini concluded that Luther's statements were in opposition to the church's doctrine on indulgences, which had been set by Pope Clement VI (1291–1352) in 1343 in a papal bull, or an official letter from the pope. He labeled Luther a heretic, which is a person who disagrees with official church teachings. As a heretic Luther could be excommunicated, or forced to leave the church. The pope demanded that Luther submit to his authority by withdrawing his heretical statements. To that end the pope sent a representative to confront Luther at Augsburg, Germany, in October 1518.

In response to the arrival of the pope's representative, Luther chose to deny the pope's absolute authority over the Catholic Church. Over the next two years, the disagreement grew more intense. In his writings and theological debates, Luther stated that the papacy, or the institution of the pope and his authority, was not a part of the original fundamental makeup of the church. Thus he began to preach what would become another key doctrine of the Protestant Reformation: that the church priesthood was in the hands not of the church hierarchy—the priests, bishops, cardinals, and pope—but of the community of the faithful. In Luther's view, people no longer needed to depend on the church's authority for guidance in spiritual matters. Rather, they could obtain such guidance on their own from sacred scripture, the sole source of revealed truth. Again, the invention of the printing press played a key role. For the first time in history a relatively affordable copy of the Bible was available to nearly all who wanted one.

In 1519 and 1520 Luther's writings continued to be published, and his name became widely known throughout Europe. In various books and sermons he openly questioned a number of basic doctrines of the Catholic Church. He denied that a person needed to be a member of the Roman Catholic Church to achieve salvation. He made a number of changes to the Catholic Church's ritual of baptism (a ritual involving the symbolic use of water that results in a person being admitted to the church community) and the Eucharist, or Holy Communion, in which bread and wine are believed to be transformed into the body and blood of Christ, during a church ceremony known as Mass. In particular he urged that laypersons be allowed to share in the cup of wine rather than just the bread, a practice contrary to that of the Catholic Church.

Laypersons are those who are common worshippers and are not a part of the priesthood. He argued that confirmation (the ritual that follows a baptism, admitting a person to full membership in the church), marriage, holy orders (the ordaining of priests), and extreme unction (the applying of oil or ointment to the dying) were not true religious rites or rituals, seeing them instead as simply extensions of the ritual of baptism because they were continuations of God's grace as bestowed in baptism.

Luther also challenged what he saw as abuses of the church. He wanted the church to reduce the number of cardinals, who were the highest-ranking members of the church other than the pope. He called for reform of the universities and the priestly orders. He believed the church should promote people based on their abilities rather than on their personal connections, only concern itself with spiritual matters, and not excommunicate all those who disagreed with church doctrine. He also called for an end to celibacy, the requirement that priests cannot have sexual intercourse. He called for complete freedom of thought and conscience on the part of Christians. Luther wrote to the pope, "I submit to no laws on interpreting the Word of God."

The Diet of Worms

In 1520 the pope threatened Luther with excommunication unless he recanted, or denied, his views. In response Luther burned the papal bull that contained the warning. On January 3, 1521, the pope finally issued a bull excommunicating Luther.

That same month, Charles V (1500–1588), the emperor of the Holy Roman Empire, a loose grouping of nations of which the German states and cities were a part, assembled the Diet of Worms. A *diet* (pronounced DEET) is an assembly similar to a parliament, while Worms is a small German city on the Rhine River. On April 16 Luther appeared before the diet and was confronted with a table covered with his books and writings. He was asked whether he still believed in the things that they taught. Luther asked for time to consider his answer. When he appeared the next day, he reportedly replied to the diet "Unless I am convicted by Scripture and plain reason—I do not accept the authority of popes and councils, for they have contradicted each other—my conscience is captive to the Word of God. I cannot and will not recant anything, for to go against conscience is neither right nor safe." He then said, "Here I stand. I can do no other. God help me. Amen."

On May 25, 1521, the Diet of Worms issued the Edict of Worms. This edict, or ruling, labeled Luther a heretic and an outlaw. As such, he would have been subject to civil punishments, including imprisonment or even burning at the stake. He had left Worms, however, and taken refuge in the Wartburg Castle at Eisenach, where he lived for the next year under the protection of a German prince. He occupied his time by translating the New Testament, the second half of the Bible, into simple German that ordinary people could understand. This was another step in his efforts to free the faithful from dependence on church authority. He would wander into the nearby town to overhear people talk so that he could capture the words and rhythms of ordinary speech in his translation. Many historians and students of language credit Luther with standardizing the German language through his Bible, which was published in full in 1534.

Luther's later years

During his time in Wartburg Castle, Luther received letters from groups all over Europe asking him to comment on various matters of church doctrine or to lend his support to their own reform movements. Reformism seemed to be spreading rapidly. In many European countries, particularly in Germany, various groups rejected church doctrine and formed new Protestant branches. Luther, however, grew concerned that the revolution he had sparked would grow out of control. He preached to his followers to proceed with more caution, especially after he left Wartburg Castle and took up residence in Wittenburg, Germany.

In the final years of his life, Luther continued to preach and write. He suffered from a number of health problems and became more stubborn, rude, insulting, and bad tempered. The death of one of his daughters in 1542 was a blow from which he never recovered. Some historians believe that his unsettled state of mind is suggested by the titles of some of his late works: *On the Jews and Their Lies* (1543) and *Against the Papacy at Rome Founded by the Devil* (1545).

In January 1546 Luther traveled to his birthplace, Eisleben, to help his family negotiate an agreement with a group of German counts who were attempting to take over the family's copper business. He began complaining of chest pains and died early in the morning on February 18, 1546. On February 22 he was buried at the Castle Church in Wittenberg.

Passages from the Ninety-five Theses

Martin Luther distributed the Ninety-five Theses to start a discussion about the practices of the Catholic Church that he believed went against the faith and how it should be practiced. Among them was an important matter of his day, indulgences. Indulgences were granted by the priesthood to absolve people of their sins. In Luther's day, indulgences had become something that could be bought. Luther felt that if people believed they could buy their way out of sin, they would never repent and gain salvation in heaven. He spoke strongly on the matter in his Ninety-five Theses.

1. Our Lord and Master Jesus Christ, when He said Poenitentiam agite ["Repent,"], willed that the whole life of believers should be repentance.

6. The pope cannot remit any guilt, except by declaring that it has been remitted by God and by assenting to God's remission; though, to be sure, he may grant remission in cases reserved to his judgment. If his right to grant remission in such cases were despised, the guilt would remain entirely unforgiven.

7. God remits guilt to no one whom He does not, at the same time, humble in all things and bring into subjection to His vicar, the priest.

16. Hell, purgatory, and heaven seem to differ as do despair, almost-despair, and the assurance of safety.

21. Therefore those preachers of indulgences are in error, who say that by the pope's indulgences a man is freed from every penalty, and saved;

22. Whereas he remits to souls in purgatory no penalty which, according to the canons, they would have had to pay in this life.

31. Rare as is the man that is truly penitent, so rare is also the man who truly buys indulgences, i.e., such men are most rare.

36. Every truly repentant Christian has a right to full remission of penalty and guilt, even without letters of pardon.

44. Because love grows by works of love, and man becomes better; but by pardons man does not grow better, only more free from penalty.

45. Christians are to be taught that he who sees a man in need, and passes him by, and gives [his money] for pardons, purchases not the indulgences of the pope, but the indignation of God.

52. The assurance of salvation by letters of pardon is vain, even though the commissary, nay, even though the pope himself, were to stake his soul upon it.

94. Christians are to be exhorted that they be diligent in following Christ, their Head, through penalties, deaths, and hell;

95. And thus be confident of entering into heaven rather through many tribulations, than through the assurance of peace.

Luther, Martin. "Disputation of Doctor Martin Luther on the Power and Efficacy of Indulgences." *Internet Christian Library.* http://www.iclnet.org/pub/resources/text/wittenberg/luther/web/ninetyfive.html.

Luther's influences

Luther's conflicts with the Catholic Church helped inspire the Peasants' War of 1524–25. Throughout Luther's lifetime, Europe was in a state of unrest. European peasants had been revolting against their masters since at least the fourteenth century. They saw Luther's attack on the church as an attack on the social order that oppressed, or mistreated, them as well. They believed that if they rebelled, Protestant reformers such as Luther would support them. The peasants were also aided by poor nobles who had no way to repay the debts that they owed to the Catholic Church.

Luther supported the peasants until the revolts turned into a bloody war. Many of Luther's critics blamed him for the uprisings. As a result he felt increasing pressure to criticize the peasants, which he did in 1525 in *Against the Murderous, Thieving Hordes of Peasants*. He was motivated in part by his desire to support the German nobility who, like him, resisted the authority of the pope and had offered him protection. The revolt was put down in 1525, though parties of peasants continued to loot churches, kidnap church officials, and commit other criminal acts.

The Peasants' War was only the beginning of a long conflict. For centuries after the Protestant Reformation, Catholicism and Protestantism would battle with each other. Violence broke out in 1606 when Catholics and Protestants clashed in the German city of Donauwörth. Elsewhere, most of the European nations—many of them, such as Spain and Italy, still Catholic—eyed the growing influence of Protestant Germans with fear and distrust. In 1618 these tensions led to the outbreak of the Thirty Years' War. The war involved most of Europe and led to the deaths of nearly one-third of the German population.

These kinds of clashes continued to occur. In England a seventeenth-century uprising ended when the Catholic king, Charles I, was beheaded by Protestant revolutionaries in 1649. Later, in 1688, the Catholic James II fled England into exile and was replaced by King William and Queen Mary, both Protestants. Catholics in England were not allowed to hold public office or attend universities until the nineteenth century. Similar anti-Catholic prejudice was common in the largely Protestant United States throughout the nineteenth century and much of the twentieth. Even in the early twenty-first century, Catholics and Protestants in Northern Ireland continued to attack one another in bombings and assassinations.

Despite the bloodshed, conflict, and prejudice that took place during the Protestant Reformation, historians agree that the revolution launched by Luther and others contributed significantly to the development of Europe. The continent's nations were freed from the iron grip that the Catholic Church had on most aspects of life, including government, education, scientific research, and the publication of books. The emphasis on personal belief rather than church authority gave rise to a renewed interest in learning. In turn, this new interest contributed to the rapid intellectual, social, and artistic advancement of Europe.

For More Information

BOOKS

Bainton, Roland H. "The Gospel," *Here I Stand: a Life of Martin Luther*. New York: New American Library, 1950.

Luther, Martin. *On the Jews and Their Lies (1543)*. Translated by Martin H. Bertram. *Luther's Works* Volume 47: The Christian in Society IV. Philadelphia: Fortress Press, 1971.

Marty, Martin E. *Martin Luther*. New York, NY: Viking Penguin, 2004.

Nichols, Stephen J. *Martin Luther: A Guided Tour of His Life and Thought*. Phillipsburg, NJ: P&R Publishing, 2003.

WEB SITES

Luther, Martin. "Disputation of Doctor Martin Luther on the Power and Efficacy of Indulgences." *Internet Christian Library*. http://www.iclnet.org/pub/resources/text/wittenberg/luther/web/ninetyfive.html (accessed June 5, 2006).

Whitford, David M. "Martin Luther (1483–1546)." *The Internet Encyclopedia of Philosophy*. http://www.iep.utm.edu/l/luther.htm (accessed on June 5, 2006).

Madhva

BORN: c. 1199 • Pajakaksetra, Karnataka, India
DIED: c. 1276

Indian religious leader

"There is one God, the embodiment of positive Divinity. . . .
You can address Him by any name."

Sri Madhvacharya was born with the name Vasudeva. He eventually took the name Madhva and later became known as Madhvacharya, one of the great *acharyas,* or revered teachers, of Hinduism. During the thirteenth century he founded a sect (religious division) of Hinduism called Madhvism, whose followers are known as Sad-Vaisnavas. This sect was still in existence in the early twenty-first century, centered at a monastery at Udupi, India, as well as at two other Indian monasteries in Madhyatala and Subrahmanya, near Mangalore.

Birth and early life

Scholars disagree about the date of Vasudeva's birth, with some placing it as early as 1197 or 1199, and others claiming it was as late as 1238. He was born in a village called Pajakaksetra, near the town of Udupi, in the Karnataka region of southwest India. His father was named Madhyageha Bhatta, and his mother was named Vedavati.

Madvha was considered to be an incarnation, or living form, of the son of the god Krishna. This 108-foot tall statue of Krishna is similar to the one Madvha installed at the temple in Udupi, India. © BALDEV/ CORBIS.

As a child Vasudeva had many talents. He had a good memory and was able to learn his lessons quickly. He was also a powerful athlete and spent much of his time swimming, weight lifting, running, hiking, and wrestling. He had a pleasing voice, and many people enjoyed listening to him give religious discourses at the local temple. Some legends also attribute miraculous powers to him. One account claims he quieted the waves of the ocean so that he could bathe in peace.

Vasudeva showed interest in spiritual matters from a young age. When he told his parents that he wanted to become a monk, they were disappointed because he was then their only surviving son, and they had hoped that he would take care of them in their old age. He respected their wishes and waited until another son was born before turning his focus to spiritual matters and taking the name Madhva. The younger brother, Vishnuchitta, cared for their parents and later became a monk himself. He went on to become one of the most important teachers of his older brother's religious views.

At the time of Madhva's birth, a community of Christians lived in the nearby town of Kalyanpur. This group represented the first followers of Christianity in India. In his youth Madhva may have absorbed some of the teachings and traditions of these Christians. Many scholars note a number of significant similarities between the early life of Madhva and the story of **Jesus Christ** (c. 6 BCE–c. 30 CE; see entry) as recorded in the Bible, the sacred text of Christianity. For example legend holds that Madhva's birth was foretold by a messenger, just as the archangel Michael visited Jesus's mother, Mary, to inform her of the coming birth of her child. Another tale claims that as a child, Madhva disappeared for three days before his parents found him preaching to his elders in the temple, a story similar to one told about Jesus. Other stories with parallels in the Christian Bible include Madhva's ability to walk on water and to multiply food for his followers, as Jesus did when he multiplied fish and loaves of bread to feed a crowd that had gathered to hear him speak. Madhva also shared

Holy Men of Hinduism

The various titles of respect given to prominent practitioners of Hinduism can be confusing to those who are unfamiliar with them. The meanings of some of these terms overlap.

- shri: Taken from a Sanskrit word meaning "beauty," or "majesty," *shri* can be both a general term of respect, similar to "mister," or a title with deeper religious meaning, similar to "saint." It is sometimes used before the names of objects, books, and places.

- sadhu: A *sadhu* is an ascetic, meaning a person, such as a monk, who gives up earthly pleasures and leads a life of self-denial and solitude.

- sage: Among Hindus, a sage is a scholar and philosopher who is believed to be blessed with divine knowledge. Historically, sages were the authors of epic poems, and they were regarded as the bearers of ancient Hindu values and

beliefs. *Sage* is in fact an English word; in India, sages are called *rishis*.

- guru: *Guru* is a Sanskrit word that literally means "venerable" but can also mean "heavy." In Hinduism, a guru is a personal teacher or spiritual guide under whom others study the texts and principles of Hinduism.

- acharya: *Acharya* literally means "teacher." The word was added to proper names as a suffix, so that, for example, Madhva became known as Madhvacharya.

- swami: The term *swami* which comes from a Sanskrit word meaning "lord" or "owner." Swamis are scholars and philosophers, and the term is usually reserved for the heads of sects or schools of thought. Many swamis run educational or social institutions.

the Christian beliefs in eternal damnation and in the concept of heaven. Most importantly Madhva was regarded as an incarnation, or living form, of Vayu, the son of the Hindu god Krishna, just as Jesus was regarded as the son of the Christian God.

Madhva studied under a famous guru, Achyutapreksha. During his religious training he began to question the accepted ideas about the nature of God. After formulating his own set of beliefs, he went on a tour of India to share them with the people. He attracted many listeners and converts because of the clarity of his views and his skill as a public speaker.

Madhva's listeners found his views comforting, particularly those regarding caste. The caste system in India ranks people by social class according to the family they are born into. At the top are the *Brahmins,* who are mostly priests, teachers, and intellectuals. These are followed by *Kshatriyas,* or warriors and rulers; *Vaishyas,* or merchants and landowners;

and *Sudras,* or laborers and farmers. In addition, a fifth caste, the "Untouchables," includes outcasts who perform "unclean" work such as the removal of waste and of dead animals. Madhva believed that caste should be decided not by the status of one's family but of one's own nature or behavior. He believed that a spiritually enlightened Untouchable was better than an ignorant Brahmin, a view with which his followers agreed.

His ideas were considered somewhat radical, and Madhva made enemies on his journey. He often took part in debates with local religious leaders, and because his views were opposed to theirs, they became angry with him and some even threatened his life. At one point the contents of his library were stolen, although the texts were later returned after a local prince intervened.

Return to Udupi

After several years of preaching throughout India, Madhva returned to Udupi. There, he established eight *mathas,* or monasteries. A monastery is a religious place of solitude and learning, where monks and nuns may go to live. Each monastery was led by one of Madhva's disciples, or followers. Madhva also installed the image of Krishna at the temple in Udupi. (Krishna is regarded either as a god or as a godlike hero in Hinduism and is worshipped as an incarnation, or form, of Vishnu, the preserver god. All gods in Hinduism are considered to be representations of the one God, Brahma.) According to legend a shipwreck took place off the coast near the town of Malpe. Madhva had a dream in which he saw an image of Krishna aboard the ship that he felt had to be retrieved. He enlisted the help of local fishermen, dove into the sea, and rescued the image of Krishna for the temple.

Madhva's religious views became popular throughout India, particularly in the south and west. Many of the region's Hindu saints followed his teachings, and some of his disciples became highly respected themselves. Madhva wrote some thirty-seven books on palm leaves. Most were commentaries on Hindu sacred texts, such as the Upanishads, the Rig-Veda, the Bhagavad Gita, and others. He also wrote a book on iconography, or the study of images and symbols associated with certain subjects, especially religious ones, as well as a book on mathematics.

Late in life Madhva set out on a pilgrimage from Udupi to the city of Badari. One legend holds that he walked out in the middle of a sermon to

start this pilgrimage. During his journey he disappeared and was never heard from again. The
date of his death is traditionally given as 1276.

Madhva's teachings

One of the chief religious debates taking place in
India during Madhva's life concerned the nature
of God and the relationship between God and
the material world. Hindu teachers tended to
fall into one of two camps. One camp preached
a "monist" view of God. Monism refers to belief
in the basic unity, or oneness, of God with the
human soul, and indeed with all of existence,
including matter. Monism was preached by
another well-known acharya, Sankara (788–820),
and was the most common view among Indian
Hindus at the time of Madhva's birth. Monism
was also the doctrine taught by the guru under
which Madhva studied as a youth. This school
of thought is called Advaita Vedanta. The
word *Vedanta* means "end of the Vedas," referring to the Upanishads, which are the concluding
portions of Hinduism's chief sacred text, the
Vedas. The Upanishads contain the essence of the teachings of the
Vedas. "Vedanta," then, is used in the name of various Hindu schools
of thought in reference to their interpretation of the Upanishads.

*A swami bathes in the tank,
known as Madhava Sarovar,
which surrounds the Sri
Krishna Temple in Udupi,
India. Worshippers believe the
Ganga, or Ganges, River flows
into the tank every ten years.
Devotees purify themselves in
the waters before going to pray.*
© DAVID H. WELLS/CORBIS.

The other camp consisted of those who held a "dualist" view of
the world. This dualist view, which was taught by Madhva, was referred
to as *Dvaita,* and the school of thought he founded is called Dvaita
Vedanta. That term is more general than the name of his specific
sect, Madhvism. Madhva based his beliefs on his interpretations of
the Upanishads and other Hindu texts. He and his disciples taught
five main points: that God was separate from the human soul; that
God was separate from the physical universe; that the human soul
and physical matter were different; that individual human souls were
different; and that various types of matter were different. Although
these distinctions may not seem surprising to modern-day readers,
they were startling in the thirteenth century. Until this time Hinduism

had only taught a basic unity among God, the human soul, and physical matter.

Madhva also taught a view of creation that was in opposition to Hindu tradition. He did not believe that creation was ordered by the god Vishnu, as was the common theory. Rather, he believed that matter existed before Vishnu and evolved in response to his will. He believed that no one could prove the existence of Vishnu, but that he could be understood through the study of the Hindu sacred texts. By studying these texts, people could ready their minds to obtain divine grace and increase their chances of achieving salvation.

Madhva shared with his followers many thoughts on the nature of God and humanity's relationship with him. As quoted on *Kamat's Potpourri* Web site, he is said to have stated, "There is one God, the embodiment of positive Divinity. He is 'Narayana.' He is also Ishwara Brahma, Vishnu, and has many other names. You can address Him by any name." He also stated "The entire nature extols God. His existence is evident in the sounds of the sea, in the wind, in singing of birds and howls of beasts. These all pay homage to God. His existence should be recognized, which is possible after self-training."

For More Information

BOOKS

Potter, Karl. "Madhva." In *Encyclopedia of Religion*. Vol. 8. 2nd ed. Edited by Lindsay Jones. Detroit, MI: Macmillan Reference USA, 2005, 5550–1.

Sarma, Deepak. *An Introduction to Madhva Vedanta*. Aldershot, UK: Ashgate Publishing, 2003.

WEB SITES

Kamat, Jyotsna. "Path of Devotion: Bhakti Cult IX; Saint Madhvacharya (1238–1317)." *Kamat's Potpourri*. http://www.kamat.com/indica/faiths/bhakti/madhwacharya.htm (accessed on June 2, 2006).

"The Great Madhva Archya." *Dharmakshetra.com*. http://www.dharmakshetra.com/sages/Saints/madvacharya.html (accessed on June 2, 2006).

Mahavira

BORN: C. 599 BCE • Kundagrama, Bihar, India
DIED: C. 527 BCE • Papa, Bihar, India

Indian philosopher; religious leader

"Whether I am walking or standing still/whether I sleep or remain awake,/the supreme knowledge and intuition/present with me—constantly and continuously."

Mahavira was an Indian philosopher who lived a life of extreme piety, or devotion. He is regarded as the founder of a religion called Jainism, which is practiced primarily in India. Jains, however, would say that Mahavira did not "found" Jainism. They would instead say he rediscovered or reinvigorated Jain principles and beliefs that had always existed.

There are few biographical records of Mahavira in existence, and much of what is known about his life is more mythical than factual. The term *hagiography,* from the Greek word *hagios,* meaning "saint," is sometimes used to refer to a biography that idealizes saintly figures. The legends that surround the life of Mahavira fall into the category of hagiography.

Birth and early life

One major uncertainty concerns exactly when Mahavira lived. Some evidence suggests that his life overlapped with that of the **Buddha** Siddhartha Gautama (563–483 BCE; see entry), the founder of Buddhism. If this is correct, he may have been born in about 490 BCE and died in about 410 BCE. Many sources, however, give other birth and death dates. Certain Western scholars believe he was born around 540 BCE

A statue representing Mahavira. © THE BRITISH MUSEUM/HIP/THE IMAGE WORKS.

and his date of death was about 470 BCE. Jains believe that Mahavira was born "seventy-five years before the fourth descending period of the current era," referring to Jain measurements of historical time. This would put his birth date at 599 BCE and his death date at 527 BCE.

Mahavira was born in Kundagrama, a village in Bihar, a modern-day Indian state in the northeast whose capital city is Patna. His birth name was Vardhamana, which means "prospering." He was given that name because soon after he was conceived, his family and the people around him began to experience good fortune.

Vardhamana came from a royal family and was considered a member of the warrior caste, called the *Kshatriya.* Castes are hereditary Indian social classes. His mother, Trishala, was related to the ruler of the nearby city of Vaisali, and his father, Siddhartha, was a local king. According to legend Vardhamana was originally conceived by a *Brahmin* mother, Devananda. (Brahmins are the highest Indian caste and are usually priests, religious teachers, and intellectuals.) The embryo was then moved into Trishala's womb. The legends also hold that Vardhamana's conception was foretold to his mother in a series of dreams. These dreams, called "auspicious dreams" (favorable or lucky dreams) included images of a lion, the full moon, the rising sun, an ocean of milk, a white bull, and a white elephant. These dreams are described in Jain literature and are often depicted in temples.

As a child Vardhamana received an education that was suitable for a prince. According to one of the two main sects, or divisions, of Jainism, he married a princess named Yasoda, and the couple had a daughter. The other major sect of Jainism denies that he married and had a child. This sect believes that he had no ties to other people in the world.

Renunciation

The most important event in Vardhamana's life was his decision at about age thirty to renounce, or give up, his worldly possessions. After the

Jain Sects

There are two main sects, or divisions, in Jainism: the *Digambara,* which translates as "sky clad," and the *Svetambara,* which translates as "white clad." The original division between the two sects resulted from disputes over which of Mahavira's teachings were the true ones and how those teachings were to be interpreted. This problem arose in part because Mahavira's teachings were not written down until well after his death, so followers had no reliable texts to use as references.

The Digambaras are the more austere, or morally strict, sect of Jainism. Unlike Svetambaras, Digambaras do not believe that women can achieve freedom until they have been reborn as men. This is partly because Digambara monks do not wear clothing. Because they believe remaining naked would be more impractical for women, they claim women have to be reborn as men in order to lead completely austere lives.

The two sects also have different views about the nature of *Jinas,* who are godlike enlightened ones. Unlike the Svetambaras, Digambaras believe that Jinas do not require food, do not have bodily functions, nor do they carry out any functions in the world. Additionally the religious images of the two sects differ. Digambara images of the *Tirthankara,* the revered Jain teachers, always have downcast eyes, signifying meditation (deep and concentrated thinking). The figures are always plain and naked. In contrast Svetambara images are always highly decorated, and the statues of the Tirthankara have wide, staring eyes, signifying preaching.

Another difference between the two sects is their views on worldly possessions. Digambaras believe that a person can achieve spiritual freedom only by completely abandoning worldly possessions. Monks of this sect are not even allowed to own a bowl for eating. All gifts they accept have to fit in the hands. A Svetembara monk, however, is allowed to wear a simple, plain white robe and may also own a begging bowl, a broom to sweep insects from his path, and writing tools.

death of his parents, he gave away all of his property, pulled out his hair, and became a wandering ascetic, or *sadhana,* meaning that he lived a life of total self-discipline and piety. He traveled around the country begging for food. At first, his only possession was a single robe, but he eventually gave up even that and went naked. He never stayed in one village for more than a day at a time and refused to shelter himself from either cold or heat. When he walked or sat, he was careful never to injure any living thing. For this reason, he traveled less during the rainy seasons, when paths would be filled with life forms that he did not want to injure. As part of this determination, Vardhamana was a vegetarian, or a person who does not eat meat. He even strained his drinking water to ensure that no creatures were living in it.

Vardhamana supposedly lived in this ascetic fashion for twelve years, six months, and fifteen days. Then, on a summer night, he sat on the bank of the river Rjupalika under a tree and achieved omniscience, or knowledge of everything. He gained a complete understanding of the world, including its past, present, and future. According to one sacred Jain text, he saw all things about all living beings, including what they thought about, said, or did. At this point Vardhamana acquired the name Mahavira, which means "great hero."

He began to attract many followers. He preached to large crowds and engaged other religious leaders in debates about spiritual matters. He organized the Jain religion into societies of nuns, monks, female laity, and male laity. The term "laity" refers to ordinary members of a religion, or those who are not monks, priests, or nuns. According to Jain tradition, by the time of his death, Mahavira had established a community of some 14,000 monks, 36,000 nuns, 159,000 laymen, and 318,000 laywomen.

Mahavira died in the town of Papa, near Patna. His followers believe that he was alone at the time, reciting religious texts. The Jains list his death as occurring in 527 BCE. As noted earlier, however, scholars offer different dates for this event. Some place it at 467 BCE, others at about 477 or 476 BCE, and still others at 490 BCE.

Mahavira as Tirthankar

Jains regard Mahavira as the twenty-fourth *Tirthankar*. This title, the plural of which is Tirthankara, means something like "maker of the ford," or "maker of the ocean crossing." It refers to building or creating ways to cross the "ocean" of rebirth. In this way a Tirthankar can be thought of as similar to a prophet (divine messenger) in other religions such as Christianity, Judaism, Islam, or Zoroastrianism.

To understand the significance of the Tirthankara in the history of Jainism, the Jain concept of time must be understood. Jains believe that the principles of their religion have always existed. Sometimes, however, those principles become less important in the minds of the people and the religion dies out for a time before it is reborn. To Jains, therefore, the concept of time is cyclical, and can be pictured much like the rotation of a wheel. The rotation includes a series of upward movements, *utsarpini,* and downward movements, *avarsarpini.* A complete turn of the wheel is called a *kalpa* and covers an immense span of time. According to Jain beliefs, a kalpa is a unit of time equal to approximately 4.32 million years.

Each of these cycles, or kalpas, is divided into six ages, which can be thought of as divisions between spokes on the wheel. Three of the ages are considered to be a kind of golden era, which is followed by a decline that continues until Jainism dies out. The process is then reversed, as the religion is reborn and eventually reaches a new golden age. Jains believe that in the current time cycle, the world has passed through the first four ages of the cycle and is currently in the middle of the fifth age, with a sixth and final age to come. Each complete kalpa is long enough for twenty-four Tirthankara to live. These twenty-four make up a "set" of Tirthankara that Jains worship.

The present cycle is said to have witnessed the passing of all twenty-four of these enlightened ones, with Mahavira being the last. No historical records prove the existence of the first twenty-two. Some evidence suggests that the twenty-third Tirthankar, Parshva, did exist and lived about 250 years before Mahavira. Mahavira did not oppose or change the teachings of Parshva. Rather, Jains believe that he came to Earth to complete and fulfill those teachings and to renew Jainism.

This Jain cosmic wheel depicts at its center the figure of Mahavira. Jainism believes that the universe is eternal, and teachings on life within the universe are central to the religion. © CHARLES & JOSETTE LENARS/CORBIS.

Jains believe that some enlightened individuals can reach the perfection of a god. These people are called *Jina,* which means "conqueror" and is the source of the word *Jain.* Jains regard Mahavira as one of the Jina. Jina are perfectly happy, having conquered earthly desires, and their spirits live eternally, so they are worshipped as "gods." Although the Jina are thought of as gods, they are neither creators nor destroyers. They do not affect the laws of the physical universe. Humans also do not exist because of the Jina's actions and cannot have any kind of relationship with them, for the Jina do not interfere in the affairs of humans. They do not reward people for good actions or forgive their sins. Humans regard them only as a source of inspiration. Because of these characteristics, Jains are sometimes referred to as atheists, meaning that they do not believe in any gods, but this is true only in a limited sense.

Mahavira's teachings

Mahavira is referred to by two titles. As a Tirthankar, he was one of the great teachers of Jainism. He purified and organized the religion in the present age. He was also a Jina, a person who has gained enlightenment and understanding to such an extent that he is to be worshipped. Mahavira achieved this position in large part by living and teaching the Five Vows of Jainism. These vows are still practiced by Jains in the early twenty-first century. The Five Vows are as follows:

1. *Ahimsa*: neither killing nor injuring any living thing.
2. *Satya*: speaking only the truth.
3. *Asteya*: not stealing things or being greedy.
4. *Brahmacharya*: practicing celibacy, or not having sex, and giving up all sensual pleasure.
5. *Aparigraha*: being detached and being neither delighted nor disturbed by any outward experiences.

Another central belief of Jainism, related to *ahimsa,* or nonviolence, is that since all creatures contain living souls, all deserve to be treated with respect.

The Five Vows can be thought of as somewhat similar to the Ten Commandments of Judaism and Christianity and to the Five Pillars of Islam, which provide the followers of these religions with basic guidelines or laws for living. The vows provide Jains with a moral and ethical code to follow. The principle that is particularly associated with Jainism is the first, ahimsa, the vow to not injure or kill any living thing. This vow not only bans such extreme actions as murder and assault but also extends into everyday life. All Jains are vegetarians, as was Mahavira, and strict Jains go to great lengths to avoid harming anything that is alive. Some Jains even avoid eating after dark in order to be certain they do not accidentally consume small living creatures that they cannot see.

Mahavira accepted the Hindu belief in reincarnation, or being reborn into another living body after death. He taught that the *jiva,* or soul, is conscious, immaterial, and eternal. Because the soul is eternal, it is subject to the ongoing cycle of birth, death, and rebirth. Mahavira also taught the Hindu concept of karma. *Karma* refers to the effects of a person's actions in one life on the nature of his or her next life. A person who earns positive karma by doing good deeds can be reborn on a higher plane of existence, while one who earns bad karma by being immoral or unethical will likely be reborn on a lower plane of existence. Mahavira taught that karma represents a kind of bondage or entrapment. The goal of every person is to stop earning new karma and to get rid of past karma. The result of doing so is *siddhi,* or perfection. He preached that a soul that has gotten rid of all karma can become spiritually pure. Unlike Hindus, Jains believe that karma is an actual physical substance, like dust, that attaches itself to the soul.

Mahavira warned that freeing the soul from karma was not easy, and could only be accomplished by mastering the "three jewels." Like the Five Vows, the three jewels form an ethical code. They are right faith, right knowledge, and right conduct. The first of these, right faith, or *samyak darshana,* means seeing clearly. It is sometimes translated as "right perception." The term refers to avoiding superstition and preconceptions (opinions formed in advance of adequate knowledge) and being determined to find the truth. The second jewel, right knowledge, or *samyak jnana,* refers to knowing and understanding the universe. The third, *samyak charitra,* or right conduct, refers to leading one's life ethically. An ethical person avoids doing harm to living things and frees himself or herself from impure desires, attitudes, and thoughts by following the Five Vows.

Regardless of the uncertainties surrounding the facts of Mahavira's life, he was an important religious figure in India in the centuries before the start of the Common Era. Though his home village of Kundagrama no longer exists, in 1956 the government of Bihar created a memorial to Mahavira near its former location. The memorial is home to the Research Institute of Prakrit, Ahimsa, and Jainology, an institution in which the principles of Jainism are studied.

For More Information

BOOKS

Dundas, Paul. *The Jains.* 2nd ed. London, UK: Routledge, 2002.

Prime, Ranchor. *Mahavira: Prince of Peace.* San Rafael, CA: Mandala Publishing, 2006.

Singh, Narendra, ed. *Encyclopaedia of Jainism.* 30 vols. New Delhi, India: Anmol, 2001.

WEB SITES

"Jainism History." *BBC Religion & Ethics.* http://www.bbc.co.uk/religion/religions/jainism/history/index.shtml (accessed June 2, 2006).

"Mahavir." *Manas: Religions.* http://www.sscnet.ucla.edu/southasia/Religions/gurus/Mahavir.html (accessed June 2, 2006).

Shah, Pravin K. "Lord Mahavir and Jain Religion." *Jain History.* http://www.cs.colostate.edu/~malaiya/mahavira.html (accessed on June 2, 2006).

Moses Maimonides

BORN: March 30, 1135 • Córdoba, Spain
DIED: December 13, 1204 • Cairo, Egypt

Spanish rabbi; physician; philosopher; writer

Moses Maimonides.

> "Maimonides is the most influential Jewish thinker of the Middle Ages, and quite possibly of all time."
>
> — Shlomo Pines as quoted on the *Jewish Virtual Library* Web site.

Moses Maimonides, one of the most well-known scholars and theologians (people who study religion) in Jewish history, was born on March 30, 1135. Most commonly his name is given simply as Maimonides, which is Greek for "son of Maimon." He is also frequently referred to as the Rambam, a loose acronym, or short form, of his title and name, Rabbi Moshe ben Maimon.

Early life and wanderings

Maimonides was born in Córdoba, Spain. His father was a judge in the Jewish court and shared with his son his vast knowledge of the Talmud. The Talmud is a set of religious principles that explains and interprets the Hebrew Scripture, the portion of the Christian Bible called the Old Testament. These principles were first written down in the second century in a text called the Mishnah. From an early age Maimonides was

249

fascinated by the Talmud. His father also encouraged him to study science and philosophy, and his earliest ambition was to be a doctor, though he gave up that ambition for a time in the face of family misfortune. By the time he was a teenager Maimonides had acquired a broad education, covering not only Jewish law and history but also the works of classical Greek philosophers, those who seek to understand fundamental beliefs of values and reality.

The early years of Maimonides's life overlapped with the height of the golden age of Judaism in medieval Spain, when Jewish learning, art, architecture, science, and philosophy were at their peak. The region of Spain in which Maimonides lived was under Muslim (Islamic) rule. Persecution did occur at times, such as in 1066, when the Jews were forced to leave the city of Granada and many Jewish families were killed. Persecution is to harass a person or people because of their beliefs. In general, however, Jews were accepted into the region's economic, cultural, and social life. Many Jewish families enjoyed considerable wealth.

The situation changed abruptly in 1148, when a radical sect of Islam called the Almohads conquered Córdoba. The Almohads took Jewish property, shut down Jewish schools, destroyed Jewish temples, and seized Jewish women and children and sold them into slavery. Jews, as well as Christians, were given a choice: They could convert to Islam, be forced into exile (forced to leave their homes never to return), or, if they remained in Córdoba and refused to become Muslims, face death. Some stayed and pretended to become Muslims while still secretly practicing Judaism. Most chose exile. For the next ten years Maimonides and his family wandered from city to city in Spain, staying one step ahead of the Almohads, who proceeded to seize control of other cities and regions. Finally Maimonides and his family joined a group of Jews who set out for North Africa in 1159. They settled in the city of Fez, the capital of modern-day Morocco, where they remained for five years.

In Fez, Maimonides and his family continued to face persecution. They eventually left and moved to Palestine, where they stayed in such cities as Jerusalem and Hebron. The political and social climate in Palestine was not friendly to Jews, largely because of the disorder and devastation caused by the Crusades (the two centuries of continuing conflict between Muslims and European Christians fighting for control of Palestine). Maimonides's family moved once more, traveling south to Egypt. They lived for a time in Alexandria before settling in Fostat, the first capital of Egypt under Arab rule, which in modern times is part of the "Old Egypt" district in Cairo. In Fostat the family finally found a home. Although Egypt was under the control of Muslims, the Fatamid dynasty (909–1171) that then ruled Egypt was tolerant of other religious groups and allowed Jews to practice their religion with complete freedom.

Misfortune struck soon after the family reached Egypt. First Maimonides's father died. Maimonides was determined to carry on the tradition of scholarship in his family. His father and generations of ancestors had been scholars before him, so he remained devoted to his studies. Meanwhile his brother, David, a jewel merchant, became responsible for the family financially. The family then encountered more bad luck when David died at sea while on a trip to India to purchase jewels. Maimonides was so affected by David's death that he became ill and had to stay in bed for several months. When he recovered, he realized that he needed to support his family. He did not believe, however, that he should make any money from his theological studies, as he had gained his vast knowledge of the Hebrew Scriptures, or holy texts, solely for the love of God. Accordingly he resumed the medical studies that he had once begun and became a physician. In time he was so successful that he was appointed personal physician to the grand vizier, or ruler, of Egypt, as well as to other important figures in the capital city.

Physician and scholar

In addition to running his medical practice Maimonides also served as a respected *rabbi*. A rabbi is a person trained in Jewish law, ritual, and tradition who is often the head of a synagogue, or Jewish house of worship. He soon became the unofficial leader of the Jewish community in Egypt. As such, he was responsible for overseeing community administration and donations to charity. He also acted as a judge, all without accepting pay. In 1177 he was officially appointed head of Cairo's Jewish community.

For the remainder of his life Maimonides worked to balance his job as a physician with his interest in Judaism. He wrote numerous commentaries and theological works. In 1187 his son Avraham was born. Avraham himself went on to have a noteworthy career as the head of Cairo's Jewish community and wrote several works that added to his father's knowledge. Maimonides died on December 13, 1204.

A page from the Mishnah Torah, a systematic code of Jewish law that was completed by Maimonides around 1178. Any study of Jewish law includes the Mishnah Torah in some way. © NATIONAL LIBRARY, JERUSALEM, ISRAEL/LAUROS/GIRAUDON/THE BRIDGEMAN ART LIBRARY.

The thirteen principles of faith

In the twenty-first century, nearly one thousand years after his death, Maimonides is still regarded as one of the leading figures of Jewish theology and philosophy. He perhaps remains best known for his "thirteen principles of faith," one of the earliest attempts to define the meaning of being a Jew. These principles include the following:

1. God exists.

2. God has unity; that is, God does not have parts or different personifications, but exists as a single being.

3. God is spiritual and incorporeal; that is, He has no material existence or body.

4. God is eternal. He has always existed, since before He created the universe, and He will continue to exist after the end of time.

5. Only God should be the object of worship (an idea stated by Maimonides to discourage idol worship, or the worship of physical objects as gods).

6. God revealed his intentions through His prophets (divine messengers), and their prophecies were revealed in the Hebrew Scriptures, primarily in the section called Prophets (Nevi'im). This section consists of twenty-one books, including 1 Kings, 2 Kings, Isaiah, and Jeremiah.

7. **Moses** (c. 1392–c. 1272 BCE; see entry) was the greatest among the prophets. Moses was the dominant figure in the biblical book of Exodus, which details the story of the formation of the Jewish nation after he led the Jewish people out of slavery in Egypt. Moses has also traditionally been regarded as the author of the Torah, the first five books of the Hebrew Scriptures, although modern biblical scholars dispute this belief.

8. God gave His law to man in the form of the Ten Commandments and other principles. God's law was first revealed to Moses in the book of Exodus. The law is detailed in the biblical book of Leviticus, although Exodus, Numbers, and Deuteronomy also contain principles that remain part of Jewish law.

9. The Torah, as God's law, is unchangeable. (Maimonides put forth this idea in response to the growing belief that God's law could evolve or change according to current conditions. This is perhaps the one of the thirteen principles of faith that has been and remains most widely disputed.)

10. God has advance knowledge of human actions.

11. God rewards good and punishes evil.

12. A Jewish messiah, or savior, will someday appear.

13. The dead will be resurrected (brought back to life) at the end of time.

The Mishnah

Gentiles, or those who are not Jews, can sometimes find the terms used to refer to Jewish scripture and traditions confusing. The most important Jewish scripture is the Bible's Old Testament, which Jews refer to as the Tanakh. ("Old Testament" is a term used by Christians.) The most essential part of the Tanakh is the Torah, the first five books in the Tanakh: Genesis, Exodus, Leviticus, Numbers, and Deuteronomy. These books detail the principles of Jewish law, the formation of the Jewish nation, and God's covenant, or agreement, with the Israelites as his "chosen people." These five books are often referred to as the "written Torah." In addition to the written Torah is the "oral Torah," which consists of interpretations of the written Torah and methods with which to apply its laws. The oral Torah, the first part of the Talmud, was written down in the second century and called the Mishnah.

The Mishnah consists of six sections, called *seders,* which means "orders." They are:

1. *Zeraim,* or "Seeds," deals with agricultural laws.

2. *Moed,* or "Festival," concerns with festivals and Shabbat observances. Shabbat is Saturday, considered in Judaism to be the seventh day of the week and a day of rest and worship.

3. *Nashim,* or "Women," discusses such issues as marriage and divorce.

4. *Nezikin,* or "Damages," details laws regarding financial matters and torts, or wrongful acts that injure or harm others.

5. *Kodshim,* or "Holy Things," deals with temple worship and sacrifices.

6. *Tohorot,* or "Purities," provides laws regarding ritual purity.

Each of the seders includes further divisions called tractates, or *masekhtots.* The total number of tractates is sixty-three. Each tractate deals with specific issues in Jewish law. Thus, when rabbis want to examine and rule on a particular issue regarding any aspect of Jewish life, they turn for guidance to the tractate that discusses that issue.

These principles were not universally accepted among Jews, particularly during the first few centuries after Maimonides created them. In modern times, however, they have been reworked as poetic prayers appearing in the Jewish prayer book. They remain important because they define the basic beliefs of Judaism. These thirteen principles of faith are still followed by Orthodox Jews, who strictly follow religious laws and beliefs as traditionally held.

Commentary on the Mishnah

While the thirteen principles of faith are of major significance, Maimonides's most important works, especially to Talmudic scholars, are the *Commentary on the Mishnah,* the *Mishneh Torah,* and *Guide of the Perplexed.* Writing the first of these, the *Commentary,* occupied Maimonides from about 1158 to 1168. He wrote the work in Arabic, and it was translated into Hebrew in sections over the next two centuries. Because of this, it did not have an immediate impact on Jewish thought. In later centuries, however, the *Commentary* became the starting point for virtually every study of the Mishnah, the first part of the Talmud, which explains Jewish tradition. The *Comentary* consists of an in-depth examination of the Mishnah and discussions on a wide range of theological problems. The central problem addressed is the nature of oral law, which originated on Mount Sinai when God established His covenant, or agreement, with the Jewish people through the Ten Commandments and other principles. Maimonides was especially concerned with how that law was to be passed on and interpreted.

Another problem discussed by Maimonides in the *Commentary* is that of the Old Testament prophecies, particularly whether the words of prophets after Moses could be considered as having the force of law in Judaism. Maimonides believed they could not. Elsewhere in the text, he tries to reconcile (make compatible or consistent) the findings of science with the biblical account of Creation in the book of Genesis. Similarly, he tries to reconcile notions of free will with belief in predestination, or fate. He rejects any fields of study, such as astrology, which he claims undermine, or take away, free will. (Astrology is the study of the movement of the stars and their affect on events on Earth.)

Within the *Commentary* Maimonides also reflects on the nature of reward, punishment, and immortality in the afterlife, offering his thoughts on ethics in a section entitled "Ethics of the Fathers." In this section he explains his idea of the golden mean, or a balance between extremes. His theory of the golden mean led him to reject asceticism (living a life without worldly possessions or earthly pleasures) and to criticize Jews who gave up the joys of life, which he believed were gifts from God. He also wrote about such matters as medicine, magic, the history of religion, and the nature of miracles.

The *Mishnah Torah* and *Guide*

Maimonides completed his second major work, the *Mishnah Torah,* in about 1178. The *Mishnah Torah* is a detailed, complete explanation of Jewish law, written in a simple style that can be understood by those who are not experts in Talmudic studies. Modern-day scholars and theologians are still impressed by the work's rich combination of ethics, philosophy, and theology. Virtually all study of Jewish law in some way involves the *Mishnah Torah*.

Maimonides's *Guide of the Perplexed* was written between 1185 and 1190. While his earlier works deal with Jewish law, the *Guide* is chiefly philosophical. Maimonides discusses a wide range of complex issues, including the relationship between religious faith and reason; the relationship between philosophy and sacred scripture; the nature of God and His relationship with the world; revelation as a means of communication between God and man; free will; and the nature of human destiny.

The work had a significant influence on later thinkers such as the Italian theologian Thomas Aquinas (c. 1225–1274). It also influenced followers of Scholasticism, a philosophical method that sought to reconcile the thinking of ancient classical philosophers with medieval Christian theology. Scholastic philosophers and theologians closely examined texts such as the Bible and attempted to resolve contradictions by examining the language of the original version. Historians of philosophy regard Maimonides as one of the most important contributors to Scholastic thought.

For More Information

BOOKS

Arbel, Ilil. *Maimonides: A Spiritual Biography*. New York, NY: Crossroads, 2001.

Davidson, Herbert A. *Moses Maimonides: The Man and His Works*. New York, NY: Oxford University Press, 2004.

Mangel, Nissen. *The Rambam: A Brief Biography*. Brooklyn, NY: Kehot Publication Society, 1998.

Nuland, Sherwin B. *Maimonides*. New York, NY: Schocken Books, 2005.

WEB SITES

"The Mishneh Torah." *A Page of Talmud*. http://www.acs.ucalgary.ca/~elsegal/TalmudMap/Maimonides.html (accessed on June 2, 2006).

Telushkin, Joseph. "Maimonides/Rambam." *Jewish Virtual Library*. http://www.jewishvirtuallibrary.org/jsource/biography/Maimonides.html (accessed on June 2, 2006).

Karl Marx

BORN: May 5, 1818 • Trier, Prussia
DIED: March 14, 1883 • London, England

Prussian philosopher; economist; writer

"Religion is the groan of the oppressed, the sentiment of a heartless world, and at the same time the spirit of a condition deprived of spirituality. It is the opium of the people."

Karl Marx.
ARCHIVE PHOTOS/
GETTY IMAGES.

Karl Marx was an economist, journalist, historian, philosopher, and atheist (a person who does not believe in a God or gods) who played a major role in shaping the intellectual atmosphere of the late nineteenth and early twentieth centuries. He was born in Trier, Prussia, on May 5, 1818, to Hirschel and Henrietta Marx. Prussia was a separate kingdom that later became part of a unified Germany. Prussia's state religion was Protestant Lutheranism, a branch of Christianity, but Marx's family was Jewish, and his ancestry included rabbis (persons trained in Jewish law, ritual, and tradition) on both sides of the family. Around 1816 or 1817, the Prussian parliament passed an order saying that Jews could not practice law. Hirschel, who was a lawyer, converted to Lutheranism and changed his first name to Heinrich. His son, Karl, was then baptized as a Lutheran in 1824.

Marx's early years and education

Marx grew up in a home that was Lutheran in name but essentially non-religious. Like many liberal Protestants of that era and region, the family did not hold strong religious beliefs. From a cultural standpoint the family's conversion to a Protestant religion alienated them from their Jewish background and community. Young Karl did not think of himself as either Protestant or Jewish. He attended religious schools as a child, but only because his parents believed he would receive a better education than in a nonreligious school.

After attending school in Trier from 1830 to 1835, Marx enrolled at the University of Bonn (Germany) to study law. To his father's dismay, however, he spent most of his time socializing and getting into debt. Determined that his son should get a good education, Heinrich paid off his son's debts and forced him to transfer to Friedrich-Wilhelms-Universität in Berlin, a more academically challenging school.

Over the next few years Marx dropped his bad habits and succeeded in his studies. He focused on law at first, but soon became more interested in history and philosophy because of the influence of one of his teachers, the political radical Bruno Bauer (1809–1882). A political radical is someone who supports extreme change in views, conditions, and institutions. Bauer introduced Marx to the work of the German philosopher Georg Wilhelm Friedrich Hegel (1770–1831). Marx joined a university group called the Young Hegelians, who met to discuss and debate the philosopher's views.

Marx was especially drawn to Hegel's view of history and historical progress, which was based on his theory of the "dialectic." According to this theory, in any area of human activity, such as history, law, and economics, a thing cannot exist without its opposite. For example the upper classes cannot exist without the lower classes, poverty cannot exist without wealth, and an oppressed class (one kept down by the use of unjust force or authority) cannot exist without a class of oppressors. In Hegel's view, human history consisted of the clash of these opposites. One thing, which Hegel called the "thesis," always clashed with its opposite, the "antithesis," to create a new social order, the "synthesis." This view of the progression of history would later influence much of Marx's own writings.

Outcast journalist and writer

In 1838 Heinrich Marx died, and Karl had to support himself financially. His first goal was to become a university teacher. He had hoped that after he completed a doctorate in philosophy at the University of Jena, Bruno

Bauer would help him find a teaching post. Bauer, though, was unable to help because his radicalism had led to his being fired from his own job. Since he was unable to secure a teaching position, Marx decided to try journalism. Most magazine and newspaper editors, however, were unwilling to publish his work because of his radical political views.

After struggling as a journalist Marx moved to Cologne, Germany, where he joined the city's large population of liberals and radicals and became involved with a group known as the Cologne Circle. Among these political rebels was Moses Hess (1812–1875), who organized socialist meetings and introduced Marx to the city's working-class population. Socialism is an economic system in which the production and distribution of goods is owned collectively by the people or by a centralized government. Marx published an article in the German newspaper, the *Rheinische Zeitung,* and readers were so impressed by it that he was appointed editor of the paper in 1842. Marx proceeded to write articles that were sharply critical of the government. In reaction to this, government censors shut the newspaper down in 1843.

During the mid-nineteenth century, the lower classes of Europe began to revolt against the wealthier citizens. These clashes occasionally erupted into violence. Many people, particularly those in government and members of the upper classes, lived in daily fear of the possibility of what they called "mob rule." Government authorities attempted to suppress radicals, freethinkers, socialists, and all others who posed threats to the established order. A freethinker is someone who forms opinions independent from authority figures.

Capitalism vs. Socialism

Any discussion of Karl Marx's life and thought involves reference to certain major economic systems. The system that Marx opposed was capitalism. Capital, in this circumstance, refers to wealth stored in the hands of individuals. In a capitalist economic system, individuals own the methods of producing goods, such as factories and raw materials. Workers supply labor to capitalists for pay, which is determined by market forces of supply and demand. If supply for a particular product is high but demand for it is low, the capitalist will not make much money and will pay his workers less. If supply is low and demand is high, however, the capitalist will have more wealth to pass on to the workers.

Nineteenth-century liberals and radicals called for an end to capitalism, which they believed created unemployment and poverty. A liberal is someone who is open to new methods and does not rely on tradition to guide views or actions. A radical is someone who advocates for extreme changes in views, organizations, and ways of doing things. They supported a different form of economic organization called socialism. In a socialist economic system, the government takes over the methods of production and provides people with a wide range of social benefits, such as health care and education. The goal is to lessen the differences between the rich and the poor, especially in terms of income. Communism can be thought of as an extreme form of socialism. Under a communist economic system, there is no private property. Factories, goods, raw materials, and land are considered to be owned collectively by the people and are given out by the government according to people's needs.

Partners with Engels

As one of these freethinkers, Marx feared that he would be arrested. After he married his longtime sweetheart, Jenny von Westphalan, he fled to Paris. Given the growing radicalism of Marx's political opinions, his marriage seems a strange one, as Jenny was a member of an aristocratic, or socially privileged, family. The marriage in fact had been opposed by both their families. In Paris Marx took a position as editor of a new political journal. He also met Friedrich Engels (1820–1895), the radical communist son of a wealthy industrialist (owner of a manufacturing industry), who would become his lifelong friend and coauthor. A communist supports an economic system under which all goods are owned collectively by the people and managed by the government according to need. Engels increased Marx's awareness of the poverty and misery of the French working class, and Marx found Engels's communist views compatible with his own.

Once again, Marx's political beliefs placed him in danger, and the French government eventually ordered him to leave the country. In 1845 he and Engels moved to Brussels, Belgium, another European capital that had attracted a large number of radical thinkers. There Marx wrote some of his earliest major works, including *On the Jewish Question* and *The Poverty of Philosophy.* He also wrote *The German Ideology,* in which he outlined his theory of materialism, which was his belief that historical events were not the result of vague, theoretical (not practical) concepts, but of concrete human activity. These ideas provided a foundation for his atheism, or disbelief in God.

In 1845 Marx and Engels visited England. They observed the industrial city of Manchester, where large numbers of workers lived in slums in which poverty, disease, unemployment, alcoholism, and domestic violence were widespread. The next year Marx established the Communist Correspondence Committee to link socialist and communist leaders throughout Europe. After radicals in London established a secret organization called the Communist League, Marx formed a branch of the league in Brussels. In 1847 he returned to London to attend a meeting of the Communist League's Central Committee, where he described the aim of the movement, quoted on the Web site *Spartacus Educational,* as "the overthrow of the bourgeoisie [the classes that owned property], the domination of the proletariat [the working classes], the abolition of the old bourgeois society based on class antagonisms, and the establishment of a new society without classes and without private property."

While still living in Brussels, Marx and Engels published their most famous work, a twelve-thousand-word pamphlet entitled *The Communist Manifesto.* Engels had written an earlier draft of the pamphlet titled *Principles of Communism,* and Marx reworked it into its final form. The *Manifesto* begins with the now famous words, "The history of all hitherto existing society is the history of class struggles." Marx and Engels outlined a new way of examining history, arguing that history was made not through the activities of great individuals, nor by the clashes between states, but by the conflict between social classes. Marx and Engels believed that there were two such principal classes in the nineteenth century: the *bourgeoisie,* or the wealthy owners of factories, raw materials, and the means of production; and the *proletariat,* or those without money or goods who were forced to work for the capitalists and often lived in poverty. Marx and Engels looked forward to a revolutionary future when the proletariat would overthrow the bourgeoisie, the bourgeoisie would disappear, income inequalities would vanish, and a classless society would arise.

The year 1848 was one of great political disorder in many cities throughout Europe. In France working-class revolutionaries overthrew King Louis-Phillipe (1773–1793) and invited Marx back to Paris. He accepted the invitation in part because the Belgian government had forced him to leave that country. The new French government failed, however, and in 1849 Marx was forced to leave Paris again. He returned to Cologne, where he resurrected his old newspaper as the *Neue Rheinische Zeitung* and reported on revolutionary developments throughout Europe. He also established a Committee on Public Safety in response to what he saw as police brutality directed against the public.

No matter where he went, however, Marx was oppressed, or treated badly by authority, because of his radical views. In 1849 he was expelled from Germany and returned to Paris, but he was soon ordered to leave France as well. He then settled in the only country that would give him entry, England. French authorities tried to persuade the British government to deny Marx admission to the country, but the British prime minister, John Russell (1792–1878), was a strong defender of the right of free speech and rejected the pleas of the French.

Marx in England

Marx spent the rest of his life in England with his growing family. They had little money, and in 1850 they were evicted from an apartment in London's Chelsea district because they could not pay the rent. They

Communist supporters carry portraits of Friedrich Engels (from left), Karl Marx, and Vladimir Lenin during a rally in Europe. Marx was an atheist who believed that religion was a method used to oppress the working man. AP IMAGES.

relocated to the Soho district, where they lived for six years in cheaper accommodations. Marx spent most of his time in the reading room of the British Museum, where he studied economic journals in an effort to understand the workings of capitalism. His debts grew, and for financial support he relied on Engels, who had returned to Germany to work for his father. For years Engels mailed money to his friend in England. To prevent the funds from being stolen during the postal process, he purchased money orders, cut them in half, and mailed the halves in separate envelopes.

Marx's fortunes took an upward turn in 1852, when the editor of the *New York Daily Tribune,* Charles Dana (1819–1897), offered Marx the opportunity to submit articles. Over the next decade, Marx delivered nearly five hundred articles to Dana, some of which were actually written by Engels. Another publisher in the United States, George Ripley (1802–1880), paid Marx to write for the *New American Cyclopedia.*

This work, combined with a small inheritance from Jenny Marx's mother, allowed the family to move to more comfortable quarters in Kentish Town, near London. Marx's good fortune, however, was short-lived. In 1856 Jenny gave birth to a stillborn child, then was later left deaf and badly scarred by smallpox, a highly infectious disease. For much of the rest of his life, Marx himself endured a number of health problems, including a severe case of boils, an inflammation of the skin. He consoled himself by characterizing the problem as a "proletarian" disease.

In the 1860s Marx's financial problems returned when his work for the *New York Daily Tribune* came to an end. Engels continued to send him money, and he also received support from Ferdinand Lassalle (1825–1864), a wealthy socialist from Germany who wanted Marx to edit a new socialist journal he was planning. Marx was unwilling to return to Germany, however, so he turned the job down. Nevertheless, Lassalle continued to contribute to Marx's support until his own death in 1864.

Despite his various problems, Marx continued to work. In 1867 he published the first volume of his second major work, *Das Kapital,* a criticism of the capitalist economic system. In this book Marx presented the theory that capitalism would in time cause its own collapse. He said wealth would become concentrated in a very small number of companies. At the same time the poverty and misery of the working classes would increase. Marx looked forward to the time when the working classes would organize themselves and overthrow the capitalist system.

In 1871 Marx thought that his vision of a new economic order was coming with the formation of the Paris Commune. In March of that year socialists rose up and established a revolutionary government in Paris that introduced a number of socialist reforms. In May, however, French troops suppressed the rebellion and killed thirty thousand revolutionaries in an assault on the city. Another fifty thousand were later executed. Marx was depressed by the outcome, but he continued to work on a second volume of *Das Kapital.* Progress proved slow, and by 1881 both Karl and Jenny were ill. In December 1881 Jenny died. Two years later Marx's eldest daughter also passed away. Marx did not recover from these losses and died himself on March 14, 1883. He never completed either the second volume, or a planned third volume of *Das Kapital.* Engels later assembled the volumes from Marx's notes.

Marx and atheism

Karl Marx was an atheist nearly his entire life. As a very young man he saw himself as a child of the Enlightenment, also called the Age of Reason, a period of increasingly progressive intellectualism in Europe that covered roughly the eighteenth century. Thinkers during this period preferred reason and the scientific method to faith, especially religious faith. In a paper he wrote at the University of Jena, Marx commented on the notion that the concept of God would have no place in a "country of reason": "Take paper money to a country in which this use of paper money is not known, and everyone will laugh at your subjective representation. Go with your gods to a country in which other gods are worshipped, and you will be shown that you are the victim of fancies and abstractions. And rightly."

Later, in an 1844 book titled *Critique of the Hegelian Philosophy of Public Law*, Marx famously stated, "Man makes religion, religion does not make man. . . . Religious suffering is, at one and the same time, the expression of real suffering and a protest against it. Religion is the groan of the oppressed, the sentiment of a heartless world, and at the same time the spirit of a condition deprived of spirituality." He concluded this passage with perhaps his most quoted words: "It [religion] is the opium of the people." In other words, Marx saw religion as a drug that people created to help themselves hide their own misery and oppression.

Marx based his atheism on three principles. The first of these, related to the Hegelian concept, he called "dialectical materialism." Marx believed that physical matter, not indefinite ideas such as spirit or thought, caused everything that occurs in the world. The second principle, related to the first, revolved around his view of history, which was based on materialist notions of economics and the class divisions within society created by economic systems. The third principle was that of humanism, a system of thought which says that the condition of humankind is foremost in importance. As Marx expressed in his *Critique,* "The criticism of religion leads to the doctrine according to which man is, for man, the supreme being."

Marx's atheism was also based on more practical considerations. Throughout his written works he frequently condemned churches as being allies of government. He saw much of religion as part of a system that created privileged classes of industrial masters who used their religion to justify their worldly success. In his view, the proletarian revolution would sweep away all such institutions that contributed to inequality.

Largely influenced by Marx's views of religion, the communist states of the twentieth century were officially atheist.

For More Information

BOOKS

Bottomore, Tom, ed. *A Dictionary of Marxist Thought.* Oxford, UK: Blackwell Reference, 1991.

Marx, Karl. *Critique of Hegel's "Philosophy of Right."* Cambridge, UK: Cambridge University Press, 1970.

Marx, Karl, and Friedrich Engels. *The Communist Manifesto.* New York, NY: Signet, 1998.

Marx, Karl, and Friedrich Engels. *On Religion.* New York, NY: Random House, 1982.

Wheen, Francis. *Karl Marx: A Life.* New York, NY: Norton, 2001.

WEB SITES

"Karl Marx." *Spartacus Educational.* http://www.spartacus.schoolnet.co.uk/TUmarx.htm (accessed on May 26, 2006).

"Karl Marx." *Stanford Encyclopedia of Philosophy.* http://plato.stanford.edu/entries/marx (accessed on May 26, 2006).

Park, Wonbin. "Karl Marx." *The Boston Collaborative Encyclopedia of Modern Western Theology.* http://people.bu.edu/wwildman/WeirdWildWeb/courses/mwt/dictionary/mwt_themes_530_marx.htm (accessed on May 26, 2006).

Moses Mendelssohn

BORN: September 6, 1729 • Dessau, Anhalt-Dessau, Germany

DIED: January 4, 1786 • Berlin, Germany

German philosopher; writer

"Let everyone be permitted to speak as he thinks, to invoke God after his own manner."

Moses Mendelssohn.

M oses Mendelssohn, an eighteenth-century German philosopher, is often referred to as the "father of the Jewish Enlightenment." A philosopher is someone who searches to understand values and reality. He was the author of a large number of literary and philosophical works. Mendelssohn called for reliance on reason rather than on blind faith and mysticism (direct, mysterious communication with God) when seeking religious truth. He also played a major role in unifying Jewish and secular (nonreligious) culture at a time when many European Jews desired education but were excluded from public and professional life. In German literature, he is remembered as the model for the noble title character in Gotthold Lessing's (1729–1781) *Nathan the Wise* (1779), a dramatic poem that is essentially a plea for religious tolerance. Some Jews call Mendelssohn the "third Moses" of Judaism, following the Old Testament prophet (divine messenger) and **Moses Maimonides** (1135–1204; see entry), a well-respected scholar of Judaism.

Early life

Moses Mendelssohn was born on September 6, 1729, in Dessau, a city in what was then the German state of Anhalt-Dessau. Because his father, a poor scribe, or copier of manuscripts and other documents, was named Mendel, Moses took the surname Mendelssohn, which means "son of Mendel." As a child he suffered an illness that left him with a curvature, or curving, of the spine, and throughout his life he spoke with a stammer.

Although Mendelssohn was largely self-taught, he also took part in formal study under a local rabbi named David Fränkel. A rabbi is a person trained in Jewish law, ritual, and tradition who is often the head of a synagogue, or Jewish house of worship. Fränkel taught Mendelssohn the Hebrew Scriptures, or holy texts, commonly referred to by Christians as the Old Testament; the Talmud, which contains traditions that explain and interpret the Torah, the first five books of the Hebrew Scriptures; and the works of Moses Maimonides. One of Maimonides's most important works, *Guide of the Perplexed,* was reprinted for the first time in two centuries when Mendelssohn was thirteen. The publication of this book signaled a growing interest in Jewish thought.

In 1743 Fränkel received an appointment as rabbi in Berlin, Germany, and Mendelssohn, then fourteen years old, followed him in order to study at his *yeshiva,* or Jewish school. Mendelssohn's life in Berlin was one of extreme poverty, and although he earned small sums of money by tutoring, he was forced to accept meals from neighboring families. He did, however, receive a very thorough education at the yeshiva. In addition to studying Jewish theology (the study of religion), he became skilled in mathematics, philosophy, astronomy (the study of the stars and planets), and logic. He studied French, English, Italian, Greek, and Latin. He used his small income to purchase a Latin copy of *Essay Concerning Human Understanding,* a major work by the English philosopher John Locke (1632–1704).

Mendelssohn took a job tutoring the children of Isaac Bernhard, a silk merchant in 1750. He quickly won Bernhard's confidence, and in time Bernhard made the young scholar his bookkeeper, then his partner. In 1754 Bernhard introduced Mendelssohn to the great German philosopher, dramatist, and literary critic Gotthold Lessing (1729–1781). Lessing was one of the important figures of the Enlightenment in Germany. The Enlightenment was a philosophical movement in Europe during the eighteenth century that emphasized reason over blind faith and tradition. These ideas were expressed in Lessing's writings. He was also a strong believer in religious tolerance at a time when Europe's Jews were forced to live in isolated portions of cities and were the victims of widespread discrimination. Jews were denied citizenship and education, barred from most professions, regarded as unintelligent and greedy, and blamed for all sorts of social problems. Lessing's 1749 play *The Jews* was extraordinary at the time for its depictions of Jews acting morally and kindly.

The relationship between Mendelssohn and Lessing was first established through the game of chess, which they both loved. Soon Mendelssohn found Lessing's views entirely consistent with his own, and the two men became lifelong friends. Mendelssohn also developed a friendship with the renowned German philosopher Immanuel Kant (1724–1804). Although the two were professional rivals, Kant became one of Mendelssohn's admirers.

Mendelssohn the philosopher

During the 1750s and 1760s Mendelssohn became one of the leading philosophers in Europe and found himself at or very near the center of some of the age's fiercest philosophical debates. After he wrote his first book, *Philosophical Conversations,* he shared the manuscript with Lessing, who had it published anonymously in 1755 without telling his friend. With Lessing's encouragement, Mendelssohn continued to write philosophical treatises (papers; reports), many of them published anonymously in the 1750s.

In 1759 Mendelssohn began to write essays and letters for a journal called *Literaturbriefe.* In many of these pieces Mendelssohn defended German philosophy, especially the work of the philosopher and mathematician Gottfried Leibniz (1646–1716). Leibniz was a rationalist, but he also believed in a benevolent (kind) God who arranged the world as a harmonious and organized place. Mendelssohn believed that Leibniz had come under unfair attack by English and French philosophers. The French philosopher Voltaire (1694–1778), for example, had savagely ridiculed Leibniz in his most famous work, *Candide* (1759), and Mendelssohn offered a defense of his countryman.

Mendelssohn encountered trouble in 1760 when he published a highly unfavorable review of a volume of poetry written by the Prussian king Frederick the Great (1712–1786; ruled 1740–86). He was critical of the king's poems because they appeared to deny that the soul was immortal. Mendelssohn also criticized the king for writing in French

The Parable of the Ring

Gotthold Lessing's *Nathan the Wise* is set during the Third Crusade, which was conducted in the early 1190s as part of Christian Europe's effort to retain control of Palestine, the Holy Land, and especially Jerusalem. The play depicts representatives of the warring parties, which include Nathan, a Jewish merchant; Saladin, a Muslim general; and a Knight Templar (a Christian warrior). The parties are shown resolving the differences between Judaism, Islam, and Christianity. At the center of the play is the ring parable, which Nathan tells after Saladin asks him which religion is the true one. (A parable is a simple story that illustrates a moral or religious lesson.) Within the parable, a ring is repeatedly passed from father to most-favored son, with the belief that the ring would make the son pleasing in the eyes of God. In time the ring comes to a father who has three sons, whom he loves equally. Accordingly he has two duplicates of the ring made so that he can give one ring to each son. After the father's death, the sons quarrel about who owns the real ring. They take the matter to a judge, who gives the following decision:

> If you will take advice in lieu of sentence,
> This is my counsel to you, to take up
> The matter where it stands. If each of you
> Has had a ring presented by his father,
> Let each believe his own the real ring.

> 'Tis possible the father chose no longer
> To tolerate the one ring's tyranny;
> And certainly, as he much loved you all,
> And loved you all alike, it could not
>   please him
> By favouring one to be of two the
>   oppressor.
> Let each feel honoured by this free
>   affection.
> Unwarped of prejudice; let each endeavour
> To vie with both his brothers in displaying
> The virtue of his ring; assist its might
> With gentleness, benevolence, forbearance,
> With inward resignation to the godhead,
> And if the virtues of the ring continue
> To show themselves among your children's
>   children,
> After a thousand thousand years, appear
> Before this judgment-seat—a greater one
> Than I shall sit upon it, and decide.

The three rings, of course, represent Judaism, Islam, and Christianity, all gifts from God the Father in heaven.

Peterson, Daniel C. and William J. Hamblin. "Nathan the Wise—An Allegory of Religious Toleration?" *Meridian Magazine*. 2004. Available online at http://www.meridianmagazine. com/ideas/041003nathan.html.

rather than in German, the language of his own people. In response to this review, the king's censor banned the journal in which it was published.

Nonetheless, Frederick evidently came to set aside whatever sense of personal insult he had felt. In 1763 Mendelssohn entered a competition held by the Prussian Academy of Sciences. He had become increasingly troubled by the effect that science was having on religious belief. To address this, he wrote an essay in which he argued that certain mathematical problems could be applied to metaphysics, or the branch of philosophy that deals with reality that lies beyond the senses. After the essay won the academy's first prize, Frederick awarded Mendelssohn the status of "Jew under extraordinary protection." As such, Mendelssohn enjoyed the right to live in Berlin undisturbed.

In 1767 Mendelssohn's major work *Phädon* was published. Mendelssohn wrote the text in response to the age's growing materialism, or focus on the physical world rather than the spiritual one. He structured the book as a philosophical dialogue modeled on *Phaedo,* by the ancient Greek philosopher **Plato** (427–347 BCE; see entry). *Phädon,* which was written in German, became a huge success. Before long, it was translated into nearly all European languages and gave rise to the "Phädon movement," a number of published treatises on the same topic by various authors. Many people called Mendelssohn the "German Plato" or the "German Socrates." He became a popular figure, and anyone of intellectual stature visiting Berlin would set aside time to pay him a visit.

Controversy with Lavater

Up until this point in his career Mendelssohn had paid little attention to Judaism in his published writings. Indeed, in most of his work he engaged in the same scientific debates that preoccupied virtually all Enlightenment philosophers, regardless of religion. From his early years, he had been troubled by the popularity of Jewish mysticism in Germany, especially a movement known as Hasidism, founded by Rabbi **Israel ben Eliezer** (1700–1760; see entry). This movement featured a mystical view of Judaism, with followers focusing more on personal experience than on reason and formal education. Mendelssohn, a rationalist, opposed such mysticism, which he believed was a rejection of human reason.

Mendelssohn's largely secular approach to philosophy underwent a transformation, however, after August 1769. That month the Swiss theologian Johann Kaspar Lavater (1741–1801) published a German translation of an essay by the Swiss theologian and naturalist (a person who studies natural history) Charles Bonnet (1720–1793) entitled *Christian Evidences.* This essay argued that Christianity was superior to other religions. Lavater believed that Christians would only be able to achieve salvation if they somehow managed to convert Jews to Christianity. He was a central figure in a group of religious enthusiasts informally known as *Schwärmer,* or "fanatics."

In the introduction to Bonnet's text, Lavater, although he greatly admired Mendelssohn, issued a challenge to him: disprove Bonnet's ideas or convert to Christianity. Mendelssohn refused to engage Lavater in public debate. He believed such debate would only heighten religious passions and make the climate of intolerance worse. Instead he published pleas for open-mindedness regarding religion. Other *Schwärmer* then began to bother Mendelssohn with the same challenge. They believed that if Mendelssohn was an advocate of proving things through the use of reason, he had no alternative but to either defend his views or accept Christianity as the one true religion.

Mendelssohn felt considerable strain as a result of these and other disputes. In 1771 he experienced an illness that left him partially paralyzed. He underwent medical treatment for five years, and during these years he withdrew from public debate and did not publish. He did, however, begin to believe that he could best put his powers of reason to use by opposing the *Schwärmer* and bettering the condition of Europe's Jews. From the mid-1770s until his death, Mendelssohn devoted himself to issues that affected the welfare of the Jewish community.

The Jewish Enlightenment

Mendelssohn believed that the main problem faced by Jews in Germany and throughout the rest of Europe was that they were isolated. They were separated from the surrounding Christian culture because their children went to Jewish schools and they conducted their affairs in Yiddish, a form of German written in Hebrew and spoken mainly by northern European Jews. To improve the cultural, social, and economic status of German Jews, Mendelssohn took steps to mix them into the surrounding culture. To that end, one of the chief projects that occupied him in his later years was a new translation of the Torah, as well as other portions of the Bible, into German. While preparing the translation, Mendelssohn attracted a number of helpers, all of whom worked on various portions of the project.

The translation was published in 1783. Because of its grace and clarity, this translation has often been considered largely responsible for the standardization of the German language. More importantly, by having scripture written in the local language, German Jews began to see themselves as Germans rather than as aliens wandering in a foreign land. German Jews began to engage themselves in German culture and society by reforming education, studying secular disciplines such as the sciences, and adding their voices to Enlightenment thought. The period of the

German Jewish Enlightenment is referred to as the Haskalah, literally, "enlightenment" in Hebrew. In time the movement spread throughout much of Europe.

Mendelssohn continued to publish works that invited debate, which were then as much political as philosophical. People in Europe were paying attention to the struggle of Americans to achieve independence from the British Empire. Growing discontent in France would lead to the French Revolution late in the 1780s. In 1781 Mendelssohn published *On the Civil Amelioration of the Condition of the Jews,* a plea for religious tolerance and a call for the freedom of Jewish people from the cultural limitations that suppressed them. His most important work during this period was *Jerusalem; or, On Religious Power and Judaism* (1783). *Jerusalem* was a forcefully written work that asserted freedom of conscience and the view that the state should play no role in determining the religious beliefs of its citizens. This doctrine would become a part of the First

Amendment to the U.S. Constitution, which established "separation of church and state" in American government. In *Jerusalem*, Mendelssohn takes the position that many truths exist. Just as governments may differ depending on the needs of their people, people themselves may differ in their understandings of religious truths according to their own situations.

During his later years Mendelssohn became an outright activist on behalf of Jewish political rights. In time his writings, as well as those of other prominent figures during the Haskalah, began to have far-reaching effects. He campaigned on behalf of the Patent of Toleration, issued in Austria on October 19, 1781. This proclamation called for "better instruction and enlightenment of [Jewish] youth, and its employment in the sciences, arts, and crafts." Joseph II (1741–1790), the emperor of Austria, had come to believe that the only way to improve the condition of Jews was to ensure that they enjoyed the same political rights as other citizens of the empire.

Mendelssohn lived to see the publication of *Morning Hours; or, Lectures about God's Existence* in 1785. His final work was a book defending Lessing, who had been widely and viciously criticized for *The Jews* and *Nathan the Wise,* which called for toleration of Jews at a time when large numbers of people in Europe strongly disliked Jews. Mendelssohn carried the work to his publishers, caught a cold, and died of complications on January 4, 1786. He left behind his wife, Fromet Gugenheim, whom he had married in 1762. The couple had six surviving children, several of whom went on to distinguished careers.

Mendelssohn's views faced intense criticism during his lifetime and afterward, from both Jews and non-Jews. Mendelssohn is widely regarded as the spark behind modern Reform Judaism, which does not accept many of the traditional Jewish beliefs, such as that God gave Moses the Torah, but does adhere to the central practices of the religion. As such, conservative Orthodox Jews feared that Mendelssohn's reforms would alienate Jews from their traditional culture and law. They were partially right. In response to the Haskalah, many European Jews discontinued their practice of Jewish law. Many converted to Christianity, including all of Mendelssohn's children and his grandson, the pianist and composer Felix Mendelssohn (1809–1847). Many immigrated to the United States, while others initiated the Zionist movement, which eventually led to the formation of a Jewish state in Israel. Judaism in Europe was forever changed because of the work of Moses Mendelssohn.

For More Information

BOOKS

Altmann, Alexander. *Moses Mendelssohn: A Biographical Study*. Oxford, UK: Littman Library of Jewish Civilization, 1998.

Isaacs, Abram S. *Step by Step: A Story of the Early Days of Moses Mendelssohn*. Whitefish, MT: Kessinger Publishing, 2005.

Sorkin, David. *Moses Mendelssohn and the Religious Enlightenment*. Berkeley, CA: University of California Press, 1996.

WEB SITES

"Mendelssohn." *JewishEncyclopedia.com*. http://www.jewishencyclopedia.com/view.jsp?artid=446&letter=M (accessed on June 2, 2006).

"Moses Mendelssohn." *Stanford Encyclopedia of Philosophy*. http://plato.stanford.edu/entries/mendelssohn/ (accessed on June 2, 2006).

Peterson, Daniel C. and William J. Hamblin. "Nathan the Wise—An Allegory of Religious Toleration?." *Meridian Magazine*. 2004. http://www.meridianmagazine.com/ideas/041003nathan.html (accessed June 2, 2006).

Schoenberg, Shira. "The Haskalah." *Jewish Virtual Library*. http://www.jewishvirtuallibrary.org/jsource/Judaism/Haskalah.html (accessed on June 2, 2006).

Shavin, David. "Philosophical Vignettes from the Political Life of Moses Mendelssohn." *The Schiller Institute*. http://www.schillerinstitute.org/fid_97-01/992_mend_dms.html (accessed on June 2, 2006).

Moses

BORN: C. 1392 BCE
DIED: C. 1272 BCE

prophet; religious leader

Moses.
© CORBIS.

"May my teaching drop as the rain, my speech distill as the dew . . . / For I will proclaim the name of the Lord. / Ascribe greatness to our God."

Moses ranks as one of the major leaders, prophets (divine messengers), and lawgivers in the Jewish and Christian traditions. He is best remembered for leading the Israelites, or the Jewish people, out of slavery from Egypt in about the thirteenth century BCE. The account of this journey is detailed in the Hebrew Scriptures in the book of Exodus. The Hebrew Scriptures, or sacred texts, are often referred to by Christians as the Old Testament of the Bible. They are called the Tanakh by Jews. Jews refer to the first five books of the Tanakh, which are Exodus, Genesis, Leviticus, Numbers, and Deuteronomy, as the Torah. Orthodox Jews and conservative Christians traditionally believe that these five books were written by Moses himself, although many modern biblical scholars dispute this notion. They believe the Torah was written by a number of authors over time.

As a lawgiver among the Israelites, Moses handed down many of the beliefs, traditions, and institutions that would become part of the foundations of Western government, law, and religion. He was one of the earliest supporters of monotheism, or the belief in one supreme God. The official religions of most of the empires in the region at the time were polytheistic, meaning they worshipped many gods, and large numbers of people practiced idol worship, or the worship of physical objects as gods. Due to this monotheistic view, Islam also reveres Moses as a great prophet, one of the earliest in a line of prophets ending with **Muhammad** (c. 570–632; see entry), the founder of Islam, who likewise preached belief in one God.

Biographical information on Moses

Virtually everything known about Moses and his life comes from the Torah. No other historical or biographical records exist. Confirming the events narrated in these books is difficult, if not impossible. Jewish rabbinical scholars have primarily been responsible for reconstructing Moses's life, although many others have also contributed to the effort. Rabbinical scholars are those studying to be rabbis, or people trained in Jewish ritual, law, and tradition. Along with the Tanakh, these scholars have drawn on various sources of biblical interpretation and detailed, critical examinations of the Hebrew Scriptures. The Talmud, the authoritative body of Jewish tradition, contains many such examinations. The Talmud has two parts: the Mishnah, which consists of oral interpretations of the Torah compiled about the second century, and the Gemara, which consists of comments on the Mishnah.

Rather than simply believing the biblical accounts of Moses's life to be true or not true, rabbinical scholars analyze the text in various ways to form a more educated opinion. They take into account the geography described in scripture; the general cultural atmosphere during Moses's lifetime; the histories of other religious systems that emerged before, during, and after Moses's lifetime; and the findings of archaeologists (people who study the remains of past cultures), who have located ruins, artifacts, and other objects that can be connected to the biblical account. Despite all this, factual evidence is scarce, and separating the true stories of Moses's life from the legends is a highly difficult task.

Moses's birth and early life

Moses was born around 1392 BCE to Amram and his wife, Jochebed. According to legend, Moses lived to be 120 years old, dying in the year 2488 of the Hebrew calendar, or 1272 BCE. The story of his birth and infancy is one of the most widely known tales from the Hebrew Scriptures. During this period Egypt was a powerful nation. Upper Egypt and Lower Egypt had been united under a new line of pharaohs, or kings. Throughout much of the thirteenth century BCE Egypt was ruled by Ramses II (c. 1304–c. 1237 BCE), and many historian believe that Ramses is the pharaoh referred to in the Hebrew Scriptures.

During his reign Ramses undertook a major building program in the delta region, where the Nile River flows into the Mediterranean Sea. Prior to this, the Israelites had found refuge from a severe food shortage in Egypt along the Nile River. The river's annual floods watered the nearby land and nourished it with rich silt, creating a 4,000-mile-long area of agricultural land surrounded by harsh desert. The Egyptians considered the Israelites to be gypsies, homeless wanderers who were nuisances and disgraced their nation. Ramses did not know what to do with the Israelites until the building program began. Since he needed large numbers of laborers to dig mud and make bricks for new buildings, he enslaved the Israelites and forced them to perform the manual labor. Part of his intention was to work as many of them as possible to death, so as to shrink their numbers. Despite his efforts, the Israelite population continued to increase. Frustrated, Ramses ordered that all sons born to Israelite couples be thrown into the Nile River and drowned.

Amram and Jochebed were Israelites living in Egypt. They were members of the Levite tribe, which had traditionally been the source of the Israelites' priestly class. To save her baby, Jochebed hid him, but after three months, when she could hide him no more, she set him adrift on the Nile in a waterproof basket made of reeds, a tall grass that grows in wet areas. The pharaoh's daughter happened to discover the basket and the baby, still alive. She rescued the infant, named him Moses, which means "to draw out," and raised him as her own son. Moses's sister, Miriam, followed the basket as it traveled down the river. When the pharaoh's daughter found the baby, Miriam offered to find an Israelite woman to nurse the child; in this way, Jochebed, Moses's actual mother, became his nurse.

The pharaoh's daughter was most likely not a princess of the royal bloodline but rather the daughter of one of the concubines (women who have sexual relations with a man they are not married to) in the pharaoh's harem, or the group of women he claimed as his own. The young woman probably took Moses back to the harem, where he was raised under the supervision of all the women. There he learned to read and write Egyptian hieroglyphics (ancient pictoral script) and probably received training in other social, administrative, and military skills. Foreign children were commonly raised in this way, enabling them to enter careers in the military or the civil service.

In this way, Moses grew to manhood. One day he reportedly witnessed an Egyptian abusing an Israelite slave. Angered, he killed the Egyptian and buried his body in the sand, thinking that no one would discover it. Later, however, as he tried to break up a fight between two Israelites, one taunted him about the Egyptian he had killed. Moses then feared for his life, particularly after he discovered that the pharaoh had also learned of his murderous act. He fled to the deserts of the Sinai Peninsula, where he lived for forty years with the Midianites, who were descendants of the prophet **Abraham** (c. 2050–c. 1950 BCE; see entry). Moses married Zipporah, the daughter of a Midian priest, and lived the life of a shepherd, learning how to survive in the harsh deserts. His son, Gershom, was born of this union.

Moses's commission from God

One day Moses was tending his flock on Egypt's Mount Horeb, the precise location of which is uncertain but may be modern-day Mount Sinai. He observed a bush that was on fire but not being destroyed. When Moses neared the burning bush, God announced his presence and commanded Moses to serve as his messenger to the pharaoh and to lead the Jews out of slavery from Egypt. This astonished the humble shepherd, and Moses expressed great reluctance. He told God that he would be unable to explain God's identity to the people, that the people would not believe him, and that he would be unable to carry out such a huge task. God answered each of Moses's objections, and Moses eventually relented.

Moses then returned to Egypt. When he arrived he met his older brother, Aaron, whom God had already informed of Moses's coming return. The two met with the elders of the Israelites and, with Aaron doing most of the talking, informed them of God's intentions. Aaron would later become Moses's chief general.

The Plagues of Egypt and Other Miracles

In claiming that a miracle has taken place, one suggests that God has chosen to involve Himself in the affairs of humans. Belief in miracles requires strong religious faith. Many people find it difficult to accept the idea that God has ever intervened in human affairs, such as with the plagues of Egypt and other events recorded in scripture.

In studying biblical history, many scholars look for natural ways to explain apparently miraculous events. In the case of the plagues, some claim that usually high flooding of the Nile River could have pulled red-tinted earth into the water, creating the impression that the water had turned to blood. Further, this flooding could have polluted the water, perhaps with microorganisms that killed the fish. In turn, the high flood tides could have swept frogs and insects into communities, where they could have multiplied rapidly, spreading disease (especially skin disease, because of the excessive moisture) and ruining crops. In addition, the sun sometimes disappears behind clouds of dust during sandstorms, which could explain the three days when the sun was not visible in the story about the plague in Egypt recounted in the Tanakh, or the Old Testament.

Several events occurred when the Israelites were fleeing the Egyptian army that again raise the issue of God's possible miraculous intervention on behalf of the Jews. According to the book of Exodus, God parted the Red Sea, allowed the Jews to escape on foot, then released the walls of water so they rushed down onto the pursuing Egyptians. Again, potential natural explanations exist. One holds that the events did not take place at the Red Sea but at the Isthmus of Suez, an arm of water that extends inland from the Mediterranean Sea. An earthquake could have caused a tsunami, a massive wave of water that engulfed the Egyptians after the Israelites passed by safely. An alternative explanation claims that the "Red Sea" as specified in Exodus was in actuality a large marsh that was thick with reeds. On foot, the Israelites would have been able to make their way through the marsh, but the Egyptians' horse-drawn chariots would have become stuck in the soggy ground, and, as the horses struggled, the Egyptians might have lost their lives.

These elders attempted to persuade the pharaoh to release the Israelites, but he refused. To show his support for the Israelites, God unleashed a series of plagues on Egypt over the course of a year. The water in the Nile turned to blood, killing the fish; frogs were driven from the river and invaded homes; gnats and flies blanketed the land; skin infections broke out on both people and their livestock; hail and storms destroyed crops; the wind carried in swarms of locusts; and the sun was blotted out for three days. The pharaoh and his magicians were not able to stop these plagues, which ended with the death of all firstborn sons of the Egyptians. (The Jewish feast of Passover honors this event, when God "passed over" the homes of the Israelites and

Moses receives the tablets containing the Ten Commandments from heaven on Mount Sinai (top). He presents these laws to the Israelites (bottom), who accept them and enter into a covenant, or agreement, with God. THE ART ARCHIVE/ BRITISH LIBRARY.

spared their sons.) The Egyptians became so terrified that they not only released the Israelites but ordered them to leave Egypt.

The Exodus

The story that dominates the book of Exodus is that of the wandering of the Israelites in the desert after their escape from Egypt. According to Exodus, the Israelite men numbered some six hundred thousand; adding in women and children would bring the total number of travelers to perhaps two million. Under the leadership of Moses the Israelites followed a route southeast to the town of Succoth, then northeast to the Isthmus of Suez, southeast again along the Sinai Peninsula to Mount Sinai, and finally northeast to Hebron, in Palestine. This journey took place over a period of forty years.

Early on in the flight of the Israelites, referred to as the Exodus, the pharaoh apparently changed his mind about ordering the Israelites out and sent his army in pursuit. The Israelites achieved a great victory at the Red Sea, which is said to have miraculously parted, allowing them to walk across safely and then swamping the pursuing Egyptian army. Another key event concerned the hunger and thirst of the people in the desert. They began to grumble and question Moses, but God met their needs by providing water and food. The source of the water was probably porous (having pores, or holes, that allow liquid through) limestone rock. No satisfactory explanation has been offered for the source of the food, called *manna,* though it has been speculated that it was the juice of a plant or perhaps a lichen, a kind of moss.

God's covenant with the Israelites

After the Israelites crossed the Egyptian frontier, Moses became their chief lawgiver. At Mount Sinai he climbed the slopes and met God. God then gave Moses the Ten Commandments, written on two stone tablets. In a section of Exodus called the "book of the covenant," God, through Moses, outlined his covenant, or agreement, with the Israelites and established a basic code of law. This code provided instructions regarding worship and a number of other matters. The code included many civil laws, such as those relating to the rights of slaves; to manslaughter and other injury to human life; to theft and damage of property; to social and religious duties; and to justice and human rights. It also included laws regarding major feasts, such as the requirement that Jews eat unleavened bread, or bread made without yeast, to celebrate the feast of Passover and the Jews' Exodus from Egypt. (Presumably, they left too quickly to be able to bring leaven for their bread.) The book after Exodus, Leviticus, lists in further detail God's laws for his people. These laws governed most aspects of life as it would have been lived in an agricultural society, covering such matters as rules for priests; the treatment of food; hygiene; medicine; sexual behavior; and other topics. While Leviticus is the chief law book, the books of Numbers and Deuteronomy outline additional Jewish laws.

The Israelites remained at Sinai for about a year. During that time Moses communicated with God frequently. As a sign of his covenant with his people, God gave Moses instructions for constructing the tabernacle, a elaborate tent that served as a shrine and signified that God lived among them.

The last chapters of the book of Exodus detail the continued wanderings of the Israelites. From Sinai, Moses led the people to Kadesh in modern-day northern Lebanon. From there, at the urging of the people, he sent scouts ahead to the promised land of Canaan, on the other side of the river Jordan, which was the Israelites' ultimate goal. The promised land was the land that God had promised to Abraham would belong to his people, the Jews. The scouts, however, returned with terrifying tales about what they observed, such as that Canaan was a land of giants who devoured their own people, and the Israelites refused to move on. The Israelites then remained in the area around Kadesh for thirty-eight years. During these years Moses faced challenges to his leadership, including one from his own brother, Aaron, and one from his sister, Miriam. He survived these challenges until his people resumed their journey. They detoured around the kingdom of the Edomites and the land of Moab, both of which refused to allow the Israelites passage. When they encountered the land of the Amorites, they fought, conquering the Amorites and seizing their territory.

Moses had been warned by God that he would never be able to lead his people on the final stage of their journey, when they would cross the river Jordan and enter the promised land. As the people approached the end of their travels, Moses assembled the tribes of Israelites and delivered a parting address, recorded in Deuteronomy, chapter 32, verses 1–3, which begins as follows:

> Give ear, O heavens, and I will speak:
> and let the earth hear the words of my mouth.
> May my teaching drop as the rain, my speech distill
>   as the dew, as the gentle rain upon the tender grass,
> and as the showers upon the herb.
> For I will proclaim the name of the Lord.
> Ascribe greatness to our God.

Moses then climbed Mount Nebo, where he looked out over the country before him and died.

For More Information

BOOKS

Kirsch, Jonathan. *Moses: A Life.* New York, NY: Ballantine, 1999.

Swindoll, Charles R. *Moses: A Man of Selfless Dedication.* Nashville, TN: Word Publishing, 1999.

Wildavsky, Aaron, and Yoram Hazony. *Moses as Political Leader.* Lanham, MD: Shalem Press, 2005.

WEB SITES

Hirsch, Emil G., Benno Jacob, and S. R. Driver. "Exodus, Book of." *JewishEncyclopedia.com.* http://www.jewishencyclopedia.com/view.jsp?artid=551&letter=E&search=Exodus (accessed on June 2, 2005).

Moberly, R. W. L. "More about Moses: Biography." *The Good Book.* http://www.bbc.co.uk/religion/religions/christianity/features/thegoodbook/moses/biog.shtml (accessed on June 2, 2006).

OTHER SOURCES

The Story of Moses. Directed by James L. Conway. Worcester, PA: Vision Video, 1998.

Muhammad

BORN: c. 570 • Mecca, Saudi Arabia
DIED: June 8, 632 • Medina, Saudi Arabia

Arabian prophet; religious leader

"The merciful are shown mercy by the All-Merciful. Show mercy to those on earth, and God will show mercy to you."

The world's one billion Muslims believe that Muhammad, the founder of Islam, was sent to Earth by Allah (God) as his final prophet, or divine messenger. His name can also be spelled Mohammad, Mohammed, or Mahomet, but he is generally referred to as the Prophet. He was born Muhammad ibn Abdullah in the city of Mecca, in the Hejaz region of modern-day Saudi Arabia. The exact date of his birth is uncertain. Some believe he was born on April 20, but Muslims belonging to the Shi'a sect, or division, believe the date was April 26. The year is variously given as 570 or 571 CE, although some scholars have argued for both earlier and later dates, 567 and 573, respectively.

Biographical information

Islamic scholars are uncertain of many of the details of Muhammad's life. The main sources of information on the subject include Islam's sacred scripture, the Qur'an; the sayings of Muhammad, called the *hadiths,* which were written down by his closest followers; and the *sira,* more formally referred to as the *sirat nabawiyya.* The sira are the traditional Muslim biographies of Muhammad, written during the golden age of Islam, from about 750 to 1500.

Problems exist with all of these sources. The Qur'an is not meant to be biographical, although it does contain some biographical details. During

Muslim pilgrims on the haj circle around the Ka'aba in Mecca, Saudi Arabia. All Muslims are expected to make the haj to Mecca at least once in their lifetime. AP IMAGES.

the era when the hadiths were written down, Islam was breaking into different sects and schools of thought, each with its own traditions. This leads modern Muslim scholars to agree that some of the hadiths might be unreliable. Qur'anic Muslims, also known as "Qur'an alone" Muslims, reject the authenticity of the hadiths entirely. The most famous compiler of hadiths, Muhammad ibn Isma'il Bukhari (810–870), gathered 600,000 supposed sayings of Muhammad, but he was able to confirm the authenticity of only about 2,600. Finally, some of the sira were written more than a century after Muhammad's death, so determining what is fact and what is based on possibly unreliable oral tradition is difficult.

Muhammad's early life

Muhammad was born into a relatively wealthy Meccan family. His father, Abdullah, died before he was born, and he was raised by his paternal grandfather, Abd al-Mattalib. His mother, Amina, who had continued to live with her own family after her marriage to Abdullah, died when Muhammad was six. After Muhammad's grandfather died when he was eight, responsibility for his care fell to his uncle, Abu Tālib. Abu Tālib had recently become head of the most powerful tribe in Mecca, the Quraysh.

During the sixth century Mecca was an important center on the east–west trade routes. Many merchants and traders stopped in Mecca to visit the Ka'aba, a shrine controlled by the Quraysh in which many idols were worshipped. Idols are objects, such as statues, that are worshipped as divide, or god-like. Meccans had a financial interest in encouraging this idol worship, for it kept travelers in the city, where they made donations and spent money on food and lodging. During these pilgrimages, warfare between tribes was forbidden so merchants could visit the Ka'aba and conduct business safely. As a result, while he was growing up Muhammad had contact with people who came from many different cultures and who practiced many different religions.

When still in his teens, Muhammad became a merchant himself. He soon gained a reputation for complete honesty, and his nickname became al-Amin, meaning "the trusted one." One of his employers was a wealthy widow, Khadijah, who may have been as much as fifteen years older than he. Khadijah offered Muhammad her hand in marriage, and the two were wed in 595. It was this marriage that made Muhammad a wealthy man, since, as a minor child, he had not been able to inherit from his father. Some stories say that Khadijah bore Muhammad four daughters and a son who died in infancy. Shi'a Muslims, however, claim that the only daughter of this marriage was Fatima and that the others either had been born during a previous marriage or were the children of Khadijah's sister.

The seeds of Islam

Muhammad often withdrew to a nearby cave called Hira to meditate (engage in quiet and focused reflection) and pray for guidance in religious matters. After spending a night in the cave in about 610, Muhammad returned to his family with an astonishing story. He said that during the night he had been visited by the archangel Jabra'il. He also said that he heard a voice saying, "Read in the name of your Lord the Creator. Read, and your Lord is the Most Honored. He taught man with the pen; taught him all that he knew not." Other visions and visitations like this

Muhammad and the Ka'aba

Most of the traditional accounts of Muhammad's life emphasize the high regard in which he was held in his community during the years before his revelations (public expressions of divine will or truth). One legend addresses his role in the renovation of the Ka'aba, a shrine that contained idols worshipped by the people, although the story has likely been exaggerated. According to the legend, the Ka'aba was in great need of repair, but no one wanted to perform the necessary work out of fear that the idols contained in the shrine would somehow release their supernatural powers against the people of Mecca. In addition, materials and skilled workmen were unavailable. This changed, however, when a capsized Greek ship washed ashore carrying high-quality wood and a skilled carpenter who had survived the wreck.

Work began on the Ka'aba and proceeded quickly. In one corner of the Ka'aba was a sacred stone called the Black Stone. During the repairs this stone had to be moved to a different location, and each of the four most powerful tribes in Mecca desired the honor of moving it. A heated argument broke out, but eventually all agreed to abide by the decision of the first man to enter the Ka'aba. That man turned out to be Muhammad. Muhammad settled the dispute by calling for a large cloak. He placed the Black Stone in the center of the cloak, then had a representative of each of the tribes grasp one corner of the cloak and carry the stone to its new position. In this way, he preserved peace among the four tribes.

supposedly continued until Muhammad's death. At first, Muhammad was puzzled by these revelations and was not sure that he wanted to take on the role of a prophet. With the encouragement of his wife, however, he eventually accepted his mission.

With these visitations Muhammad claimed there was only one true god, Allah, and that he, Muhammad, was the last of several prophets that Allah had communicated with. According to Muhammad, when previous prophets had failed to follow Allah's instructions to reform the religious and social beliefs of their nations, those nations had been destroyed. Khadijah became the first convert to Muhammad's new religion, which was called Islam. The second was a ten-year-old cousin, and the third was Muhammad's closest friend, Abu Bakr (c. 543–634). Beginning in about 613, Muhammad began to preach his beliefs and to recite verses from his revelations. These verses became the Qur'an, a word that literally means "the recitation." Over time he attracted a small but growing number of followers.

Many members of the community ridiculed Muhammad and his followers, often beating them and throwing garbage at them. They strongly disagreed with Muhammad's views about social justice, including his claim that the condition of slaves needed to be improved. Social justice is an ideal in which all people have the same rights and opportunities. They also objected to his belief that people should replace their deeply held tribal and clan loyalties with the Islamic faith. He was seen as a threat by local religious leaders, who depended on the Ka'aba for their power and income. If the people did as Muhammad preached and stopped worshipping the idols in the shrine, the city would lose trade from traveling merchants. Making matters more difficult for Muhammad was the fact that his own tribe held the position of guardian of the Ka'aba. Despite these pressures from the community, Abu Talib, Muhammad's uncle, continued to support him, although he did try to restrain his nephew somewhat.

In 620, a decade after Muhammad's first revelation, he reportedly made an announcement to his followers. He said that the previous night, Jabra'il had appeared to him with a winged horse called the Buraq and had escorted him on a miraculous journey. The first part of his journey, the Isra, took him to the holy city of Jerusalem and to the Dome of the Rock on the city's Temple Mount. During the second part of the journey, the Miraj, he was taken to heaven, where he toured paradise and spoke with Allah and some previous well-known prophets. Tradition holds that Allah instructed Muhammad to tell his followers to pray fifty times each day. The Prophet Moses, however, told Muhammad that no one would agree to pray that often and that he should go back to Allah and ask if the number could be lessened. Muhammad persuaded Allah to reduce the requirement to five times each day, a practice that Muslims still follow in the early twenty-first century.

Departure from Mecca

Muhammad and his followers endured more than a decade of persecution, with life for them becoming increasingly dangerous. Persecution is when a person or persons are harassed for their beliefs. A number of the chapters of the Qur'an, often referred to as the Meccan revelations, date from this period and document this ill treatment. In 615 Muhammad ordered a number of Islamic families to migrate to Ethiopia for their safety. Six years later, after he learned of a plot to kill him, Muhammad decided to relocate to Yathrib, some 186 miles (299 kilometers) to the north, where a number of converts to Islam lived. This city would later become called Medina. Muslims call this event the *hijrah,* which translates as "emigration" or "flight." The Muslim calendar begins with this event. Muslim dates include the letters AH, meaning *anno hegirae,* or "year of the hijrah." After Muhammad and his followers fled, the Meccans seized all the property they left behind.

Life in Yathrib was an improvement for Muhammad. He had been approached by a delegation from that city about moving there to help settle disputes between tribes. Given considerable authority, he put an end to the disagreements and absorbed the tribes into Islam, forbidding Muslims to shed the blood of other Muslims. Yathrib was also home to a number of Jewish tribes that Muhammad hoped to convert to Islam,

THERE IS NO GOD BUT ALLAH

MUHAMMAD IS HIS MESSENGER

A sign above a mosque reads in both English and Arabic, "There is no God but Allah and Muhammad is His messenger."
© ARKRELIGION.COM/ALAMY.

but his efforts were unsuccessful. Around this time, tradition holds, Muslims began to turn to Mecca during prayer rather than to the Jews' historical homeland, Jerusalem.

As he established his Islamic community in and around Yathrib, Muhammad taught that tolerance should be extended to all "people of the book." This term was used to refer to Jews and Christians, and the book referred to was the Bible, including its two halves, the Old and New Testaments. In contrast to many of the region's empires, Islam was tolerant of other religious faiths, although their members were heavily taxed. Muhammad established the specific terms by which Jews and others could live in his Islamic state in a constitution written in 622–623.

Khadijah, Muhammad's first wife, had died in 619, and in Yathrib Muhammad married A'isha, the daughter of his friend Abu Bakr. Abu Bakr would assume the leadership of Islam as caliph, which means "successor" of Muhammad after Muhammad's death. Muhammad also took a second wife, Hafsa, the daughter of a man named Umar, who would in time become Abu Bakr's successor. Muhammad's daughter Fatima married Muhammad's cousin ʿAlī ibn Abī Tālib (c. 600–661; see entry), who also became a leader of Islam after Muhammad. In this way, Muhammad created a network of family ties that not only strengthened his own position but, he believed, ensured the continuation of the religion he had founded.

Warfare

Relations between the residents of Mecca and Yathrib continued to worsen. Although Muhammad strengthened his power around Yathrib by signing treaties with various other tribes, the Muslims who had relocated from Mecca had no source of income. They relied on charity and some payment they received for manual labor. Eventually they began to assault caravans headed toward Mecca and to take control of the goods being carried. In March 624 Muhammad himself led a party of three hundred followers on one such raid, but they were driven off. The Meccans then sent an army of eight hundred to eliminate the ongoing threat to the caravans. Despite being badly outnumbered, the Muslims emerged victorious in a battle that took place on March 15. This was the first in what would be a long line of military victories for Islam.

The conflict continued, and in 625 a Meccan general named Abu Sufyan led a force of eight thousand men against Yathrib. A battle took place in Uhud on March 23, ending with no winner. In 627 Abu Sufyan attacked again, but Muhammad had ordered a trench dug around the city, and the Muslims successfully repelled the Meccan invaders. By this time the surrounding tribes and cities understood that Islam was a source of strength. The religion grew rapidly as more and more people converted.

By 628 Muhammad's forces were strong enough to reclaim Mecca. Muhammad marched on the city with sixteen hundred troops. Meccan leaders met him at the border and negotiated a treaty that would bring an end to the hostilities. Just two years later, however, Mecca violated the treaty. Muhammad then marched on the city with ten thousand men. Faced with such an overwhelming force, the city leaders surrendered without a fight. Muslims took the city, cast the idols out of the Ka'ba, and converted most of the city's residents to Islam. The Ka'ba was turned into a place of Islamic worship. It remains a central part of Islam that all Muslims are expected to make a *hajj,* or pilgrimage to Mecca, at least once during their lives.

Final years

In the years that followed, Muhammad secured power over the entire Arabian Peninsula. Muhammad's authority was not the result of formal agreements or treaties. He ruled through personal relationships, and Islam was the institution that cemented the growing empire.

Late in life, Muhammad took more wives. In addition to A'isha and Hafsa (and the deceased Khadijah), he married eight other women, for a total of eleven wives, ten of whom were living at the time of his death. Some of these women were the widows of followers of Muhammad who had died in battle. Others were the daughters of political allies. Muhammad's marriages have been the subject of considerable debate. Some historians believe that Aʾisha was only nine years old when he married her. Others have noted that he violated Islamic law by marrying the ex-wife of one of his adopted sons and by taking more than the four wives allowed by the Qurʾan.

Muhammad died unexpectedly at about noon on June 8, 632, in Yathrib. His death touched off a disagreement about who would succeed him. According to Sunnis, who constitute the largest sect of Islam, Abu Bakr was chosen as caliph (leader successor) freely and openly by the leaders of the Islamic community. Members of the Shiʾa sect, however, dispute this, arguing that Muhammad had promised leadership to ʿAli, the husband of his daughter Fatima, and that Abu Bakr and others conspired to deny ʿAli the position. The dispute continues to divide Sunni and Shiʾa Muslims into the twenty-first century.

For More Information

BOOKS

Armstrong, Karen. *Muhammad: A Biography of the Prophet*. San Francisco, CA: HarperSanFrancisco, 1993.

Esposito, John L. *The Oxford History of Islam*. New York, NY: Oxford University Press, 2000.

Esposito, John L. *What Everyone Needs to Know about Islam*. New York, NY: Oxford University Press, 2002.

Rogerson, Barnaby. *The Prophet Muhammad: A Biography*. Mahwah, NJ: Hidden-Spring, 2003.

Sardar, Ziauddin, and Zafar Abbas Malik. *Introducing Muhammad*. Cambridge, UK: Icon Books, 1999.

WEB SITES

"The Quran and Sayings of the Prophet Muhammad." *The Wisdom Fund*. http://www.twf.org/Sayings.html (accessed on June 2, 2006).

Nichiren

BORN: February 16, 1222 • Kominato, Awa, Japan
DIED: October 13, 1282 • Ikegami, Japan

Japanese religious leader

"If you wish to free yourself from the suffering of birth and death you have endured through eternity and attain supreme enlightenment in this lifetime, you must awaken to the mystic truth which has always been within your life."

Nichiren was a Buddhist prophet (divine messenger) and monk who lived in thirteenth-century Japan. He gave his name to a sect, or subgroup, of Buddhism called Nichirenshu, or the Nichiren sect. He did not, however, think of himself as its founder. Nichiren is best known for his belief in the importance of one of Buddhism's sacred texts, the Lotus Sutra. This text describes the virtues of the Buddha and teaches that all people can attain enlightenment. (Enlightenment is the realization of the true nature of reality and the universe.) He helped to unite Buddhists in Japan by calling for the establishment of Buddhism, especially Nichiren Buddhism, as the Japanese state religion. In the twenty-first century many schools of Buddhism continue to practice the form of the religion that Nichiren taught.

Birth and early life

Born in 1222, Nichiren was the son of a fisherman who lived in the village of Kominato in the Awa Province of Japan. At birth his name was Zennichimaru (or sometimes just Zennichi). In addition to fishing Nichiren's father worked at a manor house, or a house occupied by the owner of an agricultural estate. Nichiren was such a talented student that the lord of the manor encouraged him to begin his formal

Nichiren leads a boat of followers as he calms the sea.

education at the Tendai monastery called Kiyosumidera in 1233. Tendai refers to a sect, or subgroup, of Buddhism practiced by the monks who lived there and their followers. After he was ordained, or officially made a monk, in 1237, Nichiren changed his birth name to Rencho. He left the monastery for the city of Kamakura, where he continued his studies, focusing on other forms of Buddhism.

He moved from Kamakura to Mount Hiei, the center of the Tendai sect of Buddhism, and then to Mount Koya, the center of another school of Buddhism. He studied in each of these places, learning more about Buddhism and its various practices in Japan. In 1253 he returned to Kiyosumidera, where he began a mission to bring to Japan what he believed was true Buddhism. It was at this time that he took the name Nichiren. The name Nichiren comes from the Japanese word *nichi,* meaning "sun." He interpreted this name to mean "standing for the Light of Truth as well as for the Land of the Rising Sun," wherein the Land of the Rising Sun was Japan. The syllable *ren* means "lotus" and refers both to the lotus flower and to the Lotus Sutra.

On April 28, 1253, Nichiren publicly declared that all other forms of Buddhism were false. He claimed that only by following the teachings of the Lotus Sutra could one practice true Buddhism. The Lotus Sutra is the most popular Mahayana text. Mahayana Buddhism is one of the two main branches of Buddhism. Nichiren Buddhism is a subgroup of Mahayana. The Lotus Sutra discusses the importance of realizing one's essential Buddha-nature. Buddha-nature is present in every person and allows him or her to grow and obtain greater understanding and ultimately achieve enlightenment.

That same year, Nichiren was banned from Kiyosumidera, and he traveled to Kamakura to spread his teachings. This marked the start of a life filled with banishments and pardons. Nichiren would spend the rest of his life traveling around Japan, in conflict with other schools of Buddhism and with the government.

Banishment

In 1260 Nichiren presented to the government a treatise, or essay, titled "Establish the Right Law and Save Our Country." He wrote the document in the form of a dialogue between an ordinary citizen and a visitor. The dialogue examined the nature of the times in Japan. Nichiren claimed that floods, famine, political conflicts, and other difficulties were increasing because of the government's refusal to accept the Buddha's true teachings as detailed in the Lotus Sutra. He proposed that his version of Buddhism become the state religion of Japan. He also warned that rebellions and foreign invasions would occur if the government did not adopt the true Buddhism.

In the treatise Nichiren divided Japanese history into three eras since the time of the **Buddha,** Siddhartha Gautama (563–483 BCE; see entry), the founder of Buddhism. Nichiren saw the world of the thirteenth century as the third age, an age of collapse called End of the Law. He believed that only by following the teachings of the Lotus Sutra could Japan survive and prosper.

The government responded in 1261 by exiling Nichiren to the province of Izu, in Japan's main island of Honshu. Two years later, however, he was pardoned and continued to preach his form of Buddhism. From 1264 to 1268 Nichiren traveled around Japan preaching and winning converts, but he continued to have conflicts with government authorities.

In 1268 Mongols from Central Asia arrived in Japan and demanded tribute, or payments one government makes to another for protection or to acknowledge submission to the other country, to the Mongolian ruler Kublai Khan (1215–1294). Nichiren had predicted in his 1260 essay that such an event would take place. Once again he called on the government to establish his form of Buddhism as the state religion. He believed that by doing so, the government could unite the Japanese people and protect itself from foreign invaders such as the Mongols.

The government ignored both Nichiren and the Mongols. Many Japanese people, however, were alarmed that Japan was under threat from foreign invaders. They turned increasingly to Nichiren's teachings. In 1271 he was arrested after Buddhist monks from other groups brought charges against him. He was put on trial, convicted, and sentenced to banishment again. In December of that year he was taken to the island of Sado, where he remained until 1274.

Nichiren Practices

Nichiren Buddhists continue to practice many of his teachings. For example they believe that the benefits of this sect of Buddhism can be achieved by chanting the title of the Lotus Sutra, "Myoho Renge Kyo." By this and other words from the Lotus Sutra, a person can supposedly reach "Buddhahood," which is an awakening to the true nature of life. He or she can then see how all of creation is connected and how people have the ability to change and influence the world.

Additionally, Nichiren Buddhists respect the Gohonzon. This is a scroll, written in Chinese characters, that contains the laws of the sect. Many individuals have such a scroll in their homes, and it becomes a focal point for their daily rituals and prayers. The Gohonzon is thought of as a spiritual mirror. By sitting before it and chanting words from the Lotus Sutra, a person is said to be able to recognize his or her own Buddhahood. A devout Nichiren Buddhist does this chanting each morning and evening.

While on Sado, Nichiren wrote *Kaimoku Sho* (Eye-Opener or Liberation from Blindness), in which he continued to express his views about religion and the state. In the book he made three vows: that he would be the pillar, or support, of Japan; that he would be the eyes of Japan; and that he would be the "vessel" of Japan, meaning that he would contain the truth in the form of his teachings.

Final years

Nichiren was released from Sado in 1274. He returned to Kamakura, where he continued to preach his views about the Lotus Sutra and about the need for a more militant state religion. The government of Kamakura by this time was willing to be more tolerant towards him, so he was left alone. He settled near Mount Fuji, and in his final years he built temples there and in other locations. These temples continue to be sacred sites for Nichiren Buddhists into the early twenty-first century. He died in 1282 in the town of Ikegami while he was reciting verses from the Lotus Sutra.

On October 12, 1922, the emperor of Japan conferred on Nichiren the posthumous (after death) title of Rissho Daishi, which can be translated as "Master of the Establishment of Righteousness" or "Great Teacher of the Right Dharma." "Dharma" refers to the path to enlightenment detailed in the Buddha's teachings. Nichiren is also called Daishonin, which means "Great Holy Man."

Nichiren Buddhism

To understand the significance of Nichiren and his teachings, it is necessary to have some understanding of Buddhist sects in Japan and the place of the Lotus Sutra in Buddhist thought. During the Buddha's lifetime none of his teachings were written down. After his death his followers gathered on at least three occasions to refresh their memories of these teachings. Only after one century had passed did the Buddha's words begin to be written down in texts called *sutras*. Because the lessons had

Nichiren Buddhist followers, called Sokagakkai, engage in a display of gymnastics during an annual cultural festival in Tokyo, Japan. Nichiren Buddhists believe the Lotus Sutra to be among the most important of the Buddha's teachings. © BETTMANN/ CORBIS.

been passed along orally for so long, each of the sutras begins with the words "Thus have I heard."

During the early centuries of Buddhism, people began to interpret the Buddha's teachings in different ways. This was another reason that Buddhists were determined to write down the Buddha's teachings, to avoid reinterpretation. Nevertheless, the differences that had already emerged resulted in a split in the religion, and two major branches emerged. These are Theravada and Mahayana. Although each individual Buddhist varies, some rough distinctions can be made between the two branches.

Theravada Buddhism is the most traditional form of Buddhism. Its practices and beliefs are based on a literal interpretation of the original, early teachings of the Buddha. Theravada places great emphasis on self-awareness and meditation. Theravada monks were the first to write down the Buddha's teachings, and they believe these to be the most accurate accounts of his lessons.

The other main branch of Buddhism is called Mahayana Buddhism. Mahayana Buddhists are less strict in their interpretation of the Buddha's teachings, and they recognize more sutras, or sermons, than do Theravada Buddhists. While Theravada Buddhists give reverence, or great respect, only to the Buddha, Mayahana Buddhists recognize many enlightened beings, called *bodhisattvas,* who help people on the path to enlightenment.

Nichiren Buddhism is a subgroup of Mayahana, as are the other schools of Buddhism that Nichiren studied before he started spreading the teachings of the Lotus Sutra. These other schools include Pure Land Buddhism, which is ruled over by the Buddha Amitabha. Buddhists who do not achieve *nirvana,* or the end of suffering, upon their death can be reborn into the Pure Land, where they will be helped on their path. Another subgroup studied by Nichiren is Zen Buddhism. Zen places great emphasis on meditation and simplicity. Zen Buddhists learn by a question-and-answer session between masters and students, called *koans.* The koans often seem illogical and require intense thought and self-examination to understand. They are believed to help people achieve greater spiritual knowledge and move closer to enlightenment.

The Lotus Sutra, which is a shorthand name for the text, is a sacred writing of Mahayana Buddhists, although different Mahayana subgroups may place greater emphasis on other teachings. In the original Sanskrit language, the Lotus Sutra is called the Suddharma-Pundarika Sutra. In Japanese it is called Myohorengekyo, often written as separate words: Myoho-renge-kyo. This name is often shortened to Hokekyo. In English the translation of the title would be "White Lotus of the True Dharma."

Nichiren believed that the Lotus Sutra contained the essence of the Buddha's wisdom. He accepted the teachings of Tendai Buddhism, the sect popularized by the Chinese philosopher and teacher Chih-i (538–597). Tendai Buddhists claim that the teachings of the Buddha, and therefore the sutras, can be divided into five groups, ranging from the earliest to the latest. The earlier sutras are followed by Theravedan Buddhists, but the Mahayana branch believes that only the later sutras, including the Lotus Sutra, contain the truth that the Buddha wanted people to follow.

One of the chief doctrines, or principles, of the Lotus Sutra is that any person can achieve "Buddhahood." This means that enlightenment and salvation are open not just to monks, but to any person who follows the teachings of the Lotus Sutra and other late sutras. One reason that Nichiren accepted the Lotus Sutra as the true teaching of the Buddha was that in the previous sutra, the Innumerable Meaning Sutra, the Buddha had said, "In the past forty odd years, I (Sakyamuni Buddha) had not yet expounded [given or set forth] the truth." Nichiren and his followers believed that the Lotus Sutra, which followed this declaration, then must represent the truth about enlightenment that the Buddha was finally revealing to his followers.

Two additional points about the Lotus Sutra should be noted. One has to do with the significance of the lotus flower. For Buddhists, the lotus flower represents purity. The flower became a symbol in Buddhism because it thrives in clear water, so it is never muddied or soiled. The belief is that a Buddhist, like the lotus flower, should avoid being "soiled" by the circumstances of life. The second has to do with the structure of the Lotus Sutra. The sutra consists of twenty-eight chapters. The first fourteen deal with the "historical" Buddha, that is, the real human being who lived in the physical world. The last fourteen chapters deal with the "enlightened" Buddha, the Buddha who is eternal because his teachings will live forever.

Nichiren Buddhism in modern life

The early twentieth century was a difficult time for Nichiren Buddhism, and Buddhism in general in Japan. Beginning in the late nineteenth century Shinto was declared the state religion. The purpose of this was to unite Japanese culture and society as the country tried to establish an empire in Southeast Asia and throughout the Pacific. This desire for empire eventually led to Japan's involvement in World War II (1939–45; a war in which Great Britain, France, the United States, and their allies defeated Germany, Italy, and Japan). Buddhists had little choice but to go along with the government's decision. Some dealt with the new order by creating a form of Buddhism called Imperial Way Buddhism. This form of Buddhism supported the Japanese state and the nation's emperor, partly by declaring Japanese Buddhism superior to all other forms of the faith, such as those practiced in China.

After World War II ended, Buddhists in Japan were able to reassert their religion. In the decades that followed, Nichiren Buddhism became primarily a lay movement, or one practiced more by ordinary people than by monks and other religious devotees. The term *Nichirenshu* is generally used to refer to some forty religious institutions, lay associations, and new religious movements in Japan and throughout the world that follow the teachings of Nichiren. Little focus is placed on ritual or formal teachings. Nichiren Buddhists put more emphasis on making a difference in the world through social action, such as campaigning for world peace.

For More Information

BOOKS

Christensen, J. A. *Nichiren: Leader of Buddhist Reformation in Japan.* Fremont, CA: Jain Publishing, 2001.

Kirkpatrick, Marge. *Waking the Lion: The Writings of Nichiren Daishonin.* Bloomington, IN: Authorhouse, 2004.

Watson, Burton, trans. *The Lotus Sutra.* New York, NY: Columbia University Press, 1993.

WEB SITES

"What Is the Buddhism of Nichiren?" *Soka Gakkai International-USA.* http://sgi-usa.org/buddhism/bofnd.html (accessed on May 26, 2006).

Saint Paul

BORN: 3 • Tarsus, Cilicia

DIED: c. 67 • Rome

Cilician theologian; preacher

Saint Paul.
© CHRISTIE'S IMAGES/
CORBIS.

"So, as much as is in me, I am eager to preach the Gospel to you also. ... For I am not ashamed of the Gospel of Christ, for it is the power of God for salvation for everyone who believes."

Saul of Tarsus, better known to Christians as Saint Paul, was born a Jew. He later came to believe in the teachings of **Jesus Christ** (c. 6 BCE–c. 30 CE; see entry) and converted, or changed his religious affiliation, to Christianity. Paul played a central role in the development of Christianity. He composed many doctrines (principles or rules) of the church and interpreted the words and teachings of Jesus for his followers throughout Asia Minor, Greece, and other areas around the Mediterranean Sea. Some historians suggest that the early Christian Church might not have survived had it not been for Paul's tireless efforts on its behalf. In the late twenty-first century Christian churches continued to assert that "Pauline Christianity" is the official Christianity, rather than a number of competing forms of the religion preached by other groups during Paul's lifetime. Included among these groups were the Ebionites, who denied the divinity of Christ, and various other sects.

Paul is perhaps best known as the undisputed author of several important books of the New Testament of the Bible, the sacred book of Christianity. These books are generally referred to as the Epistles, which means "letters." They include Romans, 1 and 2 Corinthians, Galatians, Philippians, 1 Thessalonians, and Philemon. Traditionally Paul has also been regarded as the author of other books in the New Testament, including Ephesians, Colossians, 2 Thessalonians, 1 and 2 Timothy, and Titus. A number of biblical historians, however, suspect that someone else wrote some or all of these books.

It is virtually impossible to construct an accurate picture of Paul's life. This is mainly because the only two sources of information known to exist on his life are Paul's own Epistles, mostly written from the years 50 to 58 CE, and the New Testament book, Acts of the Apostles. The Acts contain a number of passages informally referred to as the "we passages," which were apparently narrated by an observer, likely one of Paul's followers. Most modern-day biographers regard Paul's Epistles as their primary source but also draw on information contained in Acts. Two other books from the New Testament, Acts of Paul and Thecla, also contain information on Paul's life. Elements within these books, however, are considered less reliable by scholars, or researchers. As a result, no reliable timeline of the events in Paul's life can be constructed.

Early life

Saul was born in the year 3 CE in the town of Tarsus, Cilicia (pronounced ki-LIK-ya), a region on the southwestern coast of Asia Minor along the Aegean Sea in what is now modern-day Turkey. Saul identified himself as an Israelite from the tribe of Benjamin, and his name was a common one among that tribe because it honored the first king of the Jews. People who lived within the Roman Empire typically had two names. In the case of Jews, one name would be Hebrew and the other either Latin or Greek. Thus, Saul also had the Latin name of Paul. He referred to himself as a Pharisee, or a member of a major sect, or division, of Judaism that placed great emphasis on tradition and biblical scholarship, or study of the Tanakh. He had one brother, Rufus, and was unmarried. Saul may have suffered from epilepsy, a brain disorder that at the time was thought to produce religious visions.

Saul received a Jewish education and may have studied in Jerusalem under Gamaliel, a famous scholar of Jewish law. As a young man Saul

Was Paul the First Protestant?

The Protestant Reformation was a religious reform movement in sixteenth-century Europe. Many Protestant Christian groups emerged from this period, such as Lutherans, Methodists, and Baptists, in response to criticism of the Catholic Church. Much of the opposition to the Catholic Church was based on the greed of the church's institutions and their focus on worldly rather than spiritual matters. There was also debate over basic Christian doctrines, or policies, and beliefs. One of the chief points of disagreement concerned the manner in which a person can achieve salvation, or deliverance into heaven.

The Catholic Church had traditionally taught that salvation was achieved through a combination of faith and good works. The key biblical text in support of this view is contained in the second chapter of the New Testament book of James: "man is justified by works, and not by faith alone." **Martin Luther** (1483–1546; see entry), a German Catholic monk and one of the leaders of the reform movement, disputed this point of view. He instead preached a doctrine called justification by grace through faith, often shortened to "justification through faith." According to this view, people cannot earn a place in heaven through good works. Salvation is an unconditional gift of God's love and grace that one receives through Jesus Christ by faith

alone. In support of this view, Protestants cite several biblical texts, particularly the first chapter of one of Paul's major Epistles, Romans:

> But now the righteousness of God has been manifested apart from law, although the law and the prophets bear witness to it, the righteousness of God through faith in Jesus Christ for all who believe. For there is no distinction; since all have sinned and fall short of the glory of God, they are justified by His grace as a gift, through the redemption which is in Christ Jesus.

Through statements such as this, Paul provided support for one of the major doctrines of Protestantism and helped to spark a revolt against the very church he helped establish. The Catholic Church, meanwhile, holds that these words can only be understood in the context of the debate over Jewish law. During Paul's lifetime Judaism was a religion based on "works," meaning that Jews believed that they could achieve salvation only by strictly following Jewish law as outlined in the Hebrew religious texts. Paul, the church argues, was simply trying to lessen the role of following Jewish law and focus instead on belief in Christ's atonement, or punishment, for the sins of humanity through his death and resurrection.

supported himself by making tents and working as a traveling preacher. Some historians believe he had a patron, or financial supporter, named Phoebe, who may have been a deaconess in the early Christian Church and delivered some of his letters to the church in Rome. A deaconess, or deacon, is someone who assists the bishops and priests in the Christian faith. Saul may have acquired citizenship in the Roman Empire, and later relied on that citizenship to defend him when he encountered legal difficulties. Some Christian sects believe that he was actually a Greek-born Roman citizen and that he tried to convert to Judaism so that he could court and marry a Jewish woman, the daughter of a high priest. This theory, however, is not widely accepted.

Saul's conversion

A key event in Saul's life was his conversion to Christianity. In his youth he had been an enthusiastic supporter of, and participant in, the oppression and harassment of Christians. In his letter to the Philippians in the New Testament of the Bible, Paul describes how he had "laid waste to the Church, arresting the followers of Jesus, having them thrown into prison, and trying to get them to blaspheme [curse]" the name of the Hebrew God. He had also taken an active part in the trial and execution of Saint Stephen (died c. 36), the first Christian martyr, or one who willingly dies rather than reject his religious faith.

One day Saul was traveling along the major road to Damascus, Syria. He carried letters that gave him the authority to apprehend any people he found practicing Christianity and bring them to Jerusalem for trial and probable execution. His goal, he said, was to wipe out the "sect of the Nazarene," referring to Jesus of Nazareth. (Nazareth is the town from which his mother, Mary, and her husband, Joseph, traveled before Jesus was born.) Along the road, however, Saul had a miraculous experience, as described in the ninth chapter of Acts of the Apostles:

> Now as he journeyed he approached Damascus, and suddenly a light from heaven flashed about him. And he fell to the ground and heard a voice saying to him, "Saul, Saul, why do you persecute [mistreat] me?" and he said, "Who are you, Lord?" and he said, "I am Jesus, whom you are persecuting; but rise and enter the city, and you will be told what you are to do." . . . Saul arose from the ground; and when his eyes were opened, he could see nothing.

Although some biblical scholars dispute that Paul, as he then called himself, underwent such a dramatic experience, he was nonetheless transformed from a strongly loyal Hebrew into one of the most enthusiastic leaders of the new Christian faith.

After his conversion, which probably took place sometime around the year 35, Paul lived in a trading kingdom along the border between Syria and Arabia. He later returned to Damascus. After perhaps three years he was forced to flee the city again when he heard of a plot by Jews there to kill him for preaching that Christ had been the long-awaited savior, that is, the messiah whose coming had been predicted by the Old Testament prophets. He then traveled to Jerusalem, where he met Saint Peter (died c. 64) and Saint James the Just (died c. 62). Peter was the leader of the Christian church. In effect, he could be considered the first pope. He and James, who some believe was Christ's brother, were two of Christ's twelve apostles. The apostles were followers that Jesus Christ had chosen to help him spread his teachings.

Paul's travels may have then taken him to Antioch, a city in Asia Minor, then to Cyprus, a Mediterranean island south of Asia Minor. During this journey, often referred to as his first missionary journey, Paul preached Christianity and established Christian communities. Over the course of this and later missionary journeys, he endured many hardships, faced persecution, and was imprisoned. On at least one occasion he was almost murdered. On some of these trips, he took along a number of his followers.

Saint Paul is depicted spreading the Gospel to others in this illuminated manuscript. Saint Paul was a Jew who converted to believe in the teachings of Jesus. PUBLIC DOMAIN.

The Council of Jerusalem

In the year 49 Paul traveled back to Jerusalem, where he met with leaders of the Christian Church, including Peter, James, and another apostle, Saint John (died c. 100). This meeting is generally called the Council of Jerusalem. The precise purpose of the council remains unclear. It most likely revolved around the ongoing issue of the relationship between Judaism and Christianity. In the early decades of the Common Era (the years after Jesus's birth and death), Christianity was a sect of Judaism. Christ himself was born a Jew, as were most of his followers. As a result, considerable thought was given regarding the extent to which Christians were obligated to obey Jewish law. Indeed, some early Christians believed that one could not be saved without following Jewish law, a belief that persisted until at least the fourth century.

At the council Paul took the position that the death and resurrection of Christ freed people from Jewish law. (The resurrection is the belief that Christ rose from the dead three days after being crucified on the cross.)

He believed that the emphasis of the Christian Church should be the preaching of Christ's words, not following Jewish law. After considerable debate the council took a middle position, concluding that Gentiles, or those not born Jews, should follow some restrictions of Jewish law but should not place great emphasis on doing so. Some Jewish laws made sense in purely practical terms, such as those dealing with hygiene and health in an agricultural community.

Despite the agreement of the council Paul later had an argument with Peter, an event sometimes referred to as the "incident of Antioch." Paul believed that Peter placed too much emphasis on Jewish law, to the degree that Peter refused to share a meal with Gentile Christians. Perhaps because of this disagreement, Paul set out on his second missionary journey, revisiting some of the towns that he had visited on his first journey. His travels took him through Asia Minor and into Macedonia, where he established the first Christian church in Philippi. In this city he was imprisoned for theft because he supposedly exorcized, or drove out, a demon from a slave woman. The woman's owner claimed this reduced her value to him because she had supposedly been able to read fortunes before the exorcism, but could not afterwards. After his release Paul traveled to Athens, Greece, and then to the Greek region of Corinth, where he wrote 1 Thessalonians, the first of his surviving Epistles.

In Corinth, Paul once again encountered legal difficulties, as Jews brought charges against him for preaching Christianity. In the year 52 he was called before an official named Gallio, who concluded that the matter was unimportant and dismissed the charges. The event is of some significance because it is one of the few in Paul's life actually documented with archaeological evidence as having taken place. Archaeological evidence are physical remains from history, such as ancient records. Afterward Paul began his third missionary journey, which again took him through Asia Minor to Macedonia and Antioch. In Ephesus, a region of Greece, he caused an uproar when he spoke out against the practice of worshipping statues of the Greek goddess Artemis. Many of the city's silversmiths earned their living making and selling such statues. Paul and his companions almost lost their lives to an angry mob of Ephesians.

Final years

Paul eventually arrived back in Jerusalem, bringing money that he had gathered on his travels for victims of a food shortage in the region. Outside the Jewish temple, he was recognized and nearly beaten to death by a mob of people who believed that he had made the temple unclean by entering with a Greek companion. The Romans rescued Paul from the mob, only to imprison him, and for two years he remained in custody awaiting trial. He insisted that as a Roman citizen he had the right to be tried in Rome. After a new governor took office, the governor agreed and ordered Paul sent back to Rome.

Paul's journey to Rome by ship was unpleasant. The voyage was made difficult by uncooperative winds, and the ship floated aimlessly for two weeks before being wrecked in a storm off the coast of Malta. The ship's party spent three months there before resuming the journey in the spring. Finally they arrived in Rome, probably in the year 61. Paul appears to have spent two years in a Roman prison, during which time some historians believe he wrote the books of Ephesians and Philemon. After being released from prison, he may have traveled to Spain and Britain on a fourth missionary journey, although the evidence for this is inconclusive.

Information about Paul's death is equally uncertain. A fourth-century bishop named Eusebius of Caesarea (c. 260–c. 341), often called the "Father of Church History" because he was one of the first Christians to document events involving the early church, wrote that Paul was beheaded by the Roman emperor Nero in either 64 or 67. (The later date is traditionally given for Paul's death.) A third-century writer named Gaius wrote that Paul was buried in Rome in a cemetery on the Via Ostiensis, an important road in the city. Neither of these claims can be confirmed. According to the Venerable Bede (c. 672–735), a prominent historian and author of *The Ecclesiastical History of the English People,* in 665 the pope, Vitalian, gave Paul's remains to Oswy, the king of Britain.

Paul's theology

For hundreds of years Christian theologians (people who study religion) have attempted to explain and interpret the teachings of Paul. These teachings essentially created the primary doctrines of the Christian faith. The chief belief of Pauline Christianity is the importance of religious faith in and through Christ. Paul vocalized the central beliefs that Christ suffered and died to atone for humanity's sins and that people could achieve spiritual salvation through faith in Christ. Indeed, Paul was one of the first New Testament writers to comment on the nature of

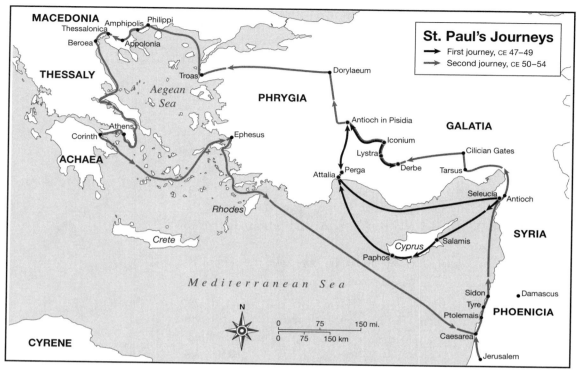

Saint Paul traveled throughout the Middle East and parts of Europe, seeking to spread the word of God and gain followers to Christianity. THOMSON GALE.

Original Sin, the concept that all of humanity is born in a state of sin due to the disobedience of Adam and Eve, the first humans, in the Garden of Eden. He stated that people could achieve salvation in heaven only by overcoming their basic sinfulness through faith in Christ.

Paul was a principal figure in the debate over Jewish law and the extent to which followers of Christ were obligated to obey it. While Paul himself followed some elements of Jewish law, he argued that salvation was to be achieved through faith in Christ, not through the law. Related to this issue was the question of whether Christianity was intended just for Jews or also for Gentiles, many of whom at the time practiced polytheism, or the belief in more than one god. Paul took the position that Christianity provided a new path to God for Gentiles, earning him the nickname "Apostle to the Gentiles."

Paul also gave prominence to the Holy Spirit. He said that the Holy Spirit, a representation of God's divinity, became part of a person with conversion to or baptism into the faith. Baptism is a religious ritual marked by a symbolic use of water that results in a person being admitting into the church community. By insisting on the Holy Spirit's divinity, Paul was in large part responsible for the Christian doctrine of the Trinity, the concept that God exists in three "persons": the Father in heaven; the Son, Jesus Christ; and the Holy Spirit.

For More Information

BOOKS

Conybeare, W. J., and J. S. Howson. *Life and Epistles of St. Paul.* Grand Rapids, MI: Eerdmans, 1949.

May, Herbert G. and Bruce M. Metzger. *The Holy Bible.* New York: Oxford University Press, 1962.

Stalker, James A. *The Life of Saint Paul.* Grand Rapids, MI: Zondervan Press, 1984.

Wilson, A. N. *Paul: The Mind of the Apostle.* New York: Norton, 1998.

WEB SITES

Prat, F. "St. Paul." *Catholic Encyclopedia.* http://www.newadvent.org/cathen/11567b.htm (accessed on March 25, 2006).

Plato

BORN: c. 427 BCE • Athens, Greece
DIED: 347 BCE • Athens, Greece

Greek philosopher; writer; teacher

Plato.
© GIANNI DAGLI
ORTI/CORBIS.

"Until philosophers rule as kings or those who are now called kings ... until political power and philosophy entirely coincide ... cities will have no rest from evils ... nor I think will the human race."

Plato was one of the most influential philosophers of the Western world. A philosopher is someone who studies logic, ethics (moral values), and other subjects for greater wisdom and experience. Along with his teacher, Socrates (469–399 BCE), and his student, **Aristotle** (384–322 BCE; see entry), Plato pioneered the classical philosophy of ancient Greece. He was the first to write about the legend of the mythical lost continent of Atlantis. He formulated the well-known concept of platonic love, or love that is spiritual rather than physical. In such works as *The Republic,* he wrote about a wide range of subjects, including ethics, politics, psychology (the study of the mind and behavior), and morality (a system of right conduct). Modern readers continue to explore his works for their understanding of epistemology, the branch of philosophy that explores how people gain knowledge and arrive at the truth, and metaphysics, which examines reality that exists beyond the senses.

Platonic Love

In modern-day times, even those who know little or nothing about Plato are likely to be familiar with the expression "platonic love" or "platonic relationship." When two people, generally members of the opposite sex, say that they have a platonic relationship, they mean that they are friends and are not involved romantically. Plato, however, never used the term. It was coined in the fifteenth century in reference to the relationship between Socrates and one of his male students. Originally it referred to homosexual love, or the physical love between two people of the same sex. The concept of platonic love is taken from Plato's book *Symposium*. In this book Plato outlines the concept of love as an ideal of good. This love, then, leads to virtue and goodness. By putting aside romantic passion for another individual, a person is able to contemplate universal and ideal love.

Birth

Historians are uncertain about the exact dates of Plato's life. The traditional date for his birth is 428 or 427 BCE, and for his death, 348 or 347 BCE. The cause of this uncertainty is the lack of reliable written records. Much of what is known about Plato comes from his own works, including his books and some letters. These works are not autobiographical, however, meaning that they do not contain information about his own life, so historians can only pick up hints and suggestions from them.

One source that historians use for information about the lives of ancient Greek philosophers, including Plato, is a ten-volume work called *Lives of the Philosophers*. This work was written by Diogenes Laertius, a historian who lived in the third century BCE. Diogenes copied his information from many different sources. He particularly enjoyed recording gossip and scandalous or amusing stories about the philosophers whose biographies he wrote. Modern historians do not regard him as a reliable source, although they trust him somewhat on matters of simple fact.

Diogenes, quoting other sources, wrote that Plato was born in the same year that Pericles, an Athenian statesman, died, which was 429 BCE, and that he lived to the age of eighty-four. Diogenes also said, however, that Plato was twenty-eight when Socrates was put to death in 399 BCE, which would put his birth date at 427 BCE. These details show how difficult it can be for modern historians to create a clear and accurate biographical record for people who lived in ancient times.

Early life

Plato was born in Athens to a wealthy family. His father, according to Diogenes, was named Ariston, and was descended from a line of early kings of Athens. His mother, Perictione, likewise came from a notable line, which included the sixth-century BCE legislator Solon. Family tradition held that they were descended from the sea god Poseidon. Plato had two older brothers, Glaucon and Adeimantus, and a sister, Potone. Ariston died when Plato was a young child, and Perictione married her uncle, Pyrilampes. The couple had a son, Antiphon.

At birth Plato's name was Aristocles, the name of his grandfather. He apparently acquired the nickname Plato later in life. Plato comes from the Greek word *platos* and means "broad." It is thought that his wrestling teacher, or possibly his fellow students, may have given him the name because of his strong build, which enabled him to win the regional wrestling championship. Other theories are that he was given the name because of the wide range of his thought or even because he had a broad forehead.

Plato's family was politically active and closely involved with many of the most important events of the day. These years were exciting ones in the city-state of Athens, which was at the height of its power around the time of Plato's birth. (During this period Greece was a collection of smaller kingdoms called city-states, each organized around a major city.) Twice during the century, the Greeks, led by Athens, had defeated the feared Persian Empire under King Darius the Great (c. 550–486 BCE) and his successor, Xerxes (c. 520–485 BCE). Many of the islands and coastal cities in and around the Aegean Sea looked to Athens for protection.

The city-states of ancient Greece had a history of rivalry and armed conflict. Sparta was Athens's chief rival. Although Athens ruled the sea with its naval power, Sparta had an army that outnumbered that of Athens two to one. While the Athenians favored democracy, or rule by majority, as their form of government, the Spartans were an oligarchy, which placed power in the hands of a small number of men. The Spartans were warlike, whereas Athens was more concerned with culture and encouraged the growth of art, architecture, education, and philosophy. War broke out between the two very different powers in 431 BCE, just a few years before Plato was born. This war is known as the Peloponnesian War.

The war ended in defeat for Athens in 405 BCE. In the disorder following this loss the Athenian empire fell into a state of decline and its democratic institutions came under attack. One of Plato's uncles, Charmides, was a member of a group called the Thirty Tyrants, of which Charmides's uncle, Critias, was the leader. This group overthrew the democratic government in 404 BCE and ruled as an oligarchy, although their control lasted for just eight months. Plato's stepfather, Pyrilampes, was a leader of the democratic faction of Athens, which defeated the Tyrants and restored democratic rule to the city-state.

Finds philosophy

In response to these events and to the rapid changes they produced in Athenian society, Plato's mother and stepfather tried to persuade him to enter politics. For a time it looked as though Plato would agree to this and become a statesman and legislator. But in about 409 BCE, Plato and his brothers met the philosopher Socrates. Plato rejected a political career and, with the encouragement of Socrates, became a passionate student of philosophy. Plato was especially inspired by two of Socrates's most famous statements: "Know thyself" and "the unexamined life is not worth living."

Socrates never authored any published works or founded a school or an organized philosophical movement. He wandered about the city, stopping people on the street and engaging them in philosophical dialogue. Then, through questions and answers, he would challenge their ideas, especially with regards to ethics and morality, and expose the errors in their positions.

The Thirty Tyrants tried to involve Socrates when they seized power in Athens, but he refused to assist them. Due to their efforts, however, Socrates gained a reputation for being an opponent of democracy. After the democratic government of Athens was restored, he was tried and executed in 399 BCE on a number of charges, including corrupting the youth, atheism (not believing in any god or gods), introducing new gods, and engaging in strange religious practices. Plato watched these events closely. As an admirer of Socrates, he became increasingly displeased with the state of Athenian politics. That displeasure reached its climax with Socrates's death. Plato recorded the events surrounding the trial and death of his teacher in his book *Apologia*.

Since he was a student of Socrates, Plato feared he might be put to death as well. Additionally, he knew that he could not serve the state that had executed his teacher. He left Athens and for the next twelve years traveled widely, visiting such places as Cyrene (a city on the north coast of Africa), Italy, Sicily, and Egypt. In Egypt he came across the water clock, an invention he later brought back to Greece. In Italy he became familiar with the works of the mathematician Pythagoras (569–475 BCE). His growing interest in mathematics sparked a fascination with science. During his travels he sought out philosophers, priests,

A fresco by the painter Raphael depicts "The School of Athens," where Greek philosophy was taught. Plato established a school to teach philosophy, mathematics, astronomy, and other subjects. © SCALA/ART RESOURCE, NY.

and prophets (divine messengers) to learn all that he could about religion, morality, ethics, science, and philosophy.

During this period Plato wrote his earliest books, including *Apologia, The Crito, Charmides, Euthyphro, Laches, Lysis, Hippias Minor and Major, Gorgias, Ion,* and *Protagoras.* These books were in the form of dialogues, the method of teaching that Socrates used with his students to encourage them to search out truth for themselves through questions and answers. Socrates himself would become a leading character in all of Plato's books except one, his last, entitled *Laws.* Other philosophers also wrote their books in dialogue form, with Socrates playing a principle role. In the early twenty-first century many teachers still use the Socratic method of questions and answers in the classroom.

At one point Plato lived in Syracuse on the island of Sicily, where he became a tutor to Dion (409–354 BCE), the brother-in-law of the island's king, Dionysius I (c. 430–c. 367 BCE). Legend holds that at some point Plato offended Dion, who then made arrangements to have Plato sold into slavery. Most historians regard this story as doubtful, for Plato and Dion had very similar personalities and became good friends.

The Academy

In 387 BCE, at age forty, Plato ended his travels and returned to Athens. Just outside the city he founded a school called the Academy. This school was named after the sacred site on which it was located. The site, in turn, was named after a legendary Greek hero, Academus (sometimes spelled Hecademus). More than two thousand years later the word "academy" continues to be used in the name of some schools, and it became the source of the word "academic," the name given to those who studied at the site. Plato delivered lectures, and his students studied philosophy, mathematics, astronomy (the study of the stars and planets), political theory, and science, all with to the goal of creating a class of philosopher-kings to rule the state. During this period Plato wrote a number of important books, including *Phaedrus, Symposium, Meno, Euthydemus, Menexenus, Cratylus, Phaedo,* and much of his most important and widely read work, *The Republic.* The Academy, in effect the first university in Europe, operated for nearly a thousand years until it was shut down by the Roman emperor Justinian in 529 CE.

Later life

When he was in his sixties, Plato's quiet life at the Academy was interrupted. In Sicily, Dionysius I died and his teenage son, Dionysius II (c. 384–344 BCE), became king. At this point Dion urged the young king to invite Plato to Sicily, where he could help the ruler become a philosopher-king as modeled in *The Republic.* Because he had become disappointed with Athenian politics and was disgusted with the city's rulers, Plato had written in this work that politics could be saved only if "either true and genuine philosophers attain political power or the rulers of states by some dispensation [indulgence] of providence [preparation] become genuine philosophers." Despite being busy with teaching and the administration of the Academy, Plato agreed and made the trip. After he arrived, however, Dionysius II, who saw Dion as a rival, ordered Dion into exile for treason. Exile is the enforced removal from one's native country. Plato, because of his association with Dion, was held in Sicily under house arrest, although officially he was a "guest" of the king.

Plato was eventually released and returned to Athens, where he and Dion were reunited and remained from 365 to 361 BCE. During this time Plato refused an invitation from Dionysius II to return to Syracuse, in Sicily. A year later Dionysius sent a ship with one of Plato's close friends, Archedemus, on board. Archedemus urged Plato to accept the king's invitation. Dion agreed with the plan, so once more Plato departed for Syracuse. His goal was to resolve the rivalry between Dion and Dionysius. Again, he was held there effectively against his will and was released only after his friends spoke on his behalf with the king. Dion, by this time, had lost patience with Dionysius. He assembled an army of mercenary soldiers, or soldiers for hire, and invaded Sicily. He gained control of the island in 357 BCE, but was killed three years later.

Plato remained at the Academy for another thirteen years, until he died quietly in his sleep in 348 (or 347) BCE. During this period he wrote the last of his books, including *Sophist, Statesman, Philebus, Timaeus, Critias,* and, uncompleted at the time of his death, *Laws.* Plato's most famous student, Aristotle, entered the Academy during these later years. Diogenes claimed that Plato was buried at the Academy, but archaeologists (people who study the remains of human civilizations) have not been able to discover his grave site.

The Republic

While many students of philosophy admire Plato's dialogues, especially his later works, *The Republic* remains the most well known. It is difficult to date Plato's works, but he probably wrote the first of the ten books, or sections, of *The Republic* some time between the death of Socrates and his first trip to Sicily. He then wrote the remaining nine books between 380 and 360 BCE.

The Republic explores such topics as justice, the ideal city, the nature of heroism, poetry, money and private property, the wisdom and methods of philosophers, war, tyranny (absolute rule), and happiness. Book VII of the work is generally the most read. This book contains the "Allegory of the Cave." An allegory is a representation of abstract ideas by characters, figures, or events in story form. In this allegory, Plato described his theory of "Forms," which says that the world humans know through their senses is only an imitation of a pure, unchanging world of ideal Forms. As a philosopher might put it, a chair that can be seen and touched is only an imperfect imitation of an ideal Form, "chairness," that cannot be duplicated on Earth. A better example might be the idea of a straight line. Plato would say that ideally, there is such a thing as a line that is perfectly, absolutely straight. In the physical world, however, it is impossible to achieve this ideal; every line, no matter how precisely drawn, will deviate from an ideal of "straightness." The same holds true for any worldly phenomenon. There is an absolute "honesty," for example, that humans can never achieve. These absolutes are called Forms.

In the "Allegory of the Cave," Plato writes that people are like men who have been imprisoned in a cave since childhood. They cannot see out of the cave. Behind them is a fire, and between the fire and the men is a walkway, where objects can be carried. The fire casts a shadow of the objects on the wall of the cave that the men face. Plato's conclusion is that men lacking education would come to believe that the shadows they see are the real thing. They would believe that any voices they hear behind them are sounds made by the objects going past. Plato claimed a man allowed to leave the cave would be similar to a man who has received education and enlightenment about the real nature of the world.

For More Information

BOOKS

Jackson, Roy. *Plato: A Beginner's Guide.* New York, NY: Headway Books, 2001.

Taylor, A. E. *Plato: The Man and His Work.* Mineola, NY: Dover Books, 2001.

Voegelin, Eric. *Plato.* Columbia, MO: University of Missouri Press, 2000.

WEB SITES

Brickhouse, Thomas, and Nicholas D. Smith. "Plato." *The Internet Encyclopedia of Philosophy.* http://www.iep.utm.edu/p/plato.htm#SH1d (accessed on April 20, 2006).

"Plato and Platonism." *New Catholic Encyclopedia.* http://www.newadvent.org/cathen/12159a.htm (accessed on May 5, 2006).

Rābiʾah al-Adawiyah

BORN: c. 713 • Basra, Iraq
DIED: c. 801 • Basra, Iraq

Iraqi religious leader; poet; mystic

"If I adore You out of fear of Hell, burn me in Hell! / If I adore You out of desire for Paradise, / Lock me out of Paradise. / But if I adore You for Yourself alone, / Do not deny to me Your eternal beauty."

Rābiʾah al-Adawiyah was an eighth-century Muslim mystic, or a person concerned with religious mysteries. She is considered a saint of Islam, a virtuous and holy woman who was also able to perform miracles. Rābiʾah, a founding member of the branch of Islam called Sufism, established the principle of mystical love, or the pure love of Allah, as a path to knowing Allah. She rejected the notion that punishment or heavenly reward motivated religious devotion. Rābiʾah was also one of the most prominent early Sufi poets, leaving behind many verses and prayers that became part of the literature and oral tradition of Islam.

A Life of poverty

Rābiʾah was born about in 713 CE to the Al-Atik tribe of Qays clan and died, by most accounts, in 801. Her name means "fourth daughter" in Arabic. Other variations of her name include Rābiʾah al-Qaysiyya and Rābiʾah al Basri (Rābiʾah of Basra), after her hometown.

Little was written about Rābiʾah during her lifetime. Much of the legend in existence comes from the thirteenth century and the writings of Sufi mystic and poet Farid al-Din Attar. In his *Tadhkirat al-Awliya* or *Biographies of the Saints,* he related the words of Rābiʾah, who left no written documents herself. Attar says that Rābiʾah was "on fire with love and longing" and that she was considered "an unquestioned authority to her contemporaries."

Most sources note that Rābiʾah was born into a poor household. Indeed, the family was so poor that on the night of Rābiʾah's birth, her father was sent out to beg for oil for the lamps. He had made a promise, however, to ask for assistance from no one but Allah and came back without any oil. That night, the Prophet **Muhammad** (c. 570–632; see entry) came to Rābiʾah's father in his sleep and told him not to worry, for his newborn daughter was destined to be a great Muslim saint. The prophet also told him that the local emir (high official) had failed to pray as a good Muslim should and that Rābiʾah's father should demand money from the emir as punishment. The money was supposedly paid, but it seems that this was the last bit of good luck the family had. Soon after, Rābiʾah's parents both died, famine struck Basra, her three older sisters moved away, and Rābiʾah was left on her own.

Some time later Rābiʾah was sold into slavery as a house servant, although accounts vary as to how this occurred. Some sources claim she was traveling in a caravan when it was attacked by robbers and taken prisoner. Most others report that she was walking down the streets of Basra one day and was kidnapped. After Rābiʾah finished her daily chores, she would turn to prayers and meditation on Allah. Her religious calling was confirmed one day when she fell in the street and dislocated her wrist. She was trying to avoid allowing a stranger to see her without her veil, which was forbidden for pure Muslim women. Praying to Allah at that moment, she was answered with a voice that said on the day of reckoning she would be among the select to sit near Allah in heaven.

After this experience Rābiʾah became increasingly religious. She practiced asceticism, or self-denial, living in a very simple manner as a means of gaining higher spiritual powers. Some ascetics wore clothing that scratched their bodies in order to remind them of their duty to God. Some also fasted or ate very little. Rābiʾah, according to legend, fasted during the day while working and then prayed much of the night. On one such night, her master happened upon her in the midst of prayer. He saw her bathed in a golden light called the *sakina,* something like a halo that marks a Christian saint. The next day he gave Rābiʾah her freedom, and she left to meditate in the desert.

Life of meditation

Rābi'ah soon established herself in the desert not far from Basra, where she lived a quiet life of prayer. She did not feel it necessary to have a teacher or other holy person direct her in her quest for Allah. Rather, she went directly to Allah for such teachings and inspiration. Rābi'ah found no comfort in organized religion with its officials and rituals. She once said of the Muslim House of God, the famed Ka'aba, in Mecca, that she had no use for a house. It was the master of the house who interested her.

This belief in a direct knowledge of Allah placed her in the early ranks of mystical Sufis. From the time of the founding of the Islamic religion, there were believers who wanted a deeper experience than that provided by the simple adherence to the five pillars of Islam: professing faith, saying prayers five times daily, giving support to the poor, fasting during Ramadan, and making pilgrimage to Mecca. These people, like Rābi'ah, wanted direct communication with Allah. They attempted to establish it through continual prayer, reading of the Qur'an, and focusing on Allah. They fasted, did not engage in sex, and repented for their sins.

What makes a Sufi

The term *Sufi* most likely comes from the Arabic word for the coarse wool many of these ascetics used for their robes. It was first seen in the literature of Islam during the eighth century, during Rābi'ah's lifetime. As Sufism evolved, two main concepts came to dominate that branch of Islam: *tawakkul,* or a total reliance on God, and *dhikr,* a continual remembrance of, or focusing on, Allah. Sufism combined elements of Christianity and Hinduism with its own distinctive Islamic concepts.

Early Sufism had a harsh, gloomy tone. Rābi'ah, however, brought joy to the obedience to and love of Allah. Rābi'ah looked to Allah not only as a master but also as a friend and companion. She was the first Sufi to preach that love and only love was the key to the mystic path. She also scorned the reward and punishment system of heaven and hell. One of her poems, translated by Charles Upton and published in *Doorkeeper of the Heart: Versions of Rābi'ah,* states, "I love God: I have no time left / In which to hate the devil."

Rābi'ah was also famous for a legend in which she was reportedly seen carrying a flaming torch in one hand and a bucket of water in the

Hasan al-Basri

Rābiʾah was a resident of the city of Basra, located in the far southeast of modern-day Iraq, near the Persian Gulf. Founded in 636, the city was an important military and trading site. Also called Bassorah, the city was mentioned in *Thousand and One Nights* as the place where Sinbad the Sailor began his voyages. The city was called the "Venice of the Middle East," because of the series of canals that once flowed through the city at high tide. Basra was also a center for the cultivation of dates and date palm trees.

During Rābiʾah's lifetime, Basra was only about a century old, but was already famous in Islam as a home to many well-known Sufis. One of the most famous of these was Hasan al-Basri (642–728). Hasan was born one year after the death of the Prophet Muhammad and moved to Basra when it was still a primitive military encampment. As a young man this famous mystic scholar served as a soldier of Islam from 670 to 673 and participated in the conquest of eastern Iran.

Upon his return to Basra, Hasan quickly became a well-respected religious figure, preaching the importance of a permanent state of anxiety in the true believer. He claimed that such anxiousness was caused not by the certain knowledge of death, but by an uncertainty about what awaited a person after death. He also preached religious self-examination, which

he said led to an avoidance of doing evil and an emphasis on doing good. Most importantly, Hasan believed that humans were responsible for their own actions and could not, therefore, blame such actions on the will of Allah.

Hasan appeared in many of the legends dealing with Rābiʾah. Her belief in the importance of love was the opposite of Hasan's emphasis on fear and hope as twin motivators for the faithful Muslim. According to one legend, Hasan asks Rābiʾah to marry him. When he is unable to answer a series of questions she puts to him, she declines the offer. Another legend tells of how Hasan, seeing Rābiʾah near a lake, decides to display his miraculous powers. He throws a prayer rug onto the water and invites her to pray with him on it. Unimpressed, she responds, as quoted by Farid al-Din Attar, "Hasan, when you are showing off your spiritual goods in the worldly market, it should be things which your fellow men cannot display." Then she throws her prayer rug into the air and flies up to sit upon it, inviting him to join her. The old man simply looks at her sadly. She feels badly for him then, and says, "Hasan, what you did fishes can do, and what I did flies can do. But the real business is outside these tricks. One must apply oneself to the real business." There is little chance these tales are true, however, as Rābiʾah was only eleven at the time of the death of the older Sufi master and had not yet become an ascetic.

other. She explained in a poem published in *Doorkeeper of the Heart:* "With these things I am going to set fire to heaven / And put out the flames of hell / So that voyagers to God can rip the veils / And see the real goal." Rābiʾah meant that a person should not worship Allah out of fear of hell or in hopes of heaven. One should worship because one loved Allah. The emotions of fear and hope were like veils that kept the true vision of Allah hidden.

Rābiʾah's teaching

Such wisdom won Rābiʾah followers, though she never developed a system of teaching. Later thinkers, however, found a logical organization in Rābiʾah's way of seeking Allah. This path began with *tawba,* or repentance, asking forgiveness of one's sins and turning from wrong actions to right ones. However, such repentance deals only with individual actions: each sin is repented after being committed. Instead, Rābiʾah focused on a more general, divine *tawba,* seeing repentance as a gift from God, whom she called the Healer of Souls. "If I seek repentance myself," Rābiʾah taught, "I shall have need of repentance again."

In order to achieve real "tawba," two qualities were needed: *sabr,* or patience, and *shukr,* or gratitude. Patience, in turn, required an end to complaint and desire. Rābiʾah's prayers were free of desires and expressed a simple, grateful acceptance of whatever happened in life.

Rābiʾah put little emphasis on *rajaʾ,* or hope, and *khawf,* fear, as motivating factors on the path to spiritual enlightenment. Instead she focused on *mahabba,* or love, the ascetic principle of *faqr,* or poverty, and *zuhd,* the giving up of anything that distracted one from the path to Allah. She believed that all of this led to *tawhid,* or the joining of the personal self with Allah.

Though Rābiʾah maintained a solitary existence throughout her life, she did have conversations with some of the other Muslim thinkers of the day and advised people who came to visit her. As an old woman, she possessed only a cracked jug, a mat made from stiff plants, and a brick that served as her pillow. She slept little at night, instead praying and meditating, and became angry with herself if she fell asleep for a short time and thus lost precious minutes or hours of devotion to Allah. In one tale, Rābiʾah refused to go out and admire nature on a fine spring day, saying that she would rather contemplate the beauty of Allah in the darkness of her dwelling. She never married, though it was reported she had many proposals.

The miraculous

Despite her disregard for the rituals of Islam, Rābiʾah went on at least one pilgrimage to Mecca (now in Saudi Arabia) in order to visit the House of God, the Kaʾaba, the most sacred place in Islam. It also lies in the direction toward which Muslims face to pray each day.

According to legend, while Rābiʾah was on her way to Mecca and traveling in the company of other pilgrims, her donkey died and she was left without transportation. She told the others to continue on their way, refusing their offers of help. She said she would rely solely on Allah for assistance. One version of this tale claimed the donkey came back to life after Rābiʾah prayed for a week. Another stated that the Kaʾaba actually came to her. She was unimpressed, however, saying that she wanted the master of the house and not simply the house. Though reportedly capable of performing miracles, Rābiʾah distrusted them and believed them to be the devil's temptations.

Toward the end of her long life, Rābiʾah became recognized as a saint. Islam, like many religions, has a high opinion of such holy people. They are called *awliya,* which literally means "Friends of Allah." Unlike the Catholic Church, Islam has no official process for conferring sainthood, but there are certain beliefs as to which conditions lead to sainthood. To be considered, a person must have a strong faith, follow the traditions laid out by the Prophet Muhammad, possess an excellent moral character, display an ability to perform certain miracles or marvels, and, finally, be accepted by other Muslims as a saint.

When she died in 801, Rābiʾah passed into legend. Many stories have been told of her great deeds and the thousand times each day she knelt to pray. Movies have been made of her life. Her name is still used by followers of Islam to praise an exceptionally religious woman.

For More Information

BOOKS

al-Adawiyah, Rābiʾah. *Doorkeeper of the Heart: Versions of Rābiʾah.* Translated by Charles Upton. Putney, VT: Threshold Books, 1988.

Attar, Farid al-Din. *Muslim Saints and Mystics: Episodes from the "Tadhkirat al-Awliya" ("Memorial of the Saints").* Translated by A. J. Arberry. Ames, IA: Omphaloskepsis, 2000. Also available online at http://www.omphaloskepsis.com/ebooks/pdf/mussm.pdf.

El Sakkakini, Widad, and Nabil Safwat. *First Among Sufis: The Life and Thought of Rābiʾah al-Adawiyah, the Woman Saint of Basra.* London, England: Octagon Press, 1982.

Schimmel, Annemarie. "Rābiʾah al-ʿAdawiyah." *Encyclopedia of Religion.* 2nd ed. Edited by Lindsay Jones. Detroit, MI: Macmillan Reference USA, 2005.

Smith, Margaret. *Muslim Women Mystics: The Life and Work of Rābiʾah and Other Women Mystics in Islam.* Oxford, England: Oneworld Publishing, 2001.

WEB SITES

Lochtefeld, James G. "Stunningly Brief Introduction to Sufism." *Sufism.* http://www2.carthage.edu/~lochtefe/islam/sufis.html (accessed on May 22, 2006).

"Rābiʾah al Basri." *Poet Seers.* http://www.poetseers.org/spiritual_and_devotional_poets/sufi/rabia (accessed on May 22, 2006).

Ramanuja

BORN: c. 1017 • Sri Perumbudur, Tamil Nadu, India
DIED: 1137 • Sri Rangam, Tamil Nadu, India

Indian theologian; writer

"We uphold unity because Brahman [Brahma] alone exists with all other entities..."

Sri Ramanujacharya is the name by which one of the great Hindu teachers of medieval India is known. He was born as Ilaya Perumal around 1017. At some point he changed his name to Ramanuja. After he became one of the most admired teachers of the era, the word *acharya* was added to his name. This word means "teacher" or "guru." It was added as a term of respect to the names of only a handful of India's most prominent and respected teachers and theologians (those who study religion) during this period. The parts of Ramanujacharya's name can also be written separately, as Ramanuja Acharya. *Sri,* which means "beauty" or "fortune" in the ancient Indian language of Sanskrit, is also a title of respect.

Early life

Ramanuja was born into a *Brahmin* family in the town of Sri Perumbudur, India. Brahmins, mostly priests, teachers, and intellectuals, are the highest caste, or hereditary social class, in Indian society. Both Ramanuja's father, Asuri Kesava, and his mother, Kantimati, were descendants of aristocratic families.

At the age of sixteen Ramanuja married Rakshakambal. Soon after the wedding, Asuri Kesava died, leaving his son in charge of the household. Ramanuja decided to move the family to the city of Kanchi, which was regarded as a holy city and was well known for its many temples and scholars.

Education

In Kanchi the young Ramanuja studied under the famed guru Yadava Prakash. A guru is a teacher and guide in spiritual matters. Yadava was a supporter of the doctrines, or principles, of an earlier famous acharya, Sankara (also spelled Sankaracharya; c. 788–c. 820). Ramanuja soon became one of Yadava's best pupils. In time, however, he began to reject some of the central doctrines taught by his master. Ramanuja then set up his own school in his home and attracted a number of followers.

Yadava grew angry with his pupil and began to see Ramanuja as a threat to his beliefs and to the central teachings of Hinduism. His anger and jealousy grew until he conspired with a group of his younger and most faithful students to kill Ramanuja. He planned a pilgrimage to the sacred Ganges river and invited Ramanuja to join him and his pupils. Ramanuja agreed, but he brought along his cousin, Govinda. After the party arrived at the site, Yadava's students took Govinda aside and told him of their plan to eliminate Ramanuja. Shocked, Govinda informed his cousin of the plan and urged him to flee. Govinda returned to the group and claimed that while he and his cousin were in the forest, they had been attacked by a tiger. The tiger, he said, had dragged Ramanuja away. Yadava and his fellow conspirators were relieved that the tiger had killed Ramanuja for them.

After Govinda's deception Ramanuja made his way back to Kanchi. He later claimed that along the way he fell into a deep sleep, had a vision of God, and awoke on the outskirts of Kanchi without knowing how he had arrived. He then resumed his life in Kanchi. Several months later Yadava and his students returned from their pilgrimage and were astonished to find Ramanuja there, conducting his school as he had before. They gave up their plans to kill him.

Ramanuja, the teacher

Ramanuja continued to teach, and his fame soon spread. At one point he was approached by a saint named Yamunacharya from the town of Sri Rangam, who begged for money. The two engaged in lengthy discussion, and Ramanuja quickly recognized that Yamunacharya's religious

Sankara

Ramanuja was one of a succession of three major *acharyas,* or teachers, in medieval India. The first of these was Sankara, or Sankaracharya, while the third was Madhva, or Madhvacharya (c. 1199– c. 1276). Sankara was born around 788 and died around 820. When he was born Hinduism was at a crossroads. The religion was breaking apart into a large number of sects (divisions) and cults (religious offshoots), many of which were blending magic, superstition, and mysticism into their belief systems. They placed great emphasis on rituals and animal sacrifices. Sankara almost single-handedly reformed Hinduism and restored some of its ancient teachings and intellectual foundations. In the twenty-first century the version of Hinduism promoted by Sankara is often referred to as "intellectual Hinduism."

Sankara was born to a poor Brahmin couple in southern India. After studying under the guru Govinda Bhagavatpada, he became an ascetic, meaning he gave up all worldly comforts in pursuit of spiritual knowledge. He possessed great skill as a speaker, and he put this skill to use in winning scholars over in debates. He was able to persuade his listeners to set aside their rituals and cultish practices and place their faith in the study of the ancient Hindu scriptures, especially the Vedas, the most sacred Hindu texts. At the time, the Vedas were written in an ancient language and were not very accessible to ordinary Hindus. Sankara changed that, reinterpreting and representing the teachings of the Vedas in a way that the average person could understand.

He conducted missionary work throughout the region of India, which at the time consisted of many kingdoms. During his travels Sankara established four monasteries in the four corners of the Indian subcontinent: in Kashmir to the north, in Dwaraka to the west, in Puri to the east, and in Sringeri to the south. All of these monasteries remained in operation into the twenty-first century, and over the centuries many pilgrims have visited them. The leaders of each of these monasteries are called *Shankara-charyas,* and because of their influence, they hold a good deal of political power in India. To distinguish themselves from the original Sankara, they refer to him, their first teacher, as either Adi Sankaracharya or as Jagadguru, meaning "universal teacher."

views were compatible with his own. He asked to be accepted as Yamunacharya's disciple, or person who assists in spreading the teachings of another. Yamunacharya agreed, then left to return to Sri Rangam, the site of a temple to the Hindu god Vishnu.

A messenger arrived in Kanchi with news that Yamunacharya was ill and near death. Ramanuja immediately set out for Sri Rangam, but he failed to arrive before the guru died. Legend holds that after Ramanuja arrived at the temple where Yamunacharya's body lay, a miracle took place. Reportedly the guru's left hand was in the Hindu position for peace, with three fingers extended and the tips of the thumb and last finger joined. His right hand, however, was clenched in a fist. Yamunacharya's followers were baffled by the fist. Looking at the hands, Ramanuja concluded that the guru had three wishes he wanted Ramanuja to fulfill. Ramanuja deduced the first wish, and the first finger of the dead guru's right hand extended. The guru then extended his second and third fingers as Ramanuja guessed the other two wishes. All those in attendance were amazed and accepted Ramanuja as their teacher. Yamunacharya's wishes were vows that he wanted Ramanuja to carry out for him.

Ramanuja decided to remain in Sri Rangam, where he spent the remainder of his life. By this time his teachings had become so popular that even Yadava and his students had converted to Ramanuja's way of thinking. Ramanuja became one of the most respected teachers in India.

Final years

Until his arrival in Sri Rangam, Ramanuja was a "householder," the term Hindus used to refer to people who practiced Hinduism but were not ascetics. Ascetics are people who have given up their worldly goods and devote themselves completely to spiritual pursuits. After relocating, he led a life of renunciation, giving up worldly comforts and living as an ascetic. Although he attracted followers and disciples, he also made enemies. Some followers of the earlier views of Sankara appealed to the king of Kanchi to silence Ramanuja. The king agreed and commanded Ramanuja to come to Kanchi to take part in a theological debate with him. The king's goal was to convert Ramanuja, by persuasion if possible and by force if necessary.

One of Ramanuja's disciples, Kuresh, distrusted the king. He persuaded Ramanuja to allow him to go to Kanchi in his place, in disguise. At Kanchi the king at first treated Kuresh with respect, believing that he was Ramanuja. Yet when Kuresh refused to change his religious views, the king had him imprisoned and blinded. Later, with the help of some local people, Kuresh was able to gain his release from prison and return to Sri Rangam. There, according to legend, another miracle occurred. Ramanuja prayed to God on behalf of Kuresh, who had been willing to sacrifice his sight, and even his life, for his guru. Ramanuja prayed for his disciple's sight to be restored, and at that moment a wind blew across Kuresh's face and his sight indeed returned.

Ramanuja reportedly lived a very long life, dying in 1137 at the age of 120. According to tradition, he announced his desire to leave the world to his followers, who were very upset. Over the next three days he issued instructions to those followers, and on the third day, with his head lying in the lap of his cousin, Govinda, he died.

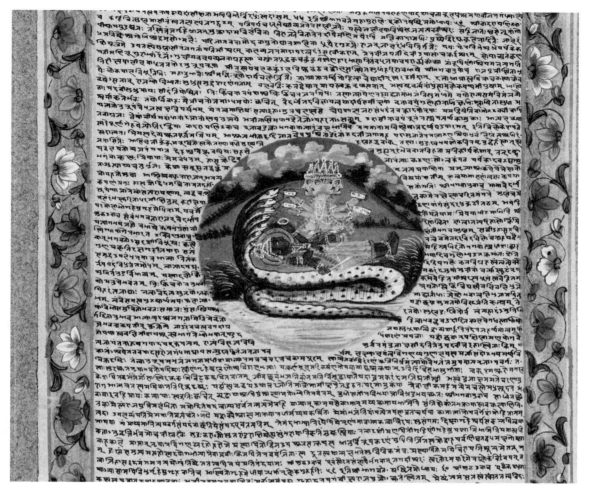

This page from the Bhagavad Purana, a part of the Vedas, depicts the gods Vishnu, Brahman, and Sesha Nag. Ramanuja wrote many essays on Hindu religious practices based on the Vedas, often challenging core beliefs. © ARCHIVO ICONOGRAFICO, S.A./ CORBIS.

Ramanuja's teachings

Ramanuja produced a number of treatises, or essays, on Hindu theology. Many of these treatises were on Hindu sacred texts, including the Bhagavad Gita and the Vedas, Hinduism's chief sacred scripture. Others were manuals for his followers. In these treatises and in his teachings Ramanuja challenged many of the core beliefs of Hinduism as it was practiced at the time. Such challenges were why such people as Yadava opposed him so vigorously.

During the twelfth century Hindu theologians debated the nature of God and the relationship between God and both the human soul and physical matter. Two major positions were taken. One was the position that had been outlined by Sankara in the late eighth and early ninth centuries. Sankara looked at the state of Hindu practice and belief and opposed what he saw as meaningless ritual and animal sacrifice. Based on his interpretation of the Vedas, he adopted a monist position about the nature of God. The monist view, called Advaita Vedanta, said that there was a fundamental oneness to everything in creation, including God.

According to the monist view, all of creation is in truth just one entity. The supreme God does not have any form or characteristics and indeed does not even have a name. Thus, monists deem it impossible to be in any meaningful way "devoted" to God, because God is both nowhere and everywhere, and humans are incapable of understanding God's nature. Further, everything in creation is alike (which to Sankara made animal sacrifice unacceptable). That is, the human belief of individuality in creation is an illusion. This view was preached by Sankara and was the most widely accepted among Hindus at the time of Ramanuja's birth. Ramanuja's rejection of this view, in particular, made his teacher, Yadava, angry.

The other major point of view taken in this era was the dualist position, which would later be taught by another acharya, **Madhva** (c. 1199–c. 1276, see entry), in the thirteenth century. The dualist view (with the prefix *duo-* meaning "two") sees a complete distinctness, or difference, between God and physical matter. The dualist view also says that the distinctions between forms of physical matter that people can see are real and not illusions. Physical matter came before the existence of God, and then the universe evolved in response to God's will. Because God was separate from creation, people could come to know His names, His characteristics, and His form. Also, because God was separate from His creation, He could become the object of worship and reverence.

The monist and dualist positions represented the most opposing views that were preached on these matters. Ramanuja's lifetime fell between those of Sankara and Madhva, so the fact that his own position was a blend of the two different opinions seems appropriate. Modern-day religious scholars refer to his views as a "modified nondualist position," or, among Hindu scholars, as Visishtadvaita, a compromise between the two opposing positions.

Ramanuja began with the belief that one cannot have knowledge about anything unless that thing has characteristics that make it different from other things. If humans claim to know something about an object, then that implies that the object has characteristics. Ramanuja applied this principle to knowledge of God. If humans are to reach God, they have to somehow know God, as much as possible. To know God implies that God has form and characteristics and is different and separate from the human soul and from physical creation.

He believed that God did have an identity and that people could on some level come to know it. For Ramanuja, the chief characteristics of God were intelligence, truth, and infinity. God was not cursed with the ignorance of humans and other living things. He was never untruthful, and he had unlimited energy. Ramanuja rejected the accepted notion that a jiva, a lesser spirit, could somehow be equal to God, as the monist position held. Yet, departing from a strict dualist position, Ramanuja also argued that a jiva or any other living thing was a "particle" of God. Its purpose was to serve God and the common whole, just as a hand is part of the body and serves the rest of the body. He concluded that if the purpose of living things was to serve God, then the physical world could not be an illusion.

Ramanuja also believed in "personality," that is, the idea that all things in creation are different. Thus, each person's soul would be different. Because each soul is different, each has to have free will. Otherwise, without freedom of will, souls could not be manifestations of God, or indications of God's existence. In Ramanuja's view the only way that God and humans could have a relationship that made any sense was if God gave people the freedom to choose. The human soul could not in any meaningful way serve God if it was not free to do so.

Both Ramanuja and his successor, Madhva, were strong supporters of the *bhakti* movement, a loosely organized movement of Hindu sects that emerged in medieval India. The word *bhakti* comes from the Sanskrit word *bhaj,* which means something like "to revere or adore." The word *bhakti,* therefore, is usually translated into English as "devotion." The meaning the word suggests is much deeper, however, signifying a total, intense devotion to God. It refers to both an attachment to God and a way of reaching God. It was through bhakti that Hindu Indians overcame divisions of birth, caste, gender, and race to become a united people.

The original bhakti movement had a significant influence on Indian religion and society. Over the centuries, many figures preached the principle that bhakti was the only way to achieve salvation, which led to several large-scale bhakti movements. One of these figures was Ramanuja. In practicing complete devotion to God, he and his Hindu followers put aside the rituals and animal sacrifices of the ancient traditions, which placed emphasis on the outward form of religion. The bhakti movements instead relied on an intense worship of a separate, identifiable God.

For More Information

BOOKS

Bartley, C. J. *The Theology of Ramanuja: Realism and Religion.* Richmond, U.K.: RoutledgeCurzon Press, 2002.

Harré, Rom. *One Thousand Years of Philosophy: From Ramanuja to Wittgenstein.* Malden, MA: Blackwell, 2000.

Lipner, Julius J. *The Face of Truth: A Study of Meaning and Metaphysics in the Vedantic Theology of Ramanuja.* Albany, NY: State University Press of New York, 1986.

Tapasyananda, Swami. *Sri Ramanuja, His Life, Religion, and Philosophy.* Chennai, India: Sri Ramakrishna Math [n.d.].

WEB SITES

Kamat, Jyotsna. "Path of Devotion: Sri Ramanujacharya." *Kamat's Potpourri.* http://www.kamat.com/indica/faiths/bhakti/ramanuja.htm (accessed on June 2, 2006).

Sri Swami Sivananda. "Ramanuja." *The Divine Life Society.* http://www.dlshq.org/saints/ramanuja.htm (accessed on June 2, 2006).

Sri Vaishnava Home Page. http://www.ramanuja.org (accessed June 2, 2006).

Mother Maria Skobtsova

BORN: December 21, 1891 • Riga, Latvia
DIED: March 30, 1945 • Ravensbrück, Germany

Latvian nun; poet

"Mother Maria is a saint of our day and for our day; a woman of flesh and blood possessed by the love of God, who stood face to face with the problems of this century."

— Metropolitan Anthony of Sourozh, as quoted in "Mother Maria Skobtsova—A Saint of Our Day."

Mother Maria Skobtsova, a saint of the Eastern Orthodox Church, a branch of Christianity, is honored for her single-minded devotion to the poor and oppressed in France in the years before and during World War II (1939–45; a war in which Great Britain, France, the United States, and their allies defeated Germany, Italy, and Japan). Near the end of the war she died in a Nazi concentration camp, possibly after offering her life in exchange for that of a Jewish prisoner. Throughout her life of service as an Orthodox nun her primary goal was to embody the Christian ideal of love for fellow human beings.

Birth and early life

Mother Maria Skobtsova was born Elizaveta Pilenko in Riga, the capital city of Latvia, on December 21, 1891. At that time Latvia was part of the Russian empire, and Pilenko grew up in Anapa, a town in southern Russia on the shore of the Black Sea. Her family was relatively wealthy and belonged to society's upper class. Her father directed a botanical garden and school, and for a time he served as the mayor of Anapa. Her mother was a descendant of the last governor of the Bastille prison in Paris, which fell at the start of the French Revolution (1789–99; a rebellion resulting in the overthrow of the monarchy and the rise of a democratic government). The home Pilenko's parents provided was a devout Eastern Orthodox one. Eastern Orthodox Christianity believes in the complete authority of the Bible, the Christian holy text, and that Jesus's teachings were preserved in them without error. After her father's death in 1906, her mother took the family to St. Petersburg, the political and cultural center of Russia at the time. The untimely death of Pilenko's father affected her deeply, and for a while she questioned her belief in God.

The early twentieth century was a time of great political unrest in Russia. During her years in St. Petersburg, Pilenko was drawn into radical and revolutionary circles. She was attracted to goals such as the overthrow of the repressive monarchy and the desire to help lift the crushing poverty of many Russians. Even as a teenager she longed to do something great with her life, in the service of others. In 1910 she married a revolutionary poet named Dimitri Kuzmin-Karaviev. Pilenko soon gave birth to a daughter, Gaiana, but the marriage proved short-lived and the couple divorced in 1913.

During this period Pilenko began to rethink her uncertainty about God and was drawn back to Christianity. She wrote a great deal of religious poetry, publishing a collection entitled *Scythian Shards* in 1912. She even applied for admission to study religion at the Theological Academy of the Alexander Nevsky Monastery. The application of a woman at that time was considered shocking, but she was nevertheless accepted.

Revolution and flight

In the mid-1910s Pilenko was growing impatient with the revolutionaries with whom she associated. In her view, they only talked about their political ideals, never actually acting on them, and these ideals had little to do with the lives of ordinary Russians. Then, in 1917, Russia's political unrest erupted into revolution and the overthrow and eventual murder of the *tsar,* the monarch of Russia, Nicholas II (1868–1918). The Russian Revolution led to the rise to power of the Bolsheviks, the extremist wing of Russia's Social Democratic Party, which later evolved into the Communist Party. Pilenko initially agreed with the party's radical views, such as the revolutionary belief that the tsar should be replaced by a more democratic government that represented the interests of common people which had led to the revolution. During the civil war that followed from 1918 to 1920, however, she came to see the revolution as an event that did more harm than good. The new political leadership seemed just as cruel as the old one. As she traveled back and forth between Anapa and St. Petersburg, she witnessed all around her signs that Russia had descended into terror, mass murder, destruction, hunger, homelessness, and criminal rule.

Pilenko was in Anapa in 1918 when the town was overtaken by the White Army, the counter-revolutionary force that opposed the Bolsheviks. When the mayor of the town fled, Pilenko took his place, but the White Army believed that she was a Bolshevik and arrested her and put her on trial for treason. She narrowly escaped a guilty verdict and execution because the judge, Daniel Skobtsov, had formerly been one of her teachers. She was cleared of the charges. That year she and Skobtsov were married and she became Elizaveta Skobtsova. (In Russian, *Skobtsov* is the masculine form of the name while *Skobtsova* is the feminine.)

People cross a snow-covered bridge near the Alexander Nevsky Monastery in St. Petersburg, Russia, where Maria Skobtsova studied theology in the 1910s. © STEVE RAYMER/CORBIS.

It soon became clear that the Bolsheviks were winning Russia's civil war. Skobtsova and her family, including her mother, decided to flee the country. Their first destination was the nearby country of Georgia, where Skobtsova gave birth to a son, Yuri. The family then went to Yugo-slavia, where a daughter, Anastasia, was born. Finally, the family landed in Paris, France, where Daniel Skobtsov took a job as a schoolteacher. After having witnessed immense suffering in Russia, Skobtsova had grown more deeply religious, and she became actively involved with the spiritual and social work of the Russian Student Christian Movement. Before long she was dedicating herself to theological (religious) studies and to helping the poor in Paris, especially refugees from Russia and other countries.

In the mid-1920s the Skobtsov family fell apart. Tragedy struck in 1926 when Anastasia died of the flu. Soon after, Gaiana left to attend school in Belgium. Then Skobtsova and her husband separated, and Yuri went to live with his father in Paris. By this time Skobtsova was devoting so much of her energy to helping the poor that the Orthodox bishop in Paris urged her to become a nun. She agreed, but only on the condition that she would not be required to live in a convent. The bishop agreed, and in 1932, after she was granted a divorce from Skobtsov, she took her vows as a nun. At this time she took the name Maria.

Service to the poor and oppressed

Throughout the 1930s Mother Maria continued her intense dedication to the welfare of the poor. As cited by Jim Forest on the *Traditional Catholic Reflections and Reports* Web site, she wrote that she wanted an "authentic and purified life" among "paupers and tramps." She saw the world as her convent and offered help and spiritual comfort to anyone who approached her. The door of her small room in central Paris was open to all those who needed help or simply wanted to talk, especially about religion. She wrote, as quoted by Forest, "If someone turns with his spiritual world toward the spiritual world of another person, he encounters an awesome and inspiring mystery. . . . He comes into contact with the true image of God in man." Indeed, perhaps in part because of the death of her daughter, she came to see herself as a universal mother figure, providing maternal comfort and aid to any who needed it. Her motto, according to Forest, was, "Each person is the very icon [representation] of God incarnate [in bodily form] in the world."

With the moral and financial support of the bishop, Mother Maria was able to expand her assistance to the community. She moved into larger quarters in a section of Paris where many Russian immigrants lived. She also rented other buildings, one to house single men, another to help families in need. She soon became a common sight around Paris, approaching street vendors and produce merchants to beg for grocery items, many nearly spoiled, that she could serve to the people in her care. In 1939 she acquired a partner, Father Dimitri Klepinin (1904–1944), who loyally served by her side during the early years of World War II.

The war years

In 1939 Germany, led by the Nazi Party, launched World War II by invading Poland. In 1940 German troops marched into France, seizing Paris on June 14 and the rest of France a week later. The German occupiers largely turned their attention to France's Russian immigrants. Many were rounded up and arrested, including one thousand on a single day in

June 1941. A number of these people had become close friends with Mother Maria and had assisted with her charitable work. Also targeted by the Nazis were Paris's Jews, many of whom were also Russian. The Nazis were sending their prisoners to concentration camps, where millions died in gas chambers or from starvation and disease. Concentration camps were locations where Germany sent Jews and other people it did not like to be contained and, eventually, put to death. Jews in Paris began showing up at Mother Maria's door, asking for certificates showing that they were Christians, with the hope that having such certificates would protect them from the Nazis. Mother Maria and Father Klepinin gladly agreed to help.

In the months that followed, conditions for Jews in Paris became steadily worse. By 1942 they were denied access to most public places. In July of that year nearly thirteen thousand were arrested, and more than one-half of them were taken to a Paris sports stadium, where they were held captive under horrible conditions. As a nun Mother Maria was still allowed some freedom of movement, so she was able to gain access to the stadium. She brought what food she could, comforted many of the prisoners, and even managed to smuggle some children out by hiding them in garbage cans. Meanwhile, she and Father Klepinin created escape routes for Jews, providing them with fake documents, food, and any other help they could.

By this time Yuri was helping his mother in her activities. On February 8, 1943, the Nazis arrested him after discovering a letter proving his involvement. The following day Father Klepinin was arrested. Then, on February 10, Mother Maria was arrested and taken to a prison in the town of Compiègne. There she met with Yuri one last time before he and Father Klepinin were taken away to the Buchenwald concentration camp in Germany. Later, the two men were transferred to the Mittelbau-Dora camp, where they died in early 1944.

Life in the concentration camp

Mother Maria was taken to the Ravensbrück concentration camp for women, located north of Berlin, Germany. As prisoner number 19,263, she managed to survive for nearly two years, toughened by the poverty she had long endured. During her time at Ravensbrück she served as a counselor and mother figure to other prisoners. She often gave away portions of her tiny food rations so that others could cling to life. As cited by Forest, one of people imprisoned with Mother Maria later recalled:

> She exercised an enormous influence on us all. No matter what our nationality, age, political convictions—this had no significance whatever. Mother Maria was adored by all. . . . She took us under her wing. We were cut off from our families, and somehow she provided us with a family.

The conditions endured by Mother Maria were terrible. Food rations were repeatedly cut. Prisoners were forcibly removed from their lice-infested beds at three o'clock in the morning and made to stand outside for hours in the cold and snow for roll call. Blankets, shoes, and socks were taken away. Medical care was nonexistent. Dozens of prisoners died each day from infectious diseases such as dysentery and typhus. Mother Maria's health began to decline, but she continued to survive with the help of other prisoners, who often had to hold her up as they stood during morning roll calls.

In March 1945 Nazi authorities ordered the camp commander to kill any prisoner who was unable to walk. Each morning the guards separated the prisoners into small groups and selected those marked for death in the gas chambers. Mother Maria continued to survive with help from friends. On some occasions guards would enter the barracks at night to make further selections. Mother Maria's friends frequently hid her in a space above the ceiling so that she would not be selected.

During the spring of 1945 the Russian army was invading Germany from the east. The German army was in retreat, and with American and other forces advancing from the west, the end of the war seemed near. Germany's defeat did not come soon enough for Mother Maria, however, and she died on March 30, 1945. According to some accounts, she was simply one of the prisoners selected for death in the camp's gas chamber that day. According to others, she volunteered to take the place of a Jewish prisoner who had been marked for death.

Canonization

During her lifetime, especially before World War II, Mother Maria was a somewhat controversial figure. Some authorities in the Eastern Orthodox Church were disturbed by her independence and outspokenness. She challenged nationalistic views about religion, meaning a nation's use of religion to encourage patriotism, and she offered aid not only to Christians but also to Jews and others in need. Her refusal to live in a convent and her active involvement with the world of the streets of Paris made some of her critics nervous.

After her death, however, Mother Maria and her life attracted widespread attention and growing respect. Biographies were written, and her many essays and poems were translated into English. In 1982 a Russian film titled *Mother Maria* was released. Orthodox Christians campaigned for her canonization as a saint. (Canonization is the term for the process a person must go through to officially be designated a saint.) On January 16, 2004, the Holy Synod of the Ecumenical Patriarchate of the Orthodox Church, the church's governing body, canonized her as Saint Mary of Paris. Later that year, her son Yuri, Father Klepinin, and one of her dedicated coworkers were also canonized. July 20 is the feast day honoring their lives.

Mother Maria the Poet

Mother Maria wrote a considerable amount of poetry, virtually all with religious themes. In 1942, while she was still living in Paris, the Nazi authorities ordered all Jews to wear yellow stars identifying them as Jews. In response Mother Maria wrote the following poem, which hints at her deep spiritual convictions about the role of suffering:

• • •

Two triangles, a star,
The shield of King David, our
    forefather.
This is election, not offense.
The great path and not an evil.
Once more in a term fulfilled,
Once more roars the trumpet of
    the end;
And the fate of a great people
Once more is by the prophet
    proclaimed.
Thou art persecuted again, O Israel,
But what can human malice mean to
    thee,
who have heard the thunder from
    Sinai?

Forest, Jim. "Mother Maria Skobtsova:
Nun and Martyr." *In Communion.*
http://ourworld.compuserve.com/
homepages/jim_forest/mmaria.htm
(accessed on May 23, 2006).

For More Information

BOOKS

Hackel, Sergei. *Pearl of Great Price: The Life and Martyrdom of Mother Maria Skobtsova, 1891–1945.* Crestwood, NY: St. Vladimir's Seminary Press, 1981.

Skobtsova, Maria. *Maria Skobtsova: Essential Writings.* Edited by Jim Forest. Maryknoll, NY: Orbis Books, 2003.

WEB SITES

Forest, Jim. "Mother Maria Skobtsova: Nun and Martyr." *In Communion.* http://www.incommunion.org/articles/st-maria-skobtsova/saint-of-the-open-door (accessed on June 2, 2006).

Forest, Jim. "Mother Maria Skobtsova: Saint of the Open Door." *Traditional Catholic Reflections and Reports.* http://tcrnews2.com/JNForest2.html (accessed on June 2, 2006).

Michal, Bonnie A. "Mother Maria Skobtsova—A Saint of Our Day." *The St. Nina Quarterly,* vol. 2, no. 2. http://www.stnina.org/journal/art/2.2.4 (accessed on June 2, 2006).

Plekon, Michael. "Maria Skobtsova: Woman of Many Faces, Mother in Many Ways." *Jacob's Well.* http://www.jacwell.org/Fall_Winter99/Plekon_Mother_Maria.htm (accessed on June 2, 2006).

Malidoma Patrice Somé

BORN: 1956 • Upper Volta

Burkinan teacher; writer

"Spirit expresses itself in a way we cannot map, cannot tell ahead of time, and has its own plan—a plan not known to us."

In the late twentieth century Malidoma Patrice Somé became well known in the United States and other Western countries as a speaker and author. Through his books and the workshops he leads, he has sought to make Westerners more knowledgeable about the indigenous religions of Africa. The term *indigenous* describes anything (people, art, culture, religion) that has been native to a geographical region over a long historical period.

Somé describes himself as a "man of two worlds." One of his worlds is the West, where he received a formal education and lives much of the time. The other is West Africa, where he is an elder and shaman, or traditional healer, of the Dagara tribe. Living in both of these worlds, Somé has tried to bridge the gap between them.

The religion practiced by Somé is called shamanism, a term that can refer to any faith featuring an unseen world of spirits and demons that respond only to shamans. Shamanism places emphasis on ancestral spirits that continue to play roles in the affairs of the living, providing guidance and wisdom. The history of shamanism dates back to the earliest eras of human history. In many cultures throughout the world, including that of the Dagara, a principal role of the shaman is to cure the sick. A shaman is able to fulfill this role by obtaining secret knowledge from the spirit world.

Birth and early life

The people of the Dagara tribe live along the borders of three African countries: Burkina Faso, Ghana, and Ivory Coast. Malidoma Somé was

Malidoma Patrice Somé

born in Burkina Faso, which was then known as Upper Volta, the name given to the region by French colonists. Somé does not know the exact date of his birth, but government records list it as 1956. His father, Elie, was a farmer and miner. His mother was Colette Dabire.

French colonists, from a primarily Catholic country, did everything they could to convert the people of West Africa to their religion, which is a branch of Christianity. Thus, Somé's father followed the customs not only of his tribe but also of French Catholicism. He gave his son the Christian name Patrice. In the boy's naming ceremony, however, held shortly after his birth, his grandfather gave him the name Malidoma, which means "be friends with the stranger," or "with the enemy." This name became appropriate for the course that Somé's life later took.

Grandfathers among the Dagara are typically storytellers, sharing their knowledge of life and spirit with their communities and especially with their grandsons. Fathers begin to play important roles in their sons' lives only later. In the Dagara culture ancestors are seen as a link between people and the spirit world. Children are believed to have just come from the spirit world, while grandfathers will soon return to that world. As a result, the Dagara claim a bond is formed when the grandfather and the grandson share what they know about the soul and the spirit. Such was the case with Somé and his grandfather, an elder and spiritual leader of the community. The two enjoyed a close relationship almost to the exclusion of Somé's father.

Somé spent the first four years of his life in his village, living the traditional life of a Dagara. When he was four years old, his grandfather died, and soon thereafter he was taken from his village by French Jesuit priests living in a nearby town. (Jesuits, who belong to an order of Catholic priests called the Society of Jesus, are best known for their extensive education, especially with respect to the principles of Catholicism.) In later life Somé would say that the Jesuits had kidnapped him. He was taken to a French missionary school in Nansi, where he lived for the next fifteen years. He rose every morning at 5:30 and followed a strict schedule of study and prayer until bedtime at 10:30 in the evening. In the school he was forced to adopt the ways of thinking of white society. He recalls learning about the West's "temperamental God," whose anger the students were taught to fear. The West refers to those countries in Europe and the Americas. He claimed that he suffered years of emotional and physical abuse at the hands of priests who were determined that he should become a wholehearted Catholic and eventually a priest.

Return to the village

When he was twenty years old, Somé escaped from the boarding school and returned to his village on foot, traveling a distance of 125 miles (201 kilometers). His homecoming, however, was not without problems. While his mother and an older sister greeted him with tears of joy, the villagers looked upon him with fear and suspicion. They considered him a "white black," meaning that he had become too much like the people from the white culture in which he had lived. They believed that he had contracted the "sickness" of French colonialism. He could no longer speak the Dagara language well and found communication with the villagers difficult.

Cultural Roles in Indigenous African Communities

Members of indigenous African tribes such as the Dagara typically fulfill different roles within their communities. These roles are associated with features of the natural world, and each has its characteristic symbolic color. For example, the color of "fire people" is red. Fire people serve as important links between the people and their ancestors. They act as conduits, or channels, through which the energy of the ancestors passes to the village.

The color of "mineral people" is white. Mineral people are the storytellers who use their vast memories to remember and recite stories about the people and their history. Through these stories, they connect communities with their pasts and with their ancestors.

The color of "nature people" is green. Nature people are those who can read nature and see order in its apparent chaos. They provide the villagers with a gateway to the spirit world and help people become more conscious of themselves and their spiritual reality. They are also the medicine men who can cure disease.

"Earth people," whose color is brown, serve the community by channeling the earth's energy into the village. They are the ones who make people feel comfortable in the community. They empower the villagers and nurture them.

Finally there are "water people," whose color is blue. Somé's uncle acted in this role by "carrying water" to his nephew. The water was not actual water, but a kind of spiritual "drink" that helped Somé make peace with his return to village life and helped the villagers overcome their suspicions and fears of him.

For the first few months after his return Somé was visited each day by his "male mother," his mother's brother. In Dagara culture the maternal uncle plays the role of "water person," or peacemaker, and tries to maintain serenity and goodwill in the village. Water persons are also thought of as reconcilers, resolving conflicts and restoring friendships. In Somé's case, many hoped that his uncle could find a way to fold him back into the tribe. The elders subjected Somé to a number of divinations, which are efforts to interpret omens (signs) and uncover secret knowledge or foretell the future. The elders determined that Somé had not fully returned to the village. They claimed part of his soul was missing, still back at the school and the world of white people. They said that his only hope was to undergo an initiation ritual called a *baor,* which would restore his entire soul to the village.

Initiation

In his 1994 autobiography *Of Water and the Spirit,* Somé details his initiation experience. The purpose of the ritual, typically undergone by boys upon entering manhood, was to allow him to learn once again to see the natural world through the eyes of the Dagara. The ritual lasts a month and requires the initiate to make a journey alone, away from the village. Somé had to sleep in the jungle and find his own food. Normally this would not be a terribly frightening experience. Most Dagara boys who undergo the ritual have spent their entire lives living in the jungle, so the environment is familiar to them. For Somé, however, the journey was terrifying, as he had spent so long living in an urban area that to him the jungle was a strange and dangerous place. He stated that he almost died during the experience.

During the initiation Somé learned a great deal about his own personal abilities, as well as about the supernatural world of the Dagara. He declared that he saw spirits from the underworld and had visions of his grandfather and that he made contact with the beings that inhabit the natural world. In his autobiography he details his first night at the initiation camp, where a fire ritual gave him insight into the world of his ancestors. In a chapter entitled "Trying to See," he makes clear the importance of learning to see the world in new ways and describes his initial resistance to the elders' instructions. He admits he even tried to lie to them to convince them that he was making progress.

Eventually Somé achieved a breakthrough, as detailed in a chapter entitled "In the Arms of the Green Lady." During his experience, he had a vision of a yila tree, the "Green Lady" of the chapter's title. By intensely focusing on the tree, he came to see it in a new way, the way of the Dagara, who see little difference between the worlds of reality and imagination. In their view, only by imagining something and intensely focusing thought on it can that thing be truly brought into being. In Somé's words, "If one can imagine something, then it has at least the potential to exist." To most people a yila tree is simply a biological, or natural, specimen; to the Dagara, such a tree can become a "Green Lady." When Somé focused on and truly saw the Green Lady, his vision of the natural world was transformed.

Back to the Western world

After the initiation the village elders decided that Somé should leave the village once again in order to tell the Western world about the world of Africa. Somé was reluctant to go, but he agreed. He first enrolled at the university in Ouagadougou, the capital city of Burkina Faso, where he earned a bachelor's degree in sociology, literature, and linguistics in 1981, then a master's degree in literature in 1982. He then went to

A shaman's fly wisk and talismans, similar to the talisman that Somé carries. Somé believes that the talisman is a source of strength and power and that it helped ensure his success both as a student and in his professional life. © ROGER DE LA HARPE; GALLO IMAGES/CORBIS.

the Sorbonne, a world-famous university in Paris, France, where he earned a master's degree in political science in 1983. Finally he attended Brandeis University in Massachusetts in the United States, where he earned yet another master's degree in 1984 and a doctorate in literature in 1990. Somé later wrote that he found school easy because of his initiation ritual. He even claimed that he knew the answers to the professors' questions just by looking at their auras, or the energy fields surrounding them.

The Dagara elders wanted Somé to live in the United States. They believed that in the United States he could be fully immersed in the Western world. In fact, Somé has said that he finds he can be "more African" in the United States than he can in Africa. He explains that because of his extensive education, he has found it difficult to be accepted in Africa, as many Africans think he has turned his back on the customs and beliefs of his tribal culture. In the United States he claims he feels relatively free to be an educated man who also believes in his ancient African religion.

After completing his doctorate at Brandeis, Somé took a job teaching at the University of Michigan, where he was a professor of literature and French from 1990 to 1993. He also worked as a visiting professor at Stanford University in California during the 1992–93 school year. Afterward he earned a living as a writer, lecturer, and speaker. With his wife, Elisabeth Sobonfu, he gives workshops and conferences in which he explores African spirituality with participants and helps Westerners see the value of indigenous cultures. He also returns to the Dagara people to teach them about the West.

Elder and shaman

In Somé's view, the West suffers from a kind of spiritual sickness. He claims this sickness shows itself in many ways: materialism (desiring to have material objects), consumerism (the buying of such objects), damage to the environment, the unequal distribution of wealth, prejudice against (or mistreatment of) people of color, and, especially, a sharp divide between the physical and spiritual worlds. Somé believes that indigenous religions such as shamanism can return people to a sense of oneness and connection with the world, with nature, and with one another.

As an elder in the Dagara tribe, Somé acts as one of its spiritual leaders as well as a shaman. He points out that in contrast to Western religions, shamanism does not view the supernatural as separate from the material world. He notes, for example, that the Dagara have no word for "supernatural." The closest word, *yielbongura,* is best translated into English as "the thing that knowledge can't eat." In other words, the supernatural is that part of human experience that the logical, rational mind cannot destroy or consume. The Dagara and other practitioners of shamanistic religions resist dividing the material and spiritual worlds and instead see them as one. They believe the material world simply gives form to the spiritual world.

Somé always carries with him a talisman, an object believed to give its bearer supernatural powers or protection. He describes this talisman as an oval-shaped pouch that contains stones from the underworld and other secret objects from the wild. He believes that the talisman is a source of strength and power and helped ensure his success both as a student and in his professional life. He also uses the talisman to educate people in the West regarding his religion and culture.

For More Information

BOOKS

Harvey, Graham. *Shamanism: A Reader.* New York, NY: Routledge, 2003.

Somé, Malidoma Patrice. *Healing Wisdom of Africa.* New York, NY: Tarcher, 1999.

Somé, Malidoma Patrice. *Of Water and the Spirit: Ritual, Magic, and Initiation in the Life of an African Shaman.* New York, NY: Penguin Books, 1995.

WEB SITES

van Gelder, Sarah. "Remembering Our Purpose: The Teachings of Indigenous Cultures May Help Us Go Beyond Modernity, An Interview with Malidoma Somé." *In Context: A Quarterly of Humane Sustainable Culture.* http://www.context.org/ICLIB/IC34/Some.htm (accessed on June 2, 2006).

Somé, Malidoma. "VISIONS: Malidoma Somé." Interview by D. Patrick Miller. *Mother Jones.* http://www.motherjones.com/news/qa/1995/03/miller.html (accessed on June 2, 2006).

Mother Teresa

BORN: August 27, 1910 • Üsküb, Kosovo
DIED: September 5, 1997 • Calcutta, India

Kosovar nun

"In these twenty years of work among the people, I have come more and more to realize that it is being unwanted that is the worst disease that any human being can ever experience."

Mother Teresa.
AP IMAGES.

Mother Teresa was a Catholic missionary nun who became known for her work with the poor. Although she assisted poverty-stricken people throughout the world, she is most closely identified with her work in the crowded slums of Calcutta (modern-day Kolkata), India, which earned her the informal title "Saint of the Gutters." In 1982, during the siege of Beirut, Lebanon, she negotiated a cease-fire between Israeli and Palestinian forces. This cease-fire allowed her to evacuate mentally handicapped patients from a hospital on the front lines of the battle. During her lifetime she received several major awards, including the Nobel Peace Prize. After her death she was beatified (blessed) by the Catholic Church. Beatification is an early step in the canonization process, after which one becomes recognized as a saint. She is now formally referred to as Blessed Mother Teresa.

Early life

Mother Teresa was born Agnes Gonxha Bojaxhiu on August 27, 1910, in the town of Üsküb, in Kosovo, which at the time was a province in the Turkish Empire. (In modern times the town is called Skopje and is the capital of the Republic of Macedonia.) She was the youngest of three surviving daughters born to Nikollë Bojaxhiu, a successful contractor, and his wife, Dranafile. Both parents were Albanian. Although most Albanians are Muslims (followers of the Islamic faith) and most of the people of Kosovo Province were Christian and members of the Macedonian Orthodox Church, the Bojaxhiu family was Roman Catholic.

Agnes's early years were relatively uneventful and her family life happy. She later noted that she felt a strong religious calling at age twelve and wanted to help the poor by becoming a missionary. A missionary is someone who undertakes a religious task. At age eighteen she received permission from the Vatican, the seat of authority of the Roman Catholic Church, to join the Sisters of Loreto, more formally referred to as the Institute of the Blessed Virgin Mary. The Sisters of Loreto, located in Rathfarnham, a residential suburb of Dublin, Ireland, was an order of nuns whose chief mission was the education of girls. When Agnes completed her training, the order sent her to Darjeeling, India. At this time she was a novice, or a person who has received religious education but has not taken her vows to the order. She took her first vows in 1931, when she adopted the name Sister Mary Teresa in honor of Teresa of Avila (1515–1582) and Thérèse de Lisieux (1873–1897), both Catholic saints. In 1937 she took her final vows and became Mother Teresa.

Mother Teresa began her career at St. Mary's High School in Calcutta, where she taught catechism (the teachings and principles of the Catholic faith), history, and geography from 1930 to 1944. From 1944 to 1948 she served as principal of the school. The people she worked with at St. Mary's would later recall little about her, stressing that she seemed ordinary, quiet, and humble. During these years she would look out upon the streets and slums of Calcutta and think about her early goal of performing missionary work among the poor. In 1946 she was riding on a train when she experienced a calling from God to serve among the poorest of the poor.

Founded the Missionaries of Charity

In 1948 Mother Teresa petitioned the pope, Pius XII (1876–1958), to live as an independent nun. She resigned her position at the high school and traveled to Patna, India, where she completed a course with the Medical

Mission Sisters. She then returned to Calcutta, where she took up residence with the Little Sisters of the Poor. She established an outdoor school for poor children, and in time she attracted both volunteer help and financial support from church groups and city officials in Calcutta.

Mother Teresa's next step in her mission to help the poor was to petition the Vatican in 1950 for permission to establish a new order of nuns. The Vatican agreed, at first calling the order the Diocesan Congregation of the Calcutta Diocese. (A diocese is a district.) Soon the order took the name Missionaries of Charity. The goal of the Missionaries of Charity, according to Mother Teresa, was to provide care for the hungry, the naked, the homeless, the crippled, the blind, and those affected by the skin disease leprosy. She sought to assist all those people who were unwanted, unloved, and uncared for by society. She located an abandoned Hindu temple and, with the help of local authorities, converted it into a hospice called the Kalighat Home for the Dying. A hospice is a facility that provides care to the dying. Later she opened three additional institutions: another hospice, called Nirmal Hriday, which means "pure heart"; a hospital for lepers called Shanti Nagar, which means "city of peace"; and an orphanage.

Continued growth

By the 1960s Mother Teresa's order had attracted numerous financial donations and recruits, and maintained a full network of charitable institutions throughout India. The humble and soft-spoken nun had become, in effect, the chief executive officer of a large and growing organization in India, one that was destined to become international in scope. In 1965 Mother Teresa received permission from the pope, then Paul VI (1897–1978), to expand her order of nuns to other nations. The first Missionaries of Charity house outside of India was established in Venezuela. It was followed by houses in Tanzania and Italy. Soon the Missionaries of Charity had houses throughout Africa, Asia, and western Europe. In the early 1990s Mother Teresa was also able to introduce operations to eastern Europe. The first such house in the United States was established in the Bronx section of New York City.

As the organization's charitable work expanded, so did its influence as a religious order. In 1963 the Missionaries of Charity Brothers was established. (In the Catholic Church, brothers are members of religious orders who are not priests; usually, orders of brothers, like nuns, perform work in schools, hospitals, missions, etc.) In 1976 a contemplative branch of the nuns was formed, in which members devote themselves to prayer and penance, often maintaining silence and living in convents. Lay workers (people who were not members of the clergy) and volunteers were organized into three groups: the Co-Workers of Mother Teresa, the Sick and Suffering Co-Workers, and the Lay Missionaries of Charity. In 1981, with the support of the pope, Mother Teresa launched the Corpus Christi Movement, a movement to create spiritual renewal among diocesan priests, or priests attached to local dioceses rather than to specific religious orders. As part of the movement, nuns spiritually "adopt" priests, something Saint Thérèse de Lisieux had done in nineteenth-century France.

Mother Teresa and her work became more familiar to people throughout the world due to the 1969 documentary film *Something Beautiful for God,* which was produced by the well-known British writer and social critic Malcolm Muggeridge (1903–1990). A book by the same title followed in 1971 and remains in print in the early twenty-first century. One story told about the production of the documentary concerns filming that took place at an Indian hospice. The film crew believed that the lighting in the building was so poor that the footage they shot there would turn out to be of little use. When they developed the film, however, they found that everything appeared brightly lit. Muggeridge, who later converted to Catholicism, claimed that the lighting was the product of "divine light" from Mother Teresa herself. Some members of the crew argued that it was simply the result of a new, improved type of film. Muggeridge was not alone in his belief, however, as throughout her lifetime many people testified that they witnessed a mysterious light associated with Mother Teresa.

Awards and prizes

The 1970s and years following brought many awards and much recognition for Mother Teresa and her work. In 1971 Pope Paul VI awarded her the Pope John XXIII Peace Prize. She sold the Lincoln Continental automobile given to her by the pope and used the money to help the poor. Mother Teresa also won the Kennedy Prize in 1971, the Nehru Prize in 1972, the Albert Schweitzer International Prize in 1975, and the Nobel Peace Prize in 1979, "for work undertaken in the struggle to overcome poverty and distress, which also constitute a threat to peace." She donated all of her prize money to the poor of Calcutta. Also in 1979, she won the Balzan Prize, given to those who promote brotherhood and

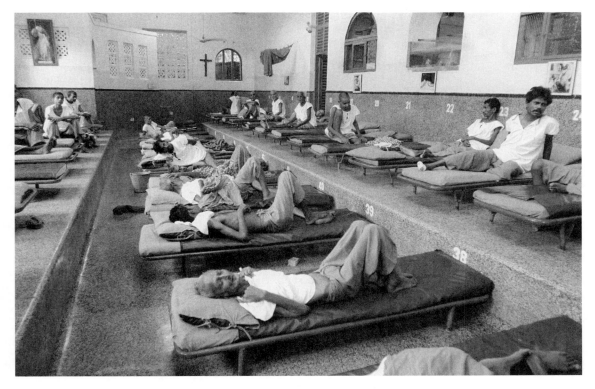

Mother Teresa's hospice Nirmal Hriday, in Kolkata, India. Mother Teresa is best-known for her work with the poor and homeless and has been called "Saint of the Gutters." © BALDEV/CORBIS.

peace among nations. Later awards included the U.S. Presidential Medal of Freedom in 1985 and the Congressional Gold Medal in 1994. In 1996 an act of the U.S. Congress made her an honorary citizen of the United States, a gesture of respect extended to only six people throughout U.S. history.

Decline and death

The 1980s marked the beginning of the final stages of Mother Teresa's life. In 1983, while visiting Pope John Paul II (1920–2005) in Rome, Italy, she suffered a heart attack. A second heart attack followed in 1989, and in 1991 she was stricken with pneumonia while traveling in Mexico. She offered to resign as head of the Missionaries of Charity, but when a vote was taken among all members of the order, the only ballot supporting her resignation was the one she cast herself.

Mother Teresa's health continued to decline through the 1990s, and she eventually became unable to continue with her work. On March 13, 1997, she resigned as the head of her order, which by then included 4,000 nuns, 100,000 lay volunteers, and 610 missions in 123 countries. The next month she fell and broke her collarbone. Later that year she contracted malaria and also had to undergo heart surgery. She died on September 5, 1997. The Indian government gave her a full state funeral, an honor usually reserved for such dignitaries as prime ministers. Religious and political leaders around the world commented on the sadness of her passing.

The twenty-first century: beatification

Mother Teresa's story continued after her death, with her beatification (blessing) and the drive mounted by Catholics to persuade the Vatican to name her a saint. In the Catholic faith a saint is a person whose admirable life makes it certain that his or her soul is in heaven. Members of the Catholic Church are said to "venerate" saints, meaning that saints are honored and are thought to be able to speak with God on behalf of the living. Catholics do not worship saints, however, as worship is given only to God.

After the death of a person such as Mother Teresa, a local bishop or other church authority begins the process of canonization (the process leading to sainthood) by conducting an investigation into the person's life. The first step toward sainthood is to be regarded as a servant of God; the second is to be regarded as venerable, or commanding of respect and reverence. Then the Vatican takes over the investigation. According to church law, for the next step, beatification, to occur, the candidate for sainthood has to have performed one documented miracle. Historically, the church has beatified many people who were not later made saints, including the emperor Charlemagne (742–814), of France. For the final step, canonization, to occur, at least one additional miracle has to be documented. The chief difference between beatification and canonization is that while beatification represents the church's "permission" for the faithful to venerate the person, canonization transforms that permission into a matter of universal church law. Therefore, beatification typically involves veneration by members of a local community, such as a region or a country, while a canonized saint is venerated worldwide as a matter of church principle.

The miracle attributed to Mother Teresa concerned a woman named Monica Besra, who is said to have been healed of cancer when a locket containing a picture of Mother Teresa was applied to her tumor. The issue of the miracle became controversial when Besra and her husband later denied that she had been healed by a miracle, and when her hospital records could not be found. Later, however, the husband supported the claim of the miraculous healing, and Mother Teresa was formally beatified by Pope John Paul II on October 19, 2003.

Controversy

Mother Teresa's life was not without controversy. Many people, including Catholics and non-Catholics alike, criticized her for her strict opposition to artificial birth control, especially in consideration of the massive overpopulation of such places as Calcutta. She also attracted some criticism for her uncompromising opposition to abortion, or terminating pregnancy. Others found fault with a statement she made in the mid-1970s, after the Indian government suspended civil liberties in the country. She said the people were happier without their liberties because there were more jobs and no strikes. Comments such as these led some observers to believe that Mother Teresa was more interested in maintaining a close relationship with the Indian government, which provided her with financial support, than in speaking out against its abuses.

Other criticisms include financial mismanagement of funds, with donations not going to the projects for which they were intended, and the number of people served by the Missionaries of Charity. Some investigators claim to have found that the largest of its missions served a few hundred people at most. While Mother Teresa received worldwide praise for her work, other religious organizations in India serve up to tens of thousands of people each day and receive little attention. Such criticism has created a level of controversy about Mother Teresa and the Missionaries of Charity, but she continued to carry out her lifelong goal of working with the poor.

For More Information

BOOKS

Muggeridge, Malcolm. *Something Beautiful for God: Mother Teresa of Calcutta.* New York, NY: Doubleday, 1977.

Scott, David. *A Revolution of Love: The Meaning of Mother Teresa.* Chicago, IL: Loyola Press, 2005.

Spink, Kathryn. *Mother Teresa: A Complete Authorized Biography.* San Francisco, CA: HarperSanFrancisco, 1998.

WEB SITES

Hunter, Michael Wayne. "Mother Teresa on Death Row." http://www.compusmart.ab.ca/deadmantalking/mhmother.htm (accessed on April 18, 2006).

"Mother Teresa: Angel of Mercy." *CNN.com.* http://www.cnn.com/WORLD/9709/mother.teresa/ (accessed on May 26, 2006).

"Mother Teresa—Biography." *Nobelprize.org.* http://nobelprize.org/peace/laureates/1979/teresa-bio.html (accessed on May 26, 2006).

"The Nobel Peace Prize 1979." *Nobelprize.org.* http://nobelprize.org/peace/laureates/1979/presentation-speech.html (accessed on May 26, 2006).

Thich Nhat Hanh

BORN: 1926 • Vietnam

Vietnamese religious leader; writer

"Meditation is about awareness of what is going on—not only in your body and in your feelings, but all around you."

Thich Nhat Hanh (pronounced tik not hawn) is often referred to as the most beloved and respected Buddhist teacher in the West (the countries of Europe and the Americas). He was forced into exile from his native Vietnam in 1966, while on a speaking tour in the United States. He was trying to promote peace between the warring parties of the U.S.-supported South Vietnam and the communist-supported North Vietnam. Communists support an economy in which all goods are owned collectively by the people and distributed by the government according to need. Communists may support the overthrow of the government by the masses, or working class. While Thich Nhat Hanh was in the United States, both Vietnams banned his return. Since his exile he has made his home in France, at the Plum Village Buddhist Center, which he founded. He has continued to travel and teach Buddhism and peace in the West, and is the author of close to one hundred books. He has also spoken and written widely about bridging the religions of Buddhism and Christianity.

Thich Nhat Hanh.
AP IMAGES.

Vietnamese roots

Thich Nhat Hanh was born in 1926 in central Vietnam. He left home as a teenager to become a Buddhist monk and was officially taken into the religious order in 1942. At that time he took the religious name of Thich Nhat Hanh. The word *thich* is a title for monks and nuns in Vietnam, which is taken as their new "family name." *Nhat* means "of the best quality," and *hanh* means "good nature" or "right conduct." Thich Nhat Hanh's followers also sometimes refer to him as Thay, or "teacher."

At the time of Thich Nhat Hanh's birth, Vietnam had been ruled by the French since the late nineteenth century. The Japanese invaded the country in 1940, during World War II (1939–45; a war in which Great Britain, France, the United States, and their allies defeated Germany, Italy, and Japan). A communist revolutionary group called the Viet Minh, under the leadership of Ho Chi Minh (1890–1969), saw this as a possible opportunity to be freed of French rule. After Japan surrendered in 1945, the Viet Minh declared the formation of the Democratic Republic of Vietnam. The French refused to leave, however, and a long period of unrest and warfare between local rebels and the French began. The French finally withdrew in 1954, and Vietnam was divided into North Vietnam, the stronghold of Ho Chi Minh's communist forces, and South Vietnam, where the French had been centered around Saigon and which was essentially democratic. The Cold War (1945–91; a period of political hostility between the United States and its allies and the Soviet Union and its allies) then brought about the involvement of the United States, which was fearful of a communist takeover of South Vietnam. The Vietnam War (1954–75), during which the United States fought with South Vietnamese forces against the North Vietnamese, was another long and bloody war in the country's history.

Thich Nhat Hanh grew up during this long period of warfare. Early in his career, he helped create a movement known as Engaged Buddhism to try to make positive changes to Vietnamese society. The movement paired nonviolent civil disobedience with more traditional Buddhist practices, such as meditation, a focusing of thoughts on a single point, usually to gain greater understanding. One result of these efforts was the 1950 founding of a major center of Buddhist studies in South Vietnam, the An Quang Buddhist Institute. Speaking in 2003 with John Malkin of the *Shambala Sun,* Thich Nhat Hanh explained the principle of engaged Buddhism: "Engaged Buddhism is just Buddhism. When bombs begin to fall on people, you cannot stay in the meditation hall all of the time.

Meditation is about awareness of what is going on—not only in your body and in your feelings, but all around you." He further explained, "When I was a novice in Vietnam, we young monks witnessed the suffering caused by the war. So we were very eager to practice Buddhism in such a way that we could bring it to society. That was not easy because the tradition does not directly offer Engaged Buddhism. So we had to do it by ourselves. That was the birth of Engaged Buddhism."

In 1961 Thich Nhat Hanh was invited to the United States to both study and teach comparative religion at Columbia University and Princeton University. Two years later, however, South Vietnamese monks asked him to return home to help try to put a stop to the warfare among the United States and Vietnamese troops. Back in his native country Thich Nhat Hanh assisted in organizing a nonviolent resistance movement. He also spread the concept of Engaged Buddhism through the 1964 creation of the School of Youth for Social Service. This program sent more than ten thousand young people to the countryside to help Buddhist monks and nuns build schools and health clinics. It was sometimes compared to the Peace Corps, established several years earlier by the U.S. president John F. Kennedy (1917–1963).

La Boi Press, which became one of Vietnam's most important publishing houses, was established by Thich Nhat Hanh in 1964. His messages of peace were then printed in books and articles. They called for an end to hostilities and a search for common ground between the warring parties. Both South Vietnam and North Vietnam, however, censored his writings.

In exile

The Fellowship of Reconciliation and Cornell University invited Thich Nhat Hanh to the United States again in 1966. He traveled and spoke at many private and public meetings, even holding conversations with officials from the presidential administration. His efforts on behalf of peace, however, resulted in his being banned from returning to either North Vietnam or South Vietnam. At forty years of age, he was effectively left without a home country.

During his extended stay in the United States, Thich Nhat Hanh became friends with civil rights activist Martin Luther King Jr. (1929–1968). King was a fellow advocate of nonviolent resistance, which he had used during his fight for equal rights for African Americans in the

Buddhism in Vietnam

Buddhism is Vietnam's primary religion and is practiced by more than half of the population. Buddhism came to Vietnam around the first century CE, from India. By the end of the second century Vietnam had developed a major Buddhist center, Luy Lau, north of modern-day Hanoi. This became a popular stopover for many Indian Buddhist monks on their way to and from China. Over time the principles of Zen and Pure Land Buddhism became dominant in Vietnam. Both of these are divisions of the Mahayana branch of Buddhism and are heavily practiced in China and Japan. The Mahayana branch of Buddhism formed after a doctrinal split (a split over beliefs) about one hundred years after the Buddha's death.

While more traditional Buddhist doctrines, or beliefs, hold that the achievement of supreme knowledge and understanding must take several lifetimes to achieve, Zen Buddhism focuses on enlightenment for the student by the most direct means possible. Followers seek to accomplish this usually through meditation and the study of koans, or question-and-answer sessions between masters and students that often seem illogical and require great effort to understand. Pure Land Buddhism also seeks enlightenment in one lifetime. In Pure Land Buddhism, a sort of heaven, Sukhavati, is ruled over by Amitabha, a buddha, or enlightened one. Pure Land Buddhism also emphasizes meditation and the saying of mantras, or chanted prayers. In Vietnam, Zen is practiced largely by monks and nuns. Pure Land is practiced mostly by the laity, or the general populace.

Because of the influence of neighboring China, both Daoism and Confucianism also became popular in Vietnam. Indeed, Confucianism became more dominant than Buddhism for several centuries. Also, the French who colonized the land in the nineteenth century discouraged the practice of Buddhism, which they saw as a threat to their authority. They imported their own religion, Roman Catholicism, a branch of Christianity. By the twentieth century, however, Buddhist revival movements began to spread across Vietnam, with many of the religion's beliefs undergoing modernization.

United States. In 1967 King nominated Thich Nhat Hanh for the Nobel Peace Prize.

Thich Nhat Hanh traveled to Europe, where he met with the Catholic pope and several heads of state. He then remained in France, forming the Unified Buddhist Church in 1969 and leading a Buddhist delegation to the Vietnam peace talks. The war finally ended in 1975, with the victory of communist North Vietnam. Thich Nhat Hanh was still denied permission to return to his homeland, and so he instead set up a small Buddhist community, Sweet Potato, about 100 miles (161 kilometers) south of Paris. He continued to work for peace and organized rescue operations for those fleeing Vietnam, which was then unsafe for anyone who had supported the south. Resistance to his operations from the governments of Thailand and Singapore, which were overwhelmed by the arrival of the Vietnamese refugees, made it impossible for him to continue his operations. Thich Nhat Hanh thereafter went into semi-retreat at Sweet Potato, where he meditated, gardened, and continued to write.

In 1982 Thich Nhat Hanh established a much larger retreat center and Buddhist community, Plum Village, in southern France. He began to travel extensively in the United States, speaking to a wide variety of groups, including environmental activists, businessmen, prison inmates, police officers, and even members of the U.S. Congress. His practice of "mindfulness," or being aware not only of world affairs but of the consequences of one's own actions, appealed to people of all faiths and nationalities. In 1993 he spoke at the National Cathedral in Washington, D.C., and attracted a crowd of twelve hundred people. Berkeley, California, named a day in his honor. He opened the Green Mountain Dharma Center and Maple Forest Monastery in Vermont in 1997 and founded the Deer Park Monastery in Escondido, California, in 1999.

Thich Nhat Hanh played an important role in getting the United Nations to pass several resolutions on peace and nonviolence. When the United States invaded Iraq in 2003, Thich Nhat Hanh's voice was again among the strongest that called for peace and an end to the fighting. He told Bob Abernathy of *Religion and Ethics Newsweekly,* "Using violence to suppress violence is not the correct way. America has to wake up to that reality."

In the interview Thich Nhat Hanh also observed, "There are ways to transform and to reduce the amount of suffering in our families, in our schools. We, as practitioners of transformation and healing, we know how to do it, how to reduce the level of violence." To this end, Thich Nhat Hanh developed fourteen rules for good living:

1. Do not be bound by doctrines and theories.
2. Do not think there is one changeless or absolute truth.
3. Do not force others to accept your views.
4. Do not close your eyes to suffering.
5. Do not become wealthy while others go without food.
6. Do not hold on to anger and hatred.
7. Do not say things that cause discord.
8. Do not say untruthful things.
9. Do not use Buddhism for personal gain.

Buddhist monks sit in peaceful protest on a street in South Vietnam during the Vietnam War. Thich Nhat Hanh was forced into exile during the war when his peace efforts took him outside of the country. He was banned from returning. © BETTMANN/ CORBIS.

10. Do not do work that is harmful to humans or nature.

11. Do not kill.

12. Do not possess things harmful to others.

13. Do not mistreat your body.

14. Finally, do not assume that your teacher, Thich Nhat Hanh, is able to follow each of these rules perfectly.

Homecoming

Thich Nhat Hanh was finally allowed to visit his native Vietnam in 2005, almost forty years after he was exiled. Writing in *Time International,* Kay Johnson called his return "a homecoming more fitting for royalty or a rock star than a monk." Indeed, Thich Nhat Hanh's work for peace and religious tolerance has made him well-known, if not famous, throughout the world. Yet his fame has not weakened the convictions he holds as a Buddhist monk.

For More Information

BOOKS

Nhat Hanh, Thich. *Going Home: Jesus and Buddha as Brothers.* New York, NY: Riverhead Books, 1999.

PERIODICALS

Gottlieb, Roger S. "Mad as Hell?" *Tikkun* (May 2002): 75.

Hey, Barbara. "Paths of Peace: The Wisdom of Thich Nhat Hanh." *Better Nutrition* (March 2003): 42.

Johnson, Kay. "A Long Journey Home." *Time International* (January 24, 2005): 47.

Lefebure, Leo D. Review of *Living Buddha, Living Christ,* by Thich Nhat Hanh. *Christian Century* (October 16, 1996): 964.

Long, Michael G. Review of *Creating True Peace: Ending Violence in Yourself, Your Family, Your Community, and the World,* by Thich Nhat Hanh. *Christian Century* (November 29, 2003): 38.

WEB SITES

Abernathy, Robert. "Thich Nhat Hanh." *Religion and Ethics Newsweekly.* http://www.pbs.org/wnet/religionandethics/week703/feature.html (accessed on June 2, 2006).

"About Thich Nhat Hanh." *Parallax Press.* http://www.parallax.org/about_tnh.html (accessed on June 2, 2006).

Howlett, Debbie. "Buddhism and the Badge." *USA Today.* http://www.usatoday.com/news/health/2003-08-19-stress-retreat_x.htm (accessed on June 2, 2006).

Nhat Hanh, Thich. "In Engaged Buddhism, Peace Begins with You: An Interview with Thich Nhat Hanh." By John Malkin. *Shambala Sun Online.* http://www.shambhalasun.com/index.php?option=com_content&task=view&id=1579&Itemid=243 (accessed on June 2, 2006).

Nhat Hanh, Thich. "Questions and Answers." *State University of New York at Stony Brook.* http://www.sinc.sunysb.edu/Clubs/buddhism/dailylife/thayq-a.html (accessed on June 2, 2006).

Schlumpf, Heidi. "Practicing Peace." *National Catholic Reporter.* http://www.natcath.com/NCR_Online/archives2/2003c/091203/091203a.php (accessed on June 2, 2006).

"Venerable Thich Nhat Hanh." *BuddhaNet.* http://www.buddhanet.net/masters/thich.htm (accessed on June 2, 2006).

"Venerable Thich Nhat Hanh." *Dharma Memphis.* http://www.dharmamemphis.com/magnolia/tnhbio.html (accessed on June 2, 2006).

Desmond Mpilo Tutu

BORN: October 10, 1931 • Klerksdorp, South Africa

South African religious leader; politician; writer

"Sometimes strident, often tender, never afraid and seldom without humour, Desmond Tutu's voice will always be the voice of the voiceless."

— Nelson Mandela as quoted on the *University of the Witwatersrand* Web site.

Desmond Mpilo Tutu.
PETER KRAMER/
GETTY IMAGES.

A s an archbishop of the Anglican Church in South Africa, Desmond Mpilo Tutu was one of the foremost opponents of the apartheid policies of that country's government in the 1970s and 1980s. *Apartheid* means "apartness" in the Afrikaans language, which is one of the official languages of South Africa. The word is most often used to refer to the former government policy of racial separation and discrimination directed against non-Europeans in the country. Discrimination is unfair treatment to a person or group because of perceived or real differences. At the time of Tutu's birth, this discrimination had been going on in South Africa since the region had become a Dutch colony in the seventeenth century. It continued after South Africa achieved independence as a nation in 1910. In 1948 apartheid became the official policy of the white South African government.

Under apartheid each person was assigned to a specific racial group: white, black, "coloured" (of mixed race), and Asian. Laws were passed to separate the races, with each assigned separate living areas and public facilities such as parks, restrooms, and beaches. A separate educational system was set up to ensure that blacks could not receive an education equal to that of whites. Travel for non-Europeans was severely restricted. Interracial marriage, or marriage between two people of different races, was strictly forbidden. Blacks had no representation in the nation's parliament, and only whites enjoyed full civil rights. The police had broad powers to arrest and imprison anyone who protested the government's policies.

Eventually the world community spoke out against apartheid. The policy officially ended in South Africa in 1990–91, when the laws were repealed and blacks were finally given an equal voice in the nation's government. One of the major figures who helped bring about this change was Desmond Tutu.

Birth and early life

Desmond Tutu was born on October 7, 1931, in the South African mining town of Klerksdorp. His father, Zachariah, was a schoolteacher. His mother, Aletta, was a domestic servant. Tutu's earliest recollections of discrimination date to his childhood, when white children regularly shouted racial insults at him and other black children. He saw firsthand the harsh results of government discrimination among the mine workers, who labored for low wages and typically lived in shacks with no running water or sanitary facilities. Tutu also felt the effects of discrimination at school, where, for example, the government provided free meals for white children, who often threw them away because they preferred the food that their mothers had packed for them. The black children, whose families lived in poverty, often went through the trash bins to scavenge the discarded food.

In 1943 Tutu's family moved to Johannesburg, South Africa's largest city, where Tutu enrolled in Johannesburg Bantu High School. (The Bantu are an African tribe.) In the city Tutu met Father Trevor Huddleston, a white priest who was an outspoken critic of racial discrimination. During this period Tutu contracted tuberculosis, an infectious disease that affects the lungs, and spent nearly twenty months in a hospital. Huddleston visited him nearly every day and would prove to be a major influence on Tutu's own opposition to apartheid. Apartheid became official after the 1948 election victories of the National Party, a political party whose members had run for office on a promise to separate the races.

Following his recovery Tutu enrolled in the school of medicine at Witwatersrand University, with the goal of becoming a doctor. He was forced to leave the university, however, because he and his family did not have enough money to pay tuition. He then enrolled at the Pretoria Bantu Normal College to train as a teacher and earned his diploma in 1953. He went on to earn a bachelor's degree from the University of Johannesburg in 1954. For the next three years he worked as a high school teacher in Johannesburg and in Krugersdorp. In 1955 he married Leah Nomalizo Shenxane, with whom he eventually had four children.

Tutu resigned from his teaching jobs in 1957 after the government revealed its Bantu Education Act, a plan to institute a new educational system for blacks that would be inferior to that provided for whites. At this point Tutu felt a calling from God and came to believe that he could best serve his people as a priest. He began to study theology (religion) with the Community of the Resurrection, the Anglican community in Johannesburg of which Father Huddleston was a member. The Anglicans are a sect, or branch, of Christianity.

Career in the Anglican Church

After being ordained, or officially made, an Anglican priest in 1961, Tutu worked in a number of small parishes (religious communities) first in South Africa, then in England. While working in England he earned a bachelor's degree in divinity in 1965 and a master's degree in theology in 1966, both from King's College in London. He then took a position in England with the Theological Education Fund, which required him to travel throughout Africa and Asia to award scholarship money from the World Council of Churches. During these years he also spent time in South Africa lecturing on theology. By the 1970s resistance to South African apartheid was growing, and in 1975 Tutu decided to return to his country permanently to help with the struggle for freedom from discrimination.

Tutu continued to rise in the Anglican Church. In 1975 he was appointed dean of St. Mary's Cathedral in Johannesburg, the first black ever to hold that position. In 1976 he became a bishop in Lesotho, a small country about the size of the U.S. state of Maryland that is entirely surrounded by South Africa. At the time the small nation was dominated by its larger neighbor so thoroughly that it was virtually a part of South Africa. Because of this it was one of the "homelands" designated by the South African government as a place where blacks could live. Throughout the late 1970s Tutu used his position to try to ease some of the racial tension that threatened both Lesotho and Soweto, a black township just outside Johannesburg. In trying to serve as a peacemaker, he took part in discussions with many different people about the racial problems dividing the country.

Opponent of apartheid

On June 16, 1976, a key event in the history of apartheid took place when a riot erupted in the Soweto township. A number of high school students protested the government's new policy requiring that classes at the schools be taught in the Afrikaans language. Afrikaans was the language of the Dutch settlers who had initiated the discrimination against black Africans, and the students rebelled against the idea of having to take classes taught in the language of their oppressors. Police arrived and responded with tear gas and gunfire. As the rioting spread, a number of government buildings were set ablaze. In the weeks that followed, protestors and government security forces clashed on numerous occasions. By the time the rioting ended, five hundred people were dead, most of them from gunshot wounds. Thousands were arrested, and thousands more fled the country.

The Soweto riots were a turning point in Tutu's life. Although he continued to call for peaceful protest and change, he became more militant in his outlook. He concluded that only intense pressure would force the government to change its policies. He resolved to use his influence and visibility to initiate talks between blacks and the government, and for the next fifteen years he spoke out publicly and forcefully against apartheid. In 1978 he became the first black secretary general of the South African Council of Churches, an organization of churches with thirteen million members collectively, 80 percent of whom were black. Tutu used his position on the council to promote antigovernment protest. In response, the government repeatedly harassed Tutu and other Council of Churches members, often charging them with small crimes they had not committed.

In 1979 Tutu challenged the government over a law called the Group Areas Act. The act gave the government the authority to forcibly move blacks from South African cities to tribal homelands. Throughout the 1980s some 3.5 million people were relocated by the government, a process that denied blacks access to better-paying jobs in the cities and left them to work on low-quality farmland. Tutu openly protested the act, comparing it to laws hostile to Jews that were passed by the Nazi leadership in Germany during the 1930s before World War II (1938–45).

In the fall of 1979 Tutu took part in a television interview in Denmark, during which he proposed that Denmark stop buying coal from South Africa as a way to protest apartheid. This was the first time that anyone had ever proposed using economic measures to try to force the South African government to change its policies. Over the next decade, people, organizations, and governments throughout the world began to boycott (refuse to buy) South African products. In the United States and other countries, many universities, local and state governments, and labor unions decided not only to stop investing funds in South African companies and companies that did business with South Africa, but also to withdraw funds that were already invested. During this period South African currency lost half of its value on the world market. In order to curb some of the unrest, the South African government allowed blacks to form labor unions for the first time.

Tutu's efforts to end apartheid were met with continued harassment. The South African government took away his passport, a move that often preceded imprisonment. Without his passport, Tutu could leave the country only with the government's permission. In 1982 he was denied permission to travel to the United States to accept an honorary degree from Columbia University in New York. In response the president of the university personally traveled to South Africa to present Tutu with the degree.

In 1984 Tutu was awarded the Nobel Peace Prize, which helped to further publicize his efforts. In the words of the commission that selected him, as quoted on the *Nobelprize.org* Web site, the prize was given "not only as a gesture of support to him and to the South African Council of Churches of which he is leader, but also to all individuals and groups in South Africa who, with their concern for human dignity, fraternity and democracy, incite the admiration of the world." Tutu used the recognition to draw more attention to the injustices committed by the South African

Blacks were forced to live in townships such as this one during the apartheid years in South Africa. Desmond Tutu protested against apartheid and used his position on the South African Council of Churches to promote antigovernment protests. © DAVID TURNLEY/CORBIS.

government. He was eventually allowed to travel to the United States, where he addressed a congressional committee and urged the country to join the fight against racism. Thousands of Americans answered his call by holding protests at South African embassies in the United States.

Tutu continued to call for peaceful solutions to South Africa's racial problems, but tensions kept building. On several occasions protests erupted into violence, and hundreds of people were killed. In response to the violence, the South African president declared a state of emergency, which deprived black citizens of what few rights they had. Among the activities that were outlawed were funeral marches to cemeteries, which the government believed could turn into riots. On one occasion armed government security guards surrounded the funeral of a young woman who had been killed in the rioting. Tutu personally appeared to conduct the funeral service and to keep tempers from rising.

In September 1986 Tutu was elected as the archbishop of Cape Town and the primate, or leader, of the Anglican Church for all of southern Africa. He continued to pressure the governments of other nations to condemn South African apartheid and to impose economic penalties. Meanwhile, the state of emergency was maintained. The government continued to ban more activities, such as the signing of petitions calling for the release of the thousands of political prisoners being held, many of whom were minors (people under age 18). Even wearing shirts with slogans opposing the confinement of the prisoners was outlawed. Nevertheless, Tutu and many of his followers defied some of these laws.

Success

By the early 1990s South Africa had become an outcast among the nations of the world, and economic pressures on the government were threatening to destroy the country. It was during this decade that apartheid crumbled. This is largely because of the leadership of Tutu and other important South African figures, such as Nelson Mandela (1918–), who had been imprisoned for twenty-six years. At last, a new government, led by F. W. de Klerk (1936–), abolished South Africa's racist policies. The country's black majority, able to vote for the first time, elected Mandela as South Africa's first democratically-elected president in 1994. Tutu's dream had become a reality.

In the years that followed, Tutu continued to speak against human rights abuses throughout the world, such as those in the African nation of Zimbabwe and the Asian nation of Burma (Myanmar). In 1995 he was appointed chair of South Africa's Truth and Reconciliation Commission. This body was formed to investigate claims of human rights abuses under the nation's apartheid system. In 1996 Tutu retired from his position as archbishop of Cape Town to devote his energies to the work of the commission. In 1998 he stepped down as commission chair to accept a position teaching theology at Emory University in Atlanta, Georgia. In 2002 he accepted a job as a visiting professor at the Episcopal Divinity School in Cambridge, Massachusetts. His name reappeared in the news that same year when he expressed his intense opposition to the invasion of Iraq planned by the United States and Great Britain.

For More Information

BOOKS

Gish, Steven D. *Desmond Tutu: A Biography.* Westport, CT: Greenwood, 2004.

Tutu, Desmond. *God Has a Dream: A Vision of Hope for Our Time.* New York: Doubleday, 2004.

WEB SITES

"Archibishop Desmond Mpilo Tutu." *University of the Witwatersrand.* http://www. wits.ac.za/histp/tutu_quotes_on.htm (accessed June 1, 2006).

"The Nobel Peace Prize for 1984." *Nobelprize.org.* http://nobelprize.org/peace/ laureates/1984/press.html (accessed on May 26, 2006).

Usuman Dan Fodio

BORN: December 15, 1754 • Maratta, Gobir
DIED: April 20, 1817 • Sokoto, Gobir

Gobirian religious leader; writer

"A kingdom can endure with unbelief, but cannot endure with injustice."

Usuman Dan Fodio was a political and Islamic religious leader during the early nineteenth century in the African city-state of Gobir, in modern-day Nigeria. He was a member of the Fulani people. The Fulani are light-skinned herders and nomads, or people who have no fixed homes and move according to the seasons in search of food, water, and grazing lands for their animals. Usuman Dan Fodio led a *jihad,* or holy war, against the state of Gobir. Gobir was part of an empire controlled by the rivals of the Fulani, the Hausa, a dark-skinned ethnic group native to the region. Usuman Dan Fodio sought to reform the religious practices of the Hausa kings and was joined by an army of Fulani who were tired of being considered second-class citizens. After winning the battle against the Hausa, Usuman Dan Fodio established a caliphate, or Islamic state, that eventually covered 200,000 square miles, making it the largest state in Africa. His empire lasted for a century, from 1804 to 1904, when it was conquered by the British. Usuman Dan Fodio was also a respected Muslim scholar who wrote more than one hundred works that influenced the intellectual, political, and religious development of West Africa.

Growth of a religious leader

Usuman (also spelled Usman or Uthman) Dan Fodio was born on December 15, 1754, in the small village of Maratta. The village was located in the ancient kingdom of Gobir, one of seven city-states that were collectively called Hausaland. Hausaland was located in the center of northwestern Africa, just south of the Sahara Desert, and its origins dated back to the eleventh century. The six other city-states in Hausaland were Daura, Biram, Kano, Katsina, Rano, and Zaria. By the late fourteenth century the region was introduced to the religion of Islam, whose followers are known as Muslims. The new religion did not become popular in Hausaland, however, until the middle of the fifteenth century, when the Fulani began immigrating into the region. They came in large numbers to escape the increasingly dry conditions to the north. The Fulani herded cattle that depended on vegetation for food, so the lack of rain had a strong impact on their livelihood. The Fulani were very faithful Muslims, and they brought along texts in order to set up Islamic schools throughout the region.

Usuman Dan Fodio was part of the educated Fulani class, as his ancestors had left the nomadic life and settled in urban areas many years before his birth. His father, Muhammad Fodio, was a religious scholar and *imam,* or Muslim spiritual leader, in the village. As a youth, Usuman Dan Fodio moved with his family southward to the town of Degel. There he studied the Islamic holy book, the Qurʾan, with his father. Usuman Dan Fodio's special spiritual abilities were evident from an early age. For example, the residents of Degel even thought he could control the *jinn* (from which the word genie is derived), supernatural beings that can change shape and influence the affairs of humans.

He was sent to Islamic scholars in the region to continue his education. One of these scholars, Jibril ibn ʿUmar, initiated him into the Sufi order, a mystical branch of Islam whose followers seek to directly experience God, known as Allah in the Islam religion. Usuman Dan Fodio also learned from Jibril ibn ʿUmar the responsibility of a religion to establish the ideal society, one free from oppression and vice, or immoral behavior.

Usuman Dan Fodio completed his education in about 1774, and began to teach and preach in his native Gobir and in the far northwest of what is modern-day Nigeria. He led a simple life of study and contemplation, or deep and concentrated thinking, as he wandered and preached about the renewal of the Islamic faith. To support himself, he occasionally made and sold rope.

At the age of thirty-six, Usuman Dan Fodio had his first mystical experience: Allah allowed him to truly see the world as it is. He felt he had power over distant objects, that he could actually reach out and grab something far away. His sense of smell, hearing, and touch all increased. He became aware of every muscle and bone in his body. Four years later, Allah supposedly gave him the Sword of Truth, with which he was to fight the enemies of Islam. Usuman Dan Fodio's fame as a scholar and a man of Allah spread throughout the region and he attracted many followers. His main aides were his son, Muhammad Bello, and his brother, Abdullahi. People began calling Usuman Dan Fodio *shehu,* or *shaykh,* a title of respect for a teacher and scholar in the Sufi tradition. Though he generally made a point of not interacting with the kings of the region, he did visit the court of Gobir, where he was able to win favors. These included the freedom to teach and spread the word of Islam and to establish a Muslim community in his hometown of Degel. Historians also believe that while at court Usuman Dan Fodio taught a youth named Yunfa, who later became king.

Religious leader to political leader

Usuman Dan Fodio created a theocracy in Degel, just as **Muhammad** (c. 570–632; see entry), the founder of Islam, had done in Medina (a city in modern-day Saudi Arabia). A theocracy is a government subject to religious authority. The community slowly became a state within Gobir, ruled by its own laws and offices. Usuman Dan Fodio used the Islamic principles of equality and justice for the benefit of all, and this attracted many followers from his own Fulani people and also from the Hausa peasantry, or poor farmers. These peasants felt they were being unfairly taxed by the king of Gobir and were happy to shift their loyalty to Usuman Dan Fodio. In time, the king of Gobir grew alarmed at the expansion of Usuman Dan Fodio's community, and he began to see it as a threat to his own rule.

When Yunfa became king of Gobir 1802, he sought to destroy the community in Degel. The final break between the new king and Usuman Dan Fodio came when Usuman Dan Fodio's followers freed some Muslims who had been taken prisoner by government forces. Usuman Dan Fodio and Degel were then directly threatened by the king's forces. These hostilities caused Usuman Dan Fodio to lead his supporters to a new home in Gudu, a small town about thirty miles to the northwest, on the border of Gobir. Usuman Dan Fodio compared this migration to that of Muhammad and his followers when they left their native Mecca in 622 to escape oppression.

Once the community was settled in Gudu, Usuman Dan Fodio was elected imam and his rule of the new Islamic state was established. He was also given the title *amirul momineen,* or "leader of the people." This

Sufi saints sit on a verandah. Usuman Dan Fodio was initiated into the mystic Sufi branch of Islam by Jibril ibn ʿUmar. © THE BRITISH LIBRARY/TOPHAM/THE IMAGE WORKS.

made him both a religious and a political leader and gave him the authority to wage a jihad, just as Muhammad had done more than one thousand years earlier. Usuman Dan Fodio gathered an army from among the Hausa and the local Fulani nomads, who were excellent horsemen. Yunfa, in Gobir, sought help from other Hausa states, telling them that Usuman Dan Fodio's jihad was a danger to them all. Indeed, such a war had the potential to topple all of the region's rulers. The Hausa governments often acted dishonestly and unfairly towards the poorer citizens, who were becoming more and more resentful of such treatment.

For the next five years, Usuman Dan Fodio's troops fought those of Yunfa in what was know as the Fulani War (1804–09). Dan Fodio himself did not participate in the battles, although he directed the military campaign while organizing his new caliphate. The word "caliphate" comes from the term *khalifatu ar-rasul*, or "deputy of the messenger." The "messenger" in this case is Muhammad, the messenger of Allah. In English, the title for the ruler of a caliphate is "caliph." After Muhammad died in 632, the leaders of Islam who came after him took this title. Usuman Dan Fodio established his caliphate to resemble that of Muhammad, imitating the political structure of that original Islamic state.

At first, things went badly for Usuman Dan Fodio's army. In December 1804 they were defeated in the first major encounter with Yunfa's forces, the battle of Tsuntua, and Usuman Dan Fodio lost two thousand of his best fighters. In 1805, however, Usuman Dan Fodio's troops captured the major regions of Kebbi and Gwandu, which gave his soldiers a permanent base. Slowly, his army gained additional support from the peasants throughout the region. Usuman Dan Fodio wrote widely about his jihad, noting that the king of Gobir had attacked him, a faithful Muslim, first. He labeled the king an unbeliever and claimed it was the duty of all true Muslims to pursue the jihad against Yunfa and anyone who aided him.

As the war proceeded, Usuman Dan Fodio continued to structure his new Islamic state. He listed its principles in one of his most famous works, *Bayan Wujub al-Hijra* (Exposition of Obligation of Emigration upon the Servants of God). He explained that the central bureaucracy, or the ruling officials, of his caliphate would be small in number and would be loyal and honest Muslims. Local administration would be in the hands of *emirs,* or governors. These would be chosen from among the class of Muslim scholars noted for their sense of justice and honesty and for their religious belief. As his state began to take shape, Muslim leaders in other Hausa states began to formally recognize the authority of Usuman Dan Fodio.

The caliphate

In 1808 Usuman Dan Fodio's men finally overran the king's forces in the Gobir capital, Alkalawa. Yunfa was killed in the fighting. After Gobir was defeated, the Fulani warriors moved against other Hausa states. Eventually they had captured all of the land from modern-day Burkina Faso in the west to the nation of Cameroon in the south. The Fulani troops

The Mahdi

Usuman Dan Fodio believed he had been chosen by Allah to bring about the renewal of Islam in order to prepare for the coming of the *Mahdi,* which translates to "he who is guided aright." Muslims believe the Mahdi is the expected messiah, or divine spiritual and political ruler, who will appear on Earth and establish a reign of righteousness over the world. They believe that this rule will last for one thousand years, until the Day of Judgment (the end of the world), when believers in Allah will go to paradise, the Islamic heaven.

Many men throughout Islamic history have claimed to be the Mahdi. One of the best-known was Muhammad Ahmad (1844–1885), a Muslim leader in the region then known as the Anglo-Egyptian Sudan, in northeastern Africa. After declaring himself the Mahdi, Muhammad Ahmad raised an army to fight the Egyptian occupiers of his land. He captured the city of Khartoum and for a time established Islamic rule. Though Muhammad Ahmad was killed in 1885, his army continued to fight for the movement. The British finally defeated these Islamic soldiers in 1898.

The Mahdi remained a powerful idea within Islam in the early twenty-first century. Dozens of books have been printed on the topic, many of them since the 1980s. As recently as 2003, the Muslim religious leader Moqtada al-Sadr, while fighting U.S. forces in Baghdad, Iraq, called his followers the Mahdi Army.

were blocked from advancing to the far south, as the cavalry was not effective in the more heavily wooded areas of southern Nigeria. The horses sickened and died from diseases carried by mosquitoes. Usuman Dan Fodio divided the rule of the immense empire between his two most loyal generals and aides. His brother, Abdullahi, was installed in the west, at Gwandu, while Muhammad Bello established his capital at Sokoto. This city soon became the center of the Fulani Empire, which was also known as the Sokoto caliphate.

The rule of Usuman Dan Fodio and his followers began a period of prosperity in the region. Government was centralized, roads were built, and trade routes were secured by troops. Education was provided for all, even women, who had formerly been denied this opportunity. The empire was particularly noted for its educational methods and teachings. Usuman Dan Fodio, Abdullahi, and Muhammad Bello were respected as writers and scholars, and all were authors of poetry and texts on religion. Soon, scholars from throughout the Islamic world came to the court at Sokoto. Arabic and local languages, including Hausa, were used in writing the laws and literature of the state, and these documents were made available to the common people so that they could know their rights. The power of the African tribal chiefs was broken under the rule of Usuman Dan Fodio, who replaced that traditional system with the laws of Islam.

As time passed, the reasons for the jihad were forgotten by many. Usuman Dan Fodio slowly withdrew into private life, leaving the day-to-day matters of ruling in the hands of his son and brother. Around 1812 he built a home in Sifawa, a town near Sokoto, where he lived simply and gathered several hundred students around him. Two years before his death in 1817, he moved to Sokoto, still preaching reform and criticizing the new bureaucracy for its tendency to oppress the common people, just as the former kings of the Hausa states had done. Usuman Dan Fodio died in Sokoto at the age of sixty-two.

Usuman Dan Fodio's legacy continued after his death. His jihad inspired similar Muslim movements in neighboring states such as Bornu and Massina, where other caliphates were later formed. He strengthened the Islamic faith throughout the region with the example of his Fulani Empire and his writings in Arabic and Fulani. These writings dealt with topics ranging from Islamic law to the establishment of just, or fair, societies.

The Sokoto caliphate lost some of its religious purity after Usuman Dan Fodio's death, and scholarship declined after his son, Muhammad Bello died in 1837. The empire remained an economic success throughout the nineteenth century, however. Additionally, although the British conquered the empire in the early twentieth century, they ultimately had to leave Usuman Dan Fodio's administrative system in place in order to rule the region's fifteen million people efficiently. After Nigeria gained independence in 1960, the caliph of Sokoto continued to influence political decisions. In 2004 the Sokoto caliphate, by then a religious confederation (a group united for a common purpose) rather than a political empire, celebrated its two-hundredth anniversary.

For More Information

BOOKS

Balogun, Ismail A. B. *The Life and Works of Uthman dan Fodio: The Muslim Reformer of West Africa* Lagos, Nigeria: Islamic Publications Bureau, 1975.

Hiskett, Mervyn. *The Sword of Truth: The Life and Times of Shehu Usman dan Fodio.* Evanston, IL: Northwestern University Press, 1994.

Johnston, Hugh Anthony Stephens. *The Fulani Empire of Sokoto.* London, UK: Oxford University Press, 1970.

Last, Murray. *The Sokoto Caliphate.* London, UK: Harlow, Longmans, 1967.

Murray, Jocelyn, and Sean Sheehan. *Africa: Cultural Atlas for Young People.* New York, NY: Facts on File, 2003.

WEB SITES

"Key Episodes in Nigerian History: The 19th Century: Usman Dan Fodio." *NigeriaFirst.org.* http://www.nigeriafirst.org/article_3847.shtml (accessed on June 2, 2006).

"Peoples." *Motherland Nigeria.* http://www.motherlandnigeria.com/people.html# Hausa (accessed on June 2, 2006).

Philips, Anza. "A Caliphate with Multiple Legacies." *Newswatch*. http://www. newswatchngr.com/editorial/allaccess/nigeria/10628125513.htm (accessed on June 2, 2006).

"Usman dan Fodio and the Sokoto Caliphate." *Country Studies: Nigeria*. http:// countrystudies.us/nigeria/9.htm (accessed on June 2, 2006).

"West African Kingdoms: Hausa States." *The Story of Africa*. http://www.bbc. co.uk/worldservice/africa/features/storyofafrica/4chapter5.shtml (accessed on June 2, 2006).

Swami Vivekananda

BORN: January 12, 1863 • Calcutta, West Bengal, India

DIED: July 4, 1902 • Calcutta, West Bengal, India

Indian religious leader; philosopher

Swami Vivekananda.

"The Hindu believes that he is a spirit. Him the sword cannot pierce—him the fire cannot burn—him the water cannot melt—him the air cannot dry."

During the nineteenth century Hinduism was largely unknown in the West (the countries in Europe and the Americas). Swami Vivekananda, one of Hinduism's great modern teachers, is credited with almost single-handedly changing that view by introducing the teachings and philosophy of the religion to the West. Philosophy is the study of ideas through which to gain a better understanding of values and reality. Originally named Narendra Nath Datta (or Narendranath Dutta), he was born into an educated, wealthy family in Calcutta (now Kolkata), India, on January 12, 1863. Indians now celebrate this date as National Youth Day in his memory. His father was Viswanath Dutta, a successful lawyer, and his mother was Bhuvaneswari Devi.

Early life and education

Narendra grew up in a home in which learning was encouraged. From childhood he showed an impressive skill for absorbing and remembering

383

what he read, including, by some accounts, the contents of the entire *Encyclopaedia Britannica*. In addition to his studies he organized a theatrical troupe and enjoyed rowing, fencing, wrestling, and other athletic pursuits. He also practiced meditation and even as a child began to ponder spiritual matters and the nature of God. Meditation is quiet, focused thought to gain greater spiritual awareness and understanding. Narendra was stubborn, temperamental, and given to playing pranks on others. Later in life he was usually seen wearing an unusual turban, which he claimed he styled after the turban worn by a poor taxi driver he had seen during his childhood.

In 1879 Narendra enrolled in Presidency College (formerly called Hindu College), a liberal arts institution associated with the University of Calcutta. After a year he transferred to another University of Calcutta organization, a Christian missionary institution called the Scottish Church College. At both of these schools he acquired a broad education in science, philosophy, European history, and religion. He learned to speak several languages, including English, and was particularly attracted to the study of Western logic. He was also an accomplished musician, singer, and poet.

During his years in college Narendra began to see many similarities between the principles and beliefs of Western science and philosophy and those found in Hindu sacred texts written thousands of years before. Indeed, he came to see little conflict between the teachings of Hinduism and the findings of modern science. For example, Hinduism sought to understand the fundamental building blocks of the universe and the energy that existed throughout all of creation. In this respect, it was seeking the same ends as scientists such as Nikola Tesla (1856–1943), the Yugoslavian physicist (a scientist who studies the interactions between energy and matter) who used Sanskrit words to refer to matter and energy because he believed that the Hindu concept was accurate. He also began to question the nature and presence of God and to reject some of the features of Hinduism, primarily its acceptance of castes, the social classes into which Indians are born.

For a while Narendra followed the system of thought of the Brahmo Samaj, a social and religious movement that had been founded in Calcutta (now Kolkata) earlier in the century. The movement rejected the caste system, believed in the authority of the Vedas, the oldest of Hindu sacred texts, and sought to bring worshippers together to read from these texts in a group setting, which was new to Hinduism. The Brahmo Samaj, however, ultimately failed to provide Narendra with the answers he was seeking.

At the feet of the master

A turning point in Narendra's life came in 1881, after one of his professors at the Scottish Church College told him about the great religious teacher Shri Ramakrishna (1836–1886). At this stage in his life, Narendra was doubtful about religion and was unsure about the existence of God. He was not prepared to accept Ramakrishna as a spiritual *guru* (guide or teacher), as he did not believe that the guru could truly experience and understand the nature of the divine. Narendra's opinions would change, however, after he underwent a dramatic experience during his second meeting with Ramakrishna. He later said, as quoted on the *Manas: Religions* Web site of the University of California–Los Angeles:

> My eyes were wide open, and I saw that everything in the room, including the walls themselves, was whirling rapidly around and receding, and at the same time, it seemed to me that my consciousness [awareness] of self, together with the entire universe, was about to vanish into a vast, all-devouring void. This destruction of my consciousness of self seemed to me to be the same thing as death. I felt that death was right before me, very close.

Narendra's words express the essence of the branch of Hindu philosophy taught by Ramakrishna, called Advaita Vedanta. As *advaita* means "not two," this school of philosophy rejected existential dualism, or the separation of the self from the universe. The school instead taught monism, or the "oneness" of the self with the universal whole, called Brahma (or Brahman). *Vedanta* means "end of the Vedas," referring to the Upanishads. The Upanishads are texts that are included within the Vedas and contain the core of Hindu beliefs. Later, in his address to

Swami Vivekananda's Thoughts on Women

Early in his life, Swami Vivekananda shared the viewpoint of many Hindu holy men regarding women, seeing them as an obstacle to purity of thought and action. Later in life, after he had examined many of the social problems that affected India and tried to help correct them, he changed his attitude, at one point saying, "The best thermometer to the progress of a nation is its treatment of its women." He believed that no country could develop and progress if it continued to treat its women badly.

He based his belief on the teachings of the Vedanta, which makes no distinction between men and women and indeed teaches that all people, of either sex, take part in the same universal soul. One reason that he changed his thinking about the role of women was that in the United States, he came to admire the greater education and achievement of women compared to women in his native India at that time.

the World Parliament of Religions in 1893, Narendra would state the principle of the unity of the self with the universe, which he had learned from Ramakrishna, in this way, as quoted on *UniversalWisdom.org:*

> The Hindu believes that he is a spirit. Him the sword cannot pierce—him the fire cannot burn—him the water cannot melt—him the air cannot dry. The Hindu believes that every soul is a circle whose circumference [boundary] is nowhere but whose center is located in the body, and that death means the change of the center from holy to body. Nor is the soul bound by the conditions of matter.

For five years Narendra studied under Ramakrishna, who recognized the remarkable abilities in his new student and patiently tried to help him "see God." To expand Narendra's knowledge, he read to him from the Christian Bible, placing emphasis on passages dealing with Mary, the mother of **Jesus Christ** (c. 6 BCE–c. 30 CE; see entry), as an example of divine love. During these years Narendra explored the basic principles of Hindu thought: Brahma, the nature of the soul, meditation, yoga (a discipline aimed at preparing the mind for perfect spiritual insight), karma (the belief that one's destiny is affected by the sum total of one's deeds), and reincarnation (the belief that one's soul is reborn in another body). He also studied the Hindu sacred texts, particularly the Vedas and the Upanishads.

After Ramakrishna's death in 1886, Narendra inherited the elder's role as a spiritual master. He and a group of Ramakrishna's followers took vows as monks and lived in a house in the Indian city of Baranagar. At this point Narendra took the monastic name Vivekananda, formed from the words *vivek,* meaning "conscience" or "mind," and *ananda,* meaning "joyous." The title *swami,* which means "owner" or "lord" in Hindi, is used to identify a teacher and ascetic, or one who gives up worldly possessions and lives a life of self-denial. During this period Vivekananda and his fellow monks survived by begging.

In 1890 Vivekananda and some of his fellow monks set out on a two-year pilgrimage throughout India. At times he stayed in palaces, and at other times he stayed in the huts of the poor. During his travels he became more aware of the poverty and hunger that affected many of his countrymen. He also came to recognize that under British rule and the forces of modernization, Indians were losing their faith in their ancient religion. (The British had established control of India in the mid-1800s.) On December 24, 1892, Vivekananda arrived at Kanyakumari, a town at the tip of southern India. According to his followers, he swam out to a small island in the ocean, where he meditated for three days. When he returned he expressed his determination not only to help improve the condition of Indians but also to preach the message of the divine unity of humankind. The island became the site of the Vivekananda Rock Memorial.

World Parliament of Religions

Vivekananda then traveled to Madras, India, where he attracted a larger number of followers. The young men of Madras had learned about the upcoming first-ever meeting of the World Parliament of Religions in Chicago, Illinois, which was scheduled for September 1893, at the same time as the Chicago World's Fair. They urged Vivekananda to attend the parliament as a representative of Hinduism. He agreed, and with the financial help of his followers he made the trip to the United States.

When he arrived in Chicago Vivekananda did not even know the exact dates when the World Parliament of Religions was scheduled to be held (September 11–27), nor did he carry any credentials, or documents establishing authority, that entitled him to speak. Nonetheless, as a highly respected guru, he was given permission on three occasions to address the seven thousand people in attendance, at times bringing his listeners to their feet in applause. In the eyes of many observers, including the newspaper reporters who covered his speeches, Swami Vivekananda was the most dominant figure at the parliament.

Vivekananda delivered his most important address on September 19, when he presented the "Paper on Hinduism." In this speech he expressed a number of views that were new to most people in the West. He explained the concept of reincarnation, in which souls are believed to last through many bodily lives, and why people are unable to remember their past lives. He stated that the universe was eternal, not something that had been created at a given point in time, which was the Jewish and Christian belief. He also stated his philosophical belief that the goal of human life was to realize the divinity that lies within and express that divinity through concern for the welfare of others. Perhaps most importantly, he rejected the concept, prominent in Christianity, that all people are naturally sinners.

Vivekananda Illam, located along the waterfront in Madras, India, is an important pilgrimage site for every student and follower of Swami Vivekananda. © CHRIS LISLE/CORBIS.

His primary goal in attending the parliament was to promote religious tolerance. In his address, Vivekananda quoted from the Bhagavad Gita, a well-known Hindu text, and recounted at *SriRamakrishna.org*: "As the different streams having their sources in different places all mingle their water in the sea, so, O Lord, the different paths which men take through different tendencies, various though they appear, crooked or straight, all lead to Thee." In later years historians would assert that Swami Vivekananda's appearance at the World Parliament of Religions, and specifically his "Paper on Hinduism," marked the beginning of Western interest in Hinduism and of the awareness that India's ancient religion had something to teach the West.

Realizing the greatness of the opportunity before him, Swami Vivekananda spent the next four years in the West, traveling and giving lectures at universities. He became a great admirer of the United States and England, and he opened centers for the study of Vedantic philosophy (the philosophy of the Vedas) in New York City and London. After returning to India he toured the West again from early 1899 to late 1900.

Vivekananda's views and actions sometimes sparked controversy: Some observers believed that he exaggerated the impact that he was having on Western thought, especially since he claimed to have "conquered" the West with Vedantic philosophy. He also attracted opposition from Christian missionaries in India, whom he fiercely criticized. Devout Hindus believed that he had discredited himself by traveling in the West, which they believed was impure and overly concerned with material goods. They felt that he had abandoned his monastic life for fame and celebrity. Indian nationalists, who were calling for independence from Great Britain, resented the fact that he was on such friendly terms with the British.

Final return to India

Despite these criticisms, Swami Vivekananda returned to India at the end of 1900 to great acclaim. Many Hindus were proud of his accomplishments in the West. During the remainder of his life he devoted himself to addressing the difficulties of the poor in India and to speaking out about social problems. With the help of the Ramakrishna Math, the order of monks formed after the death of Ramakrishna, he established the Ramakrishna Mission. Among its many other accomplishments, the mission provided care for Indians during an outbreak of the deadly infectious disease called the plague, saving many lives.

Although Swami Vivekananda died at the age of thirty-nine, on July 4, 1902, the work of the Ramakrishna Mission continued throughout the world into the early twenty-first century. Its motto, *Atmano mokshartham jagad-hitaya cha,* means "For one's own salvation, and for the good of the world." Under the alternate name of Vivekananda Vedanta Society, the organization maintains more than one hundred missions worldwide, including twelve in the United States.

For More Information
BOOKS

Ghosh, Gautam. *The Prophet of Modern India: A Biography of Swami Vivekananda.* New Delhi, India: Rupa, 2003.

Vivekananda, Swami. *Complete Works of Swami Vivekananda.* 8th ed. West Bengal, India: Advaita Ashrama, 1989.

WEB SITES

"Paper on Hinduism." September 19, 1893. *UniversalWisdom.org.* http://www.theuniversalwisdom.org/hinduism/paper-on-hinduism-vivekananda/ (accessed June 2, 2006).

"Ramakrishna Order." *Vivekananda Vedanta Network: Ramakrishna Vedanta Society of Boston.* http://www.vivekananda.org/RKOrder.asp (accessed June 2, 2006).

"Swami Vivekananda: A Short Biography." *Vedanta Society of Southern California.* http://www.vedanta.org/rko/vivekananda/sv_bio.html (accessed June 2, 2006).

"Swami Vivekananda: Chicago Address. Addresses at the Parliament of World Religions." September 11, September 15, and September 27, 1893. *SriRamakrishna.org.* http://www.sriramakrishna.org/chicago.htm (accessed June 2, 2006).

"Vivekananda." *Manas: Religions.* http://www.sscnet.ucla.edu/southasia/Religions/gurus/Vivek.html (accessed on June 2, 2006).

Vivekananda, Swami. "Complete Works of Swami Vivekananda." *Sri Ramakrishna and Swami Vivekananda.* http://www.ramakrishnavivekananda.info/vivekananda/volume_1/vol_1_frame.htm (accessed on May 26, 2006).

Isaac Mayer Wise

BORN: March 29, 1819 • Steingrub, Bohemia

DIED: March 26, 1900 • Cincinnati, Ohio,
United States

rabbi; editor; writer

Isaac Wise.
© BETTMANN/CORBIS.

"Had the Hebrews not been disbursed in their progress a thousand and more years ago, they would have solved all the great problems of civilization."

Isaac Mayer Wise was one of the most well-known Jews in the United States during the nineteenth century. He was a *rabbi,* a person trained in Jewish law and tradition who is often the head of a synagogue, a Jewish house of worship. He was also an editor and the author of several books and plays about Judaism. He created three religious organizations: the Union of American Hebrew Congregations; the Hebrew Union College, of which he served as president; and the Central Conference of American Rabbis. He is regarded as a major figure in the development and organization of Reform Judaism in the United States. Reform Judaism believes that the Torah, the Jewish holy book, was written by several authors, rather than just one. Its followers do not adhere to many of the commandments, or laws, laid out in the Torah, unlike some other branches of Judaism.

Birth and early life

Isaac Mayer Weiss was born to Leo Weiss, a schoolteacher, and Regina Weiss on March 29, 1819, in Steigrub, a town in Bohemia. Bohemia was at the time part of the Austro-Hungarian Empire but later became a part of the Czech Republic. As a youngster Weiss was a gifted student who showed interest in a range of subjects. His father tutored him in Jewish scripture, collectively known as the Tanakh, or Hebrew Bible, and the Talmud. The Talmud consists of traditions that explain and interpret the first five books of the Jewish scripture, which are referred to as the Torah.

By the time Weiss was nine, his father had taught him all he could, so Weiss then studied with his grandfather for three years. After his grandfather died, he went to the city of Prague, the capital of the modern-day Czech Republic, and enrolled at a *yeshiva,* or Jewish school. He then studied at a well-known rabbinical school, where Jews prepare to become rabbis, in the town of Jekinau. Weiss next attended the University of Prague for two years and the University of Vienna in Austria for one year. In 1842, at age twenty-three, he was ordained, or officially made, a rabbi. He married Therese Bloch two years later, and the couple eventually had ten children. A later marriage produced four more children.

A controversial rabbi

Weiss first served as a rabbi in Radnitz, Bohemia, but he found the environment there unpleasant because of the discrimination against Jews in the region. Discrimination is unfair treatment against a person or group because of differences such as religion and other characteristics. During this period European Jews were the victims of widespread religious intolerance and prejudice, or mistreatment. They were typically regarded as outsiders in the largely Christian communities. Weiss believed that the United States held the promise of more religious freedom, so he left Bohemia for and arrived in New York City on July 23, 1846. At this point he changed the spelling of his name from Weiss to Wise. He accepted a job as rabbi at an Orthodox temple in Albany, New York, where he remained for four years. Orthodox Judaism is a traditional form of the religion, based on a strict interpretation of the Torah.

Wise quickly became known as a highly controversial figure within his congregation. Orthodox Jews strictly follow the traditions and laws of Judaism. Wise, however, had already concluded that some of these traditions and laws no longer made sense in modern life. He introduced a number of reforms, which many members of the congregation resisted. A congregation is a group of worshippers who, in this instance, are members of the same synagogue. Wise ended the practice of chanting both prayers and readings from the Torah, the central part of the Orthodox service. He also formed a choir made up of both men and women and ended the practice of women and children sitting in different pews from men. He substituted confirmation, a ceremony marking the completion of a young person's religious training, for the *bar mitzvah,* a coming-of-age ceremony for Jewish boys. Many members of Wise's congregation found these and other changes disturbing.

In 1850 Wise ordered the members of the congregation's board to close their businesses on Saturday, which is considered the Jewish Sabbath, a day of rest. One of the board members, however, refused to follow the order. Many feared that the board member, whose preaching was popular, would be dismissed. The congregation became evenly split between supporters and critics of Wise. The board met and voted to fire Wise, but he refused to go. On the next Sabbath, a fight broke out in the temple between Wise and the board president. A riot eventually erupted among the congregation, and the police had to restore order.

After these events Wise resigned and started his own temple in Albany, New York, and his supporters from the previous temple followed him. Indeed, many welcomed his reforms, and his congregation grew rapidly. He remained in Albany until 1854, when a congregation in Cincinnati, Ohio, invited him to become their rabbi. He accepted and remained at the Cincinnati temple, Beth Jeshurun (also Yeshurun), for the rest of his life. This congregation, like his first Albany congregation, was somewhat traditional. Still, Wise introduced his reforms, though more slowly and tactfully than he had in the 1840s, and again his congregation grew rapidly. Under Wise's leadership, the congregation constructed an immense temple in the 1860s that remains in use in the twenty-first century.

Wise and Reform Judaism

Wise had both an impressive talent for organization and a great desire to unify Judaism in the United States. In the 1850s he began to use this talent and desire to complete several large projects. He created a Jewish prayer book and formed the Union of American Hebrew Congregations,

Denominations of Judaism

In the modern era Judaism consists of three major denominations, or subdivisions: Orthodox, Reform, and Conservative Judaism. Orthodox Judaism is the most traditional in its practice of the religion. Orthodox Jews believe that God gave Moses the Torah, part of the Jewish Old Testament, and that Moses was the Torah's only author. They also believe that the 613 *mitzvoth,* or commandments contained in the Torah, must be followed by Jews everywhere.

Reform Jews, in contrast, are less traditional and do not strictly follow all of the mitzvoth. They do not accept that God gave Moses the Torah. Instead, they believe that several different authors wrote the Torah. Reform Jews do retain the culture of Judaism and many of its values, ethics, and practices.

Conservative Judaism was established in an attempt to bridge the divide between Orthodox and Reform Judaism. Conservative Jews believe that God did reveal the Torah to Moses, but that human authors recorded and transmitted it, so it contains elements from these authors as well as from God. Conservative Jews believe that Jewish law should be followed but that it should change and adapt to the surrounding culture.

the Hebrew Union College, and the Central Conference of American Rabbis. Over time he emerged as the major spokesperson for Reform Judaism in the United States.

The prayer book In 1847 Wise was asked to become a member of an advisory board. This board was to make recommendations on various matters to Jewish congregations throughout the country, although it would not have power over them. At one board meeting Wise submitted a copy of a prayer book he had compiled. He was troubled by the common practice of rabbis compiling their own prayer books for use with their congregations. He wanted Jewish congregations in the United States to adopt a common prayer book used by all.

No action was taken on Wise's proposal until 1855. That year a committee was formed to edit Wise's prayer book, nearly all of which he had written himself. The book was then published as the *Minhag Amerika.* Although Wise had attempted to find a balance between traditional and more modern Jewish religious practices in the book, many Orthodox congregations in the East and Northeast areas of the country still found it departed from tradition too much, and they would not use it. Some Reform congregations, on the other hand, did not adopt the book because they found it to be too traditional.

Other than these few exceptions, the prayer book became widely used, primarily in the South and West, and represented a first step towards the greater unification of American Judaism.

The Union of American Hebrew Congregations Wise believed that Judaism in the United States was generally too disordered. Each congregation throughout the vast and still-growing country was taking its own direction. There was no unity in Jewish thought and teaching. As early as 1848 Wise proposed the formation of a union that would have some authority over Jewish congregations throughout the nation. For more than two decades he tried to convince others of the importance of such a union, mostly through the newspaper he founded in 1854, the *American Israelite,* which remains in publication in the early twenty-first century.

His goal was accomplished in 1873, when the Union of American Hebrew Congregations was formed in Cincinnati, Ohio. Wise avoided using the word *reform* in the name of the union because he still felt that Orthodox and Reform Jews could be united. Wise believed that Jews could enjoy religious freedom in the United States that they could not enjoy anywhere else in the world. For this reason in particular he wanted to see a strong and united American Judaism.

Hebrew Union College Wise was also behind the formation of the Hebrew Union College in Cincinnati. He believed that too many rabbis leading American congregations were not knowledgeable enough in Jewish law and tradition. For many years he published articles in the *American Israelite* calling for the establishment of a rabbinical school. Such a school would provide the intense training and education that Wise thought rabbis needed. Hebrew Union College opened its doors in 1875, with Wise acting as president.

In 1883 the college graduated its first class, and a banquet was held to celebrate the event. Wise was disappointed when the Orthodox rabbis in attendance walked out because the food served did not conform to the strictest Jewish dietary laws. Believing that Wise's college was simply too liberal, or accepting of practices that did not strictly follow traditional practices, a group of these rabbis formed the Jewish Theological Seminary of America, a more conservative school. At this point Wise realized that his hopes of unity among American Jews would never be fulfilled. From this point until his death, he was a major spokesman for Reform Judaism.

Wise played a dominant role at a conference of Reform rabbis held in Pittsburgh, Pennsylvania, in 1885. This group issued the Pittsburgh Platform, a document that defined Reform Judaism in the United States. The document noted that Judaism was not a nationality but a religion. It also claimed that nothing in Jewish belief was at odds with the discoveries of science. The platform called for the elimination of Jewish dietary laws and distinctive Jewish dress. The platform was also anti-Zionist, meaning that it opposed the formation of a Jewish state or homeland.

Central Conference of American Rabbis A final major accomplishment of Wise's was the formation of a central ruling body for American Judaism. Again, he had campaigned for such a body for years, but relations between his followers and more Orthodox rabbis from the East were strained, making it difficult to reach an agreement. Finally, in 1889 the Central Conference of American Rabbis was formed. Wise served as president of this organization for the final eleven years of his life.

Wise and American politics

Wise was outspoken on a variety of political issues, especially those affecting Jews. He had seen firsthand the discrimination against Jews that existed in Europe, and he wanted to ensure that American Jews did not suffer in the same way. In 1856 the governor of Ohio issued a Thanksgiving Day proclamation to the "Christian people" of Ohio. Wise immediately reminded the governor that the people of Ohio were neither Christian nor Jewish but free and independent. In 1862 Wise challenged General Ulysses S. Grant's (1822–1885) order that all Jews be discharged from the army department that he headed. Wise also fought efforts to bar Jewish (and Catholic) chaplains from serving with troops during the American Civil War (1861–65; a war between the Union [the North], who were opposed to slavery, and the Confederacy [the South], who were in favor of slavery). He openly opposed a U.S. treaty with Switzerland because he believed that the Swiss government discriminated against American Jews living there.

Wise was criticized for not taking a stand on the issue of slavery, which dominated political discussion in the 1850s and led to the Civil War. Some American rabbis defended slavery, citing passages from Jewish scripture that they believed supported the practice. Other rabbis strongly opposed it. Wise did not adopt a clear position. Many of those who subscribed to the *American Israelite* lived in the South, where slavery was widespread, and he may have feared offending his readers by opposing it. He may have also believed that stating a position on slavery would cause further divisions among American Jews.

Major works

In addition to all his other activities, Wise was also an author. Early in his career he wrote eleven novels, in English and in German, as well as two plays, both in German. Some of his novels were serialized, or published in parts over an extended period of time, in the journals that he edited. The earliest, published in 1854, was *The Convert.* This was followed by *The Catastrophe of Eger, The Shoemaker's Family,* and *Resignation and Fidelity, or Life and Romance,* all three of which were published in 1855. He published several other novels later in the 1850s.

Wise also wrote about history, theology (the study of religion), and Judaism. Some of his major works on these subjects include *The History of the Israelitish Nation from Abraham to the Present Time* (1854), *The Essence of Judaism* (1861), *The Origin of Christianity, and a Commentary on the Acts of the Apostles* (1868), *Judaism, Its Doctrines and Duties* (1872), *The Cosmic God* (1876), and *Judaism and Christianity, Their Agreements and Disagreements* (1883). Many of these books remain in print in the early twenty-first century.

Death

On March 24, 1900, Wise preached his last sermon at his temple. That afternoon, he suffered a stroke. Soon thereafter he slipped into a coma and died on March 26. As Wise was perhaps the most prominent Jew in the United States, his passing was widely noted, and his funeral in Cincinnati was a major public event. His legacy has since survived. The course of American Judaism was profoundly influenced by the efforts and beliefs of Isaac Mayer Wise.

For More Information

BOOKS

Temkin, Sefton D. *Isaac Mayer Wise: Shaping American Judaism.* New York, NY: Oxford University Press, 1991.

Wise, Isaac M. *Judaism, Its Doctrines and Duties.* Whitefish, MT: Kessinger Publishing, 2003.

WEB SITES

Adler, Cyrus, and David Philipson. "Wise, Isaac Mayer." *JewishEncyclopedia.com.* http://www.jewishencyclopedia.com/view.jsp?artid=214&letter=W (accessed on May 26, 2006).

Brody, Seymour. "Isaac Mayer Wise." *Jewish Virtual Library.* http://www.jewish-virtuallibrary.org/jsource/biography/IWise.html (accessed on May 26, 2006).

"Judaiac Treasures of the Library of Congress: Isaac Mayer Wise." *Jewish Virtual Library.* http://www.jewishvirtuallibrary.org/jsource/loc/Wise.html (accessed on May 3, 2006).

Zarathushtra

BORN: Persia

Persian religious leader; teacher

"Zoroastrianism is the oldest of the revealed world-religions, and it has probably had more influence on mankind, directly and indirectly, than any other single faith."

— Mary Boyce, *Zoroastrians: Their Religious Beliefs and Practices.*

Zarathushtra was a prophet, or divine messenger, who founded and gave a version of his name to the ancient Persian religion of Zoroastrianism. In the early twenty-first century the religion is practiced by an estimated 2 million to 3.5 million people, most of whom live in Iran and India, where they are called Parsis. The prophet's full original name was Zarathushtra (or Zarathustra) Spitama, although he is most widely known as Zoroaster, the Western adaptation of the ancient Greek version of his name, Zoroastres. The modern Persian version of his name is Zartosht, or Zardosht.

He is often credited with founding the world's first monotheistic religion, that is, one in which a single supreme God is worshipped. Disagreements about the era in which he lived make this conclusion uncertain, however. Some historians believe that Zarathushtra lived before the emergence of Judaism, in which case the monotheism he preached would stand first historically. If this is true, many of Zoroastrianism's principles likely had a major impact on the development of Judaism and on Christianity, which evolved from Judaism. Other historians believe that Judaism came first, and so it was Judaism that influenced Zoroastrianism.

Zarathushtra's teachings challenged the traditional religious views in ancient Persia (modern-day Iran). He promoted the belief in one God, called Ahura Mazda, which means "wise lord" or "lord of wisdom." Many other Zoroastrian concepts, such as those regarding the soul, heaven and hell, the arrival on Earth of a savior, resurrection (the act of rising from the dead), final judgment, and guardian angels, are similar to those found in Jewish and Christian traditions.

Historical uncertainty

Estimates of when Zarathushtra lived vary widely. Persian mythology places the dates of his life as early as 10,000 BCE. The writings of ancient Greek and Roman historians suggest that Zarathushtra lived some time between 7000 and 6000 BCE, which are the dates accepted by traditional Parsis. Findings by archaeologists (people who study the remains of past human cultures) suggest that he lived around 2000 BCE. One Zoroastrian text, the *Bundahism,* which means "creation," claims that Zarathushtra was alive 258 years before the defeat of Persia by the Greek conqueror Alexander the Great (356–323 BCE), which would be 588 BCE. Many nineteenth-century historians took this date as authoritative. Modern historians questioned it, however, and most now accept that Zoroaster probably lived between 1500 and 1000 BCE, perhaps more precisely around 1200 BCE.

Historians arrived at this last estimate after close examination of the language of the Gathas. The Gathas, a collection of divine songs in seventeen chapters and 241 verses, form a sacred Zoroastrian text believed to record the actual words of Zarathushtra. They are contained within a work called the Yasna, which is in turn part of the sacred Zoroastrian text called the Avesta. The Gathas were written in an ancient Persian language called Old Avestan, which was similar to Sanskrit, the classical language of India and Hinduism.

Experts have compared the Gathas to other Sanskrit writings known to have been written around 1200 BCE, especially the Rig-Veda, one of the four books that compose the Vedas, the sacred literature of Hinduism.

Language similarities suggest that the Gathas were most likely written around the same time. Some scholars, however, remain open to the later date of around 600 BCE mentioned in the *Bundahism*. These scholars note that the Old Avestan language may have been preserved solely for religious writings and was no longer in common use by 1200 BCE. An example of this would be Latin, which remained the official language of Christianity even after it was no longer spoken. Others reject this possibility by noting that the language of the Gathas suggests that they were transmitted orally and thus could not have been written in a language that was no longer spoken.

Further support for the earlier dates can be found in references in the Gathas to social customs that were followed roughly between 1200 and 1000 BCE. These social customs were those of a rural, nomadic (having no fixed home) society. If the Gathas had been written much later, they would have likely reflected a more urban lifestyle centered around the Persian court.

Many Zoroastrian religious texts were partly or entirely destroyed, some by Alexander the Great in 330 BCE, others by Arab and Mongol invaders beginning in 650 CE. As a result, very few written records of the religion and the life of its founder still exist. One of the greatest losses was that of the thirteenth section of the Avesta, the Spena Nask, which contained a summary of Zarathushtra's life.

Early life

Zarathushtra's name is composed of two words in Old Avestan that translate to something like "keeper of old camels," "keeper of feeble camels," or perhaps "keeper of yellow camels." Efforts have been made to suggest a more dignified translation for Zarathushtra's name, such as "bringer of the golden dawn." People living in ancient Persia, however, often had names composed of root words that reflected the ownership of camels or horses, which were signs of wealth and status.

Textual evidence can be used to support claims for a variety of possible birthplaces for Zarathushtra. Most historians agree he was probably was born and lived in northeast Persia, though the Greeks claimed that he was born in Bactria, an ancient Greek kingdom whose borders lay in modern-day Afghanistan and Tajikistan. His mother was named Dughdova, which means "milkmaid." His father was Pourushaspa, which means "many horses." The family name was Spitama, or "white."

According to legend, Zarathushtra was an unnaturally wise, thoughtful, and serious child, although one tale claims that he laughed at the time of his birth. He spent an extended period living in the wilderness, and by age fifteen he had decided to devote himself to contemplation and religious beliefs. Traditional accounts hold that when he was seven years old he was the target of an assassination (murder) plot. The plot was supposedly formed by some Persians who believed him to be the prophet of a new faith that would threaten already established religious beliefs.

At about age twenty Zarathushtra left his parents' house and lived for seven years in a cave, where he practiced meditation, or focused thinking aimed at attaining greater spiritual knowledge and awareness. When he returned he was prepared to preach a new religion, one that placed less emphasis on ritual and more on thought and intellect. Zarathushtra declared his religion would be inclusive of all of Ahura Mazda's people. He also stressed the purity of the earth, which has earned the religion the title "the world's first ecological [environmental] religion."

In the kingdom of Bactria

At first Zarathushtra met with little success in trying to convert people to his religious beliefs. Outside of his immediate family, his first convert was a cousin (or perhaps a nephew) named Maidhyoimangha. Many people in Zarathushtra's community thought he was insane and did all they could to keep away from him. Even the residents of his mother's hometown rejected him, a remarkable insult in the tribal culture of the time, when kinship ties were especially strong. At one point he was imprisoned, but escaped. The rejection was in large part because Zarathushtra demoted the Daevas, or evil spirits, from gods to mere workers on behalf of Angra Mainyu. Angra Mainyu is the name Zarathushtra gave to the primary evil spirit of Zoroastrianism, who is locked in an ongoing cosmic battle with Spenta Mainyu, an aspect of Ahura Mazda who represents good.

Zarathushtra tried to find acceptance for his beliefs for about twelve years. Frustrated, he finally left his community and took refuge in Bactria. In the text of the Yasna, within the Avesta, he commented with sorrow on his departure from his home:

> To what land should I turn? Where should I turn to go?
> They hold me back from folk and friends.
> Neither the community I follow pleases me,
> nor do the wrongful rulers of the land . . .

The Three Wise Men

According to Christian tradition, after the birth of **Jesus Christ** (6 BCE–c. 30 CE; see entry) he was visited by three *magi* from the east who are often referred to as the three wise men. The three had followed a bright star, the star of Bethlehem, and arrived at Jesus's birthplace bearing gifts of gold, frankincense, and myrrh. (Frankincense and myrrh are oils used to make perfume or incense.) The three magi have become a fixed aspect of modern Christmas celebrations in the West (the countries of Europe and the Americas), and most displays of the nativity scene, or the birth of Jesus, include depictions of the magi paying their respects to the Christ child.

The source of the story is one of the Gospels, the first four books of the New Testament. According to the Gospel of Matthew, the magi had been sent by Herod, the Roman governor of Judea, as spies to discover the birthplace of the prophesied Messiah, or Saviour. The Roman Empire, which occupied the region of Palestine, saw the arrival of a Jewish messiah as a threat to the established Roman control and order. In a dream, however, the magi were warned not to return to Herod, so they traveled home by another route. Herod ordered the murder of all boys in and around Bethlehem ages two and under in an effort to ensure that the child destined to be the Messiah did not live to assume his role.

The phrase "three wise men" may be a mistranslation. Many biblical scholars use the word *magi,* which comes from the Greek word for "magic." The magi may have been "magicians" in the sense that they practiced astrology, which is the study of celestial bodies in the belief that they have an influence on the lives of humans. Some historians suggest that the magi were Zoroastrian astrologer-priests. In Western custom they have been identified by the names of Caspar, Melchior, and Balthasar, but they are known by other names in other traditions. The belief that they were Zoroastrians is supported by the Syrian Christian name for one of the wise men, Hormisdas. This is a variation of a Persian name, Hormoz, later spelled Hormazd, which is the name of the patron angel of the first day of each month in Zoroastrian tradition. This name is also similar to the alternative name for Ahura Mazda, which is Ormazd.

Many biblical historians doubt that the story of the magi has any truth to it at all. They point out, for example, that Bethlehem was only a few miles from Jerusalem. Herod would not have had to send spies; he could have simply ordered his army to the area. They also note that Herod, as a high Roman official in command of Judea, would not have allied himself with people like the magi, foreigners who practiced a religion that was entirely alien to someone like Herod and whom Herod would have regarded as beneath him. Additionally, the star of Bethlehem is mentioned in no other records from the time.

I know ... that I am powerless.
I have a few cattle and also a few men.

In Bactria, King Vishtaspa and his queen, Hutosa, heard Zarathushtra debate local religious leaders. They decided to adopt his beliefs, especially after Zarathushtra was able to cure the king's horse of an illness. Zarathushtra then established close ties with the family of the king and

A Zoroastrian head priest offers prayers at a wall of stone carvings near a fire temple in Mumbai, India, during the Parsi New Year. © REUTERS/CORBIS.

queen, whose sons were named Frashaoshtra and Jamaspa. Frashaoshtra's daughter, Hvovi, would become Zarathushtra's wife, and the two would have six children: three daughters, Freni, Friti, and Pourucista, and three sons, Isat Vastar, Uruvat-Nara, and Hvare Cithra. In turn Zarathushtra's daughter, Pourucista, would become the wife of the king's son, Jamaspa.

After a time the king and queen made Zoroastrianism the official religion of the kingdom, and they named Zarathushtra court prophet. At first Zoroastrianism was as much a military order as a religion, since its members were forced to fight persecution (mistreatment towards a person or group because of differences) and fend off attacks from other tribes. Zarathushtra himself denounced the Karpans, the priests of traditional Persian religion, enraging them and perhaps leading to his murder. One legend holds that Zarathushtra died during a battle with a central Asian group called the Turanians, under the leadership of the general Arjaspa. This legend claims Zarathushtra was killed as he tended the sacred fire in a temple at Balkh, a town in modern-day Afghanistan, where he was then buried. Other legends hold that Zarathushtra died peacefully.

In the Persian Empire

The religion founded by Zarathushtra spread rapidly, and the battles ceased. Zoroastrianism became dominant in the Persian Empire, particularly during the Achaemenid dynasty (529–323 BCE). This dynasty ruled over a vast region, from eastern Europe through the Middle East and into both North Africa and central Asia. One of the most prominent Zoroastrian figures from this period was King Darius I, also called Darius the Great, who ruled from 521 to 485 BCE. When Darius secured the kingdom by seizing the throne, he introduced reforms in law, the monetary system, trade, and weights and measurements. Some stories claim that King Vishtaspa was the father of Darius the Great, which, if true, would support the estimates of Zarathushtra having lived around 600 BCE.

Alexander the Great conquered the Achaemenids beginning in the 330s BCE. The empire was then ruled by the Seleucid and Parthian dynasties, but few Zoroastrian records from this time remain. During the Sassanid Dynasty (224–651 CE), Zoroastrianism spread aggressively throughout the Persian Empire. By the sixth century it had moved into northern China, though it died out there by the thirteenth century.

In the seventh century the Sassanid Dynasty was overthrown by Arab Muslims, who were believers in the Islamic religion. Because its followers were often the victims of persecution, Zoroastrianism began to lose influence and membership in the Arab world. During the eighth and ninth centuries large numbers of Zoroastrians fled Persia for India. Zoroastrians living in modern-day Iran continue to be persecuted in the twenty-first century. Members are known as *Gabars,* meaning "infidels," or unbelievers, and the government strongly encourages Zoroastrians to marry within their own faith as a way of keeping the religion's membership from growing. Even in Iran, however, Zarathushtra is seen as a central figure in the development of the nation's culture. Many people in the central Asian republics of the former Soviet Union, including Tajikistan and Kazakhstan, began to show renewed interest in their Zoroastrian roots after the fall of the Soviet Union at the end of the twentieth century.

For More Information

BOOKS

Boyce, Mary. *Zoroastrians: Their Religious Beliefs and Practices.* Boston, MA: Routledge & Kegan Paul, 1979.

Hartz, Paula. *Zoroastrianism.* 2nd ed. New York, NY: Facts On File, 2004.

Kriwaczek, Paul. *In Search of Zarathustra: The First Prophet and the Ideas That Changed the World.* New York, NY: Knopf, 2003.

Nigosian, S. A. *The Zoroastrian Faith: Tradition and Modern Research.* Montreal, QC: McGill–Queen's University Press, 1993.

WEB SITES

Chothia, Fali S. "Getting to Know the Zoroastrians." *The Zoroastrian Associated of Metropolitan Washington, Inc.* http://www.zamwi.org/religion/Getting.html (accessed June 2, 2006).

"Zoroastrian Archives." *Avesta.org.* http://www.avesta.org/ (accessed on June 2, 2006).

Zoroastrian Kids Korner. http://www.zoroastriankids.com (accessed June 2, 2006).

"Zoroastrianism." *United Religions Initiative.* http://www.uri.org/kids/other_zoro.htm (accessed June 2, 2006).

Where to Learn More

The following list focuses on works written for readers of middle school and high school age. Books aimed at adult readers have been included when they are especially important in providing information or analysis that would otherwise be unavailable.

Books

Armstrong, Karen. *Islam: A Short History,* rev. ed. New York: Modern Library, 2002.

Bottero, Jean. *Religion in Ancient Mesopotamia.* Chicago, IL: University of Chicago Press, 2001.

Boyer, P. *Religion Explained: The Human Instincts That Fashion Gods, Spirits, and Ancestors.* London: William Heinemann, 2001.

Buswell, Robert E., Jr., ed. *Encyclopedia of Buddhism.* 2 vols. New York: Macmillan Reference, 2003.

De Lange, Nicholas. *An Introduction to Judaism.* Cambridge, U.K.: Cambridge University Press, 2000.

Dundas, Paul. *The Jains.* 2nd ed. London and New York, NY: Routledge, 2002.

Flood, Gavin D. *An Introduction to Hinduism.* Cambridge, U.K.: Cambridge University Press, 1996.

Glazier, Stephen D. *Encyclopedia of African and African-American Religions.* New York: Routledge, 2001.

Grimassi, Raven. *Encyclopedia of Wicca and Witchcraft.* St. Paul, MN: Llewellyn Publications, 2000.

Hartz, Paula. *Zoroastrianism,* 2nd ed. New York: Facts On File, 2004.

Higginbotham, Joyce. *Paganism: An Introduction to Earth-centered Religions.* St. Paul, MN: Llewellyn Publications, 2002.

Hirschfelder, Arlene, and Paulette Molin. *Encyclopedia of Native American Religions: An Introduction.* 2nd ed. New York: Facts On File, 2001.

Hoffman, Nancy. *Sikhism.* Detroit, MI: Lucent Books, 2006.

Jones, Lindsay. *Encyclopedia of Religion,* 2nd ed. Detroit, MI: Macmillan Reference USA, 2005.

Keown, Damien. *Dictionary of Buddhism.* New York: Oxford University Press, 2003.

Lace, William W. *Christianity.* San Diego, CA: Lucent Books, Inc., 2005.

Martin, Michael, ed. *The Cambridge Companion to Atheism.* Cambridge, U.K.: Cambridge University Press, 2005.

Momen, Moojan. *A Short Introduction to the Baha'i Faith.* Oxford, U.K.: Oneworld Publications, 1997.

Nasr, Seyyed Hossein. *Islam: Religion, History, Civilization.* San Francisco: Harper San Francisco, 2003.

Oldstone-Moore, Jennifer. *Confucianism: Origins, Beliefs, Practices, Holy Texts, Sacred Places.* New York: Oxford University Press, 2002.

Oldstone-Moore, Jennifer. *Taoism: Origins, Beliefs, Practices, Holy Texts, Sacred Places.* New York: Oxford University Press, 2003.

Robinson, George. *Essential Judaism: A Complete Guide to Beliefs, Customs and Rituals.* Rev. ed. New York: Pocket Books, 2000.

Roochnick, David. *Retrieving the Ancients: An Introduction to Greek Philosophy.* New York: Blackwell, 2004.

Tiele, C. P. *Comparative History of the Egyptian and Mesopotamian Religions.* New York: Routledge, 2001.

Tomkins, Steven. *A Short History of Christianity.* London: Lion Books, 2005.

Web Site

URI Kids: World Religions. United Religions Initiative. http://www.uri.org/kids/world.htm (accessed on July 24, 2006).

Religions, Faith Groups, and Ethical Systems. Ontario Consultants on Religious Tolerance. http://www.religioustolerance.org/var_rel.htm (accessed on July 24, 2006).

World Religions Index. http://wri.leaderu.com/ (accessed on July 24, 2006).

Index

Italic type indicates volume numbers; **boldface** type indicates main entries and their page numbers; Illustrations are marked by (ill.).

A

Abdal-Rahman ibn Muhammad ibn Khaldun.
  See ibn Khaldūn
Abdullah, Muhammad Ibn.
  See Muhammad
Abdullah (son of Muhammad), *1:* 199
Abimelech, *1:* 6
Abraham, *1:* 1(ill.), **1–8**
  descendants of, *1:* 6
  early life, *1:* 2
  expulsion from Egypt, *1:* 3–4
  God's promises to, *1:* 5
  influence of, *1:* 7–8
  role in major religions, *1:* 1–2
  similarities with Jesus Christ, *1:* 1
Abram. *See* Abraham
Abu Bakr, *1:* 18, 20
Abu Sufyan, *2:* 291
Abu Talib, *1:* 18, 200, 201
Academy of Plato, *2:* 316
Acharya, *2:* 235
Achyutapreksha, *2:* 235
Active learning, *2:* 215
Acts of Paul and Thecla, *2:* 302
Acts of the Apostles, *2:* 302
Advaita Vedanta school, *2:* 239, 240, 385–86
  See also Upanishads
African communities, cultural roles in, *2:* 346
Ahimsa, 2: 246
Aisha (widow of Muhammad), *1:* 30; *2:* 304

Akhenaten, *1:* **9–16,** 9 (ill.), 13 (ill.)
  life of, *1:* 10
  reign of, *1:* 11, 14
Akhenaton. *See* Akhenaten
Akhetaten (city), *1:* 12, 15 (ill.)
Akkad (city), *1:* 123
Akkadians, *1:* 123
Albert Schweitzer International Prize, *2:* 294
Alexander the Great, *1:* 36 (ill.); *2:* 405
  See also Aristotle
'Ali Abī Ibn Tālib, *1:* **17–24**
  death of, *1:* 22
  early life, *1:* 18
  fourth caliph, *1:* 21–22
  Muhammad and, *1:* 19, 200
  succession issue, *1:* 17–18
'Ali Muhammad, Siyyid, *1:* 44
"Allegory of the Cave" (Plato), *2:* 317–18
Almohads, conquest of Spain, *2:* 250
Amarna period, *1:* 11, 15
Amenhotep IV. *See* Akhenaten
America Israelite newspaper, *2:* 395
Al-Amin. *See* Muhammad
Amram, *2:* 279
An (sky god), *1:* 122
An Quang Buddhist Institute, *2:* 360
Analects (Confucius), *1:* 88, 89
Anandatirtha. *See* Madhva
Anandpur, Battle of, *2:* 355
Anandpur siege, *2:* 356
Anaxagoras, *1:* **25–31,** 25 (ill.)
  early life, *1:* 25–26

E-u-gim e-a (Hymn of Praise to Ekishnugal and Nanna on Assumption of En-ship), *1:* 126
Ea (water god), *1:* 122
Eastern Orthodox Christianity, *2:* 336, 360
Ecclesiastical Ordinances (Calvin), *1:* 79
Edict of Worms, *2:* 228–29, 230–31
Egyptian pharaoh, *1:* 4–5
Eightfold Path, *1:* 62
Ekhaka Sapa. *See* Black Elk
Electronic Text Corpus of Sumerian Literature, The, *1:* 125
Eliezer, Israel Ben, *1:* **171–78**
    early life, *1:* 172–74
    followers, *1:* 177
    spiritual awakening, *1:* 174–77
Engaged Buddhism, *2:* 360–61
Engels, Friedrich, *2:* 260–61, 262 (ill.)
Enheduanna, *1:* **121–27,** 122 (ill.)
Enlil (storm and earth god), *1:* 122
Ephriam (grandson of Jacob), *1:* 6
Episcopal Divinity School (Massachusetts), *2:* 373
Esau (son of Isaac), *1:* 6
Essay Concerning Human Understanding (Locke), *2:* 268
Essence of Judaism, The (Wise), *2:* 397
Eudemian Ethics (Aristotle), *1:* 39–40
Euphrates River, *1:* 3
Euthydemus (Plato), *2:* 316
Euthyphro (Plato), *2:* 315
Exaltation of Inanna, The, *1:* 125
Exodus story, *2:* 282–83

Fadaʿih al-BatiniyyaI (al-Ghazali), *1:* 148
Faith, declaration of, *2:* 304
Faqr, *1:* 13
Farabi, Abu al-Nasr Al-, *1:* 147
Farel, Guillaume, *1:* 78
Fatima (daughter of Muhammad), *1:* 199
    as female ideal, *1:* 20
    Hand of, *1:* 18 (ill.)
    marriage of, *1:* 19

Fellowship of Crotona, *1:* 139
Festival of Ridvan, *1:* 46
Fetterman, Lieutenant Colonel William, *1:* 53
Fihi Ma Fih (Rumi), *1:* 183
Five Ks of Sikhism, *1:* 158–59
Five Points of Calvinism, *1:* 77
Five Vows of Jainism, *2:* 246
Flower of the Saints (Loyola), *2:* 218
Fodio, Muhammad, *1:* 376
Forced conversions of Sikhs, *2:* 345
Foster, Mary E., *1:* 111
Four Nobel Truths, *1:* 70
Four Valleys (Baháʾuʾlláh), *1:* 45
Francis I, arrest of Protestants by, *1:* 77
Fränkel, David, *2:* 268
Frederick the Great, *2:* 260–70
Freud, Sigmund, *1:* 13
Fulani people, *2:* 376
Fulani War, *2:* 377–78

Gabriel (angel), *1:* 200
    See also Jabraʾil (angel)
Gad (son of Jacob), *1:* 6
Gamaliel, *2:* 302, 316
Gandhi, Mahatma, *1:* **129–36,** 129 (ill.)
    children dressed as, *1:* 132 (ill.)
    early life, *1:* 129–36
    education, *1:* 130
    racism experienced by, *1:* 130–32
    in South Africa, *1:* 131–33
Gardner, Gerald Brousseau, *1:* **137–44,** 137 (ill.)
    early life, *1:* 138
    religious explorations, *1:* 139
Gardner, Grissell, *1:* 138
Gathas, The, *2:* 400
Gaudiya Vaishnavism, *1:* 67–68, 69, 72–73
Gaura. *See* Caitanya Mahaprabhu
Gautama, Maha-Pajapati, *1:* 71, 72
Gelug. *See* Tibetan Buddhism
Geluk. *See* Tibetan Buddhism
Geneva, under Calvinism, *1:* 80
German Ideology (Marx), *2:* 260
German Jewish Enlightenment, *2:* 272–73

N